Ármin Vámbéry

Sketches of Central Asia

Additional chapters on my travels, adventures and on the ethnology of Central Asia

Ármin Vámbéry

Sketches of Central Asia

Additional chapters on my travels, adventures and on the ethnology of Central Asia

ISBN/EAN: 9783337210441

Printed in Europe, USA, Canada, Australia, Japan

Cover: Foto ©Andreas Hilbeck / pixelio.de

More available books at **www.hansebooks.com**

SKETCHES

OF

CENTRAL ASIA.

ADDITIONAL CHAPTERS

ON

MY TRAVELS, ADVENTURES,

AND ON THE

ETHNOLOGY OF CENTRAL ASIA.

BY

ARMINIUS VÁMBÉRY,

PROFESSOR OF ORIENTAL LANGUAGES IN THE
UNIVERSITY OF PESTH

PHILADELPHIA:
J. B. LIPPINCOTT & CO.
WM. H. ALLEN & CO., 13, WATERLOO PLACE,
PALL MALL, LONDON.

1868.

Lewis and Son, Printers, Swan Buildings, Moorgate Street.

PREFACE.

In the reviews of my "Travels in "Central Asia," which have issued from the European and American press, I have generally been reproached with scantiness of details and scrappiness of treatment;—in a word, with having said much less than I could have said about my journey from the Bosphorus to Samarkand,—so rich in varied adventures and experiences.

Now, I will not deny that such a charge has not been quite unfairly levelled against me.

While I was writing my memoirs, during the first three months of my stay in London, after my year-long wanderings in Asia, I had very great trouble in accustoming myself to the idea of being firmly settled down. I always kept fancying myself bound on the morrow to pack up and extend my travels with the caravan: hence my irresolution and hasty procedure. Moreover, I was quite a stranger in the domain of travelling, and deemed it my duty now to keep something back for mere decency; anon to leave out something else, as of inferior interest. Hence many an episode was left untouched, many a picture remained but a feeble sketch.

To make up for this defect—if sparingness in words be really a defect—I have written the following pages. They contain only supplementary papers, partly about my own adventures, partly on the manners and rare characteristics of the Central Asiatic peoples, linked together in no particular connection. It would naturally have been better to offer these pages in the place of the former volume; and yet the slightest notice of a country so little known to us as Turkestan, which political questions will soon bring into the front of passing questions, will always have its uses; and "meglio tardi che mai."

A. V.

Pesth,
2nd December, 1867.

CONTENTS.

	PAGE
CHAPTER I. Dervishes and Hadjis	1
CHAPTER II. Recollections of my Dervish Life	22
CHAPTER III. Amongst the Turkomans	44
CHAPTER IV. The Caravan in the Desert	62
CHAPTER V. The Tent and its Inhabitants	75
CHAPTER VI. The Court of Khiva	87
CHAPTER VII. Joy and Sorrow	98
CHAPTER VIII. House, Food, and Dress	114
CHAPTER IX. From Khiva to Kungrat and back	127

viii CONTENTS.

CHAPTER X.
My Tartar . . . 150

CHAPTER XI.
The Round of Life in Bokhara 166

CHAPTER XII.
Bokhara, the Head Quarters of Mohamedanism . . 186

CHAPTER XIII.
The Slave Trade and Slave Life in Central Asia . 205

CHAPTER XIV.
Productive Power of the Three Oasis-Countries of Turkestan 231

CHAPTER XV.
On the Ancient History of Bokhara 257

CHAPTER XVI.
Ethnographical Sketch of the Turanian and Iranian Races of Central Asia 282

CHAPTER XVII.
Iranians 313

CHAPTER XVIII.
Literature in Central Asia 339

CHAPTER XIX.
Rivalry between Russia and England in Central Asia 379

SKETCHES OF CENTRAL ASIA.

CHAPTER I.

DERVISHES AND HADJIS.

The dervish is the veritable personification of Eastern life. Idleness, fanaticism, and slovenliness, are the features which in him are regarded as virtues, and which everywhere are represented by him as such. Idleness is excused by allusion to human impotence; fanaticism explained as enthusiasm in religion; and slovenliness justified by the uselessness of poor mortals in struggling against fate. If the superiority of European civilization over that of the East was not so clearly established, I should almost be tempted to envy a dervish, who, clad in tatters and conversing in a corner of some ruined building, shows, by the twinkling in his eye, the happiness he enjoys. What a serenity is depicted in that face; what a placidity in all his actions; what a complete contrast there is between this picture and that presented by our European civilization! In my disguise as a dervish it was chiefly this unnatural composure which made me nervous, and in the imitation of which I made, of course, the greatest mistakes. I shall never forget one day at Herat, when, after reflecting on the happiness of the early termination of the painful mask I had been wearing for so many months, I suddenly jumped up from my seat, and in a somewhat excited state began to pace up and down the old ruin which gave me shelter. A few minutes afterwards I perceived that a crowd of passers by had collected at the door, and that I was the object of general astonishment. Seeing my mistake, I blushingly resumed my seat. Soon afterwards several people came up to ask me what was the matter with me, whether I was well, &c. The good people thought I was deranged; for, to oriental notions, a man must be out of his senses if, without necessity or a special object in view, he suddenly leaves his seat to pace up and down a room.

As the dervish represents the general character, so he does the different peoples of the East. It is true, Mahomedanism enforces the dogma: "El Islam milleti wahidun"—all Islamites are *one* nation; but the origin and home of the different sects are easily recognised. Bektashi, Mewlewi, and Rufai, are principally natives of Turkey; because Bektash, the enthusiastic founder of the Janissaries, Moola Djelaleddin Rumi, the great poet of the Mesnevi, lived, and are buried in Turkey; the Kadrie and Djelali are most frequently met with in Arabia; the Oveisy, and Nurbakhshi Nimetullah in Persia; the Khilali and Zahibi in India; and the Nakishbendi and Sofi Islam in Central Asia.* The members of the different fraternities are bound together by very close ties; apprentices (Murid) and assistants (Khalfa) have to yield implicit obedience to the chief (Pir), who has an unlimited power over the life and property of his brethren. But these fraternities do not in the least trouble themselves about secret political or social objects, as is sometimes asserted in Europe by enthusiastic travellers, who have even discovered Freemasons amongst the Bedouin tribes of the Great Desert. The dervishes are the monks of Islamism; and the spirit which created and sustains them is that of religious fanaticism, and they differ from each other only by the manner in which they demonstrate their enthusiasm. For instance; whilst one of these religious orders commands constant pilgrimages to the tombs of saints, the other lays down stringent rules for reflection on divine infinity and the insignificance of our existence. A third compels his votaries to occupy themselves day and night with repeating the name of of God (Zikr) and hymns (Telkin); and it cannot surprise us to learn that the greater number of a company which has continually been calling out with all its

* Sofi Islam is a sect which originated about thirty years ago. Its founder, a Tadjik from Belkh, was desirous of opposing the ever-increasing influence of the Nakishbendi. In this fraternity prevails the principle of communism and blood relationship. The Sofi Islamites wear a cap trimmed with fur, and are most frequently met with this side of the Oxus, as far as Herat, and also amongst the Turkomans.

might: "Ja hu! Ja hakk! La illahi illa hu! are seized with *delirium tremens*. The orthodox call this condition Medjzub; *i.e.*, carried away by divine love, or to be in ecstacy. A person to whom such a fortunate event happens, for as such it is regarded, is envied by everybody; and as long as it lasts, the sick and the maimed, and barren women, try to get in his immediate presence, taking hold of his dress,—as touching it is supposed to have healing powers.

What the dervishes are able to do during the ecstacy caused by *Zikr*, I had once an opportunity of witnessing in Samarkand. In Dehbid, close to the tomb of the Makhdun Aazam, one of these howling companies had grouped themselves around the Pir (chief) of that district. At first they contented themselves with repeating the formula in a natural tone of voice, and almost in measured time. The chief was lost in the deepest thought; all eyes and ears were fixed upon him; and every motion of his hand, and every breath he drew, was audible, and encouraged his followers to utter wilder and louder ejaculations. At last he seemed to awake from his sleep-like reflections, and as soon as he raised his head all the dervishes jumped up from their seats like possessed beings. The circle was broken, and the different members began to dance in undulating motions; but hardly did the chief stand upon his feet than the enthusiastic dancers became so terribly excited that I, who had to imitate all their wild antics, became almost frightened. They were flying about, constantly dancing, right and left, hither and thither, some leaving the soft meadow and getting upon the rough stones, constantly dancing, till the blood began to run freely from their feet. Still they kept on their mad excitement, till most of them fell fainting to the ground.

In a country like the East, where such social relations exist, and where we meet with such amusing extremes, the dervish or beggar, though placed at the very bottom of the social scale, often enjoys as much consideration as the prince who reigns over millions and disposes of immense treasures. Man, an unresisting plaything in the powerful hand of Fate, can, if Destiny wills it, be transported from one extreme to the other, of which history furnishes us with numerous instances; and as in fiction we see with pleasure the two antipodes—the king, Shah-ü Keda, and the beggar, brought into close propinquity—even so we often find a ragged and dirty dervish, covered with vermin, sitting on the same carpet with a magnificently-dressed prince, and engaged with him in familiar conversation, nay, often drinking with him out of the same cup. European travellers view such a *tête-à-tête* with surprise, and even sometimes with a feeling of amusement; but in the East it is considered as quite natural. For, says the oriental moralist, the king must see in the glaring contrast between him and his neighbour the vanity of earthly splendour, and banish from his mind all feeling of pride; while the dervish discovers beneath the pompous dress of the prince a mere mortal man, and mindful of the vanity of sublunary things, laughs at the farce of life.

Though perfectly conscious of their relative position, these two extremes exhibit, when they meet, an admirable degree of toleration and indulgence. The dervish, who, when received in private, behaves with the freedom and unconstraint of an intimate friend, never forgets on public occasions that he is the poorest of the poor. The man of rank suffers from him what to any other person would appear insupportable. At Kerki, the governor of the province had a dervish in his palace, who, in conformity with a precept of his order, had the agreeable office of crying aloud uninterruptedly, from sunset till break of day: Ya hu! ya hakk! La illa hu!* and that with the voice of a Stentor. As soon as darkness prevailed, and the busy hum of public life had become silent, the melancholy and monotonous exclamations became more and more audible, not only in the palace itself, but to a considerable extent around it. That his devotions disturbed many in their sleep, may be easily imagined. Nevertheless, the governor, notwithstanding the entreaties of his own family, did not venture to make any objection to this proceeding, and the dervish continued his vociferations every night as long as he sojourned in Kerki. As I lodged in the vicinity of the palace, I

---

* Yes, it is he! it is the righteous one! there is no God but he; are the usual forms of prayer which occur in the Zikr.

enjoyed my share of this nightly concert; and as the voice of the enthusiastic bawler became towards the approach of dawn weaker and weaker, I was enabled to calculate from it the distance of daybreak without stepping out of the dark cell in which I lay.

We may say, however, that we nowadays very seldom meet with a dervish in the strict sense of the word; that is, a man who, renouncing from inward conviction earthly goods and worldly comforts, is desirous only of obtaining experience of life and devoting himself to the practice of religious duties: such a man, in a word, as the poet Saadi is represented to have been. Those who embrace this vocation are either unprincipled and lazy fellows, or professed beggars, who, under the cloak of poverty, collect treasures, and when they are sufficiently enriched often adopt some lucrative trade. This is particularly the case in Persia. So long as Fortune is favourable to them they lead a life of ostentatious magnificence, and forget how transitory all is in this world. But should he be overtaken by adversity, then he retires to some modest corner, rails at the vain pursuits of men, and, inflated with pride, cries out: Men dervish em; I am a dervish.

The dervishes of India, and particularly those of Cashmere, are throughout the East pre-eminent among their Mahometan brethren for cunning, secret arts, forms of exorcism, &c. These fellows impose most impudently on the credulity of the people in Persia and Central Asia, and even men of wit and understanding sometimes fall into their snares; for, wherever such a Cashmere dervish appears, gifted as he generally is with a noble figure, striking features, bright eloquent eyes, and long dark flowing hair, he is sure of success.

The Mahometans of India and the adjoining eastern countries have always been celebrated in the Islamite world for their supernatural gifts. As soon as such a travelling saint arrives in a Mahometan country, he is entreated to cure dangerous maladies, to exorcise ghosts, or to point out where hidden treasures are buried; for, although those arts are forbidden by the Koran, they appear everywhere as the most zealous Mahometans. Count Gobineau, in his work, "Trois Ans dans l'Asie," tells us of an excellent trick, which an alchemist from Cashmere played a gold-seeking prince in Teheran. A similar trick was played on the brother of the reigning Khan of Khiva, who, wanting to have all his saddles and bridles converted into gold, was cheated in a most ridiculous manner. But they are sometimes so devoid of conscience as to rob the poorest man of his last penny. In Teheran, a Hadji, lately arrived from Central Asia, told me, with tears in his eyes, the following story. As, said he, I had heard much in Meshed of the frequent robberies that occurred on the road to Teheran, I and my companion were anxious to know what would be the best way to conceal our little capital, which was to defray our expenses to the holy grave of the Prophet. This money was the savings of five hard years, and thou knowest how difficult it is to travel without money in this land of heretics. Next to us in the caravanserai at Meshed there lodged a pious Ishan (sheikh) from Cashmere; to him we communicated our fears, and were delighted when he offered, by means of a certain form of prayer, to secure our money against all attacks of robbers. He invited us to follow him to the mosque of Iman Riza: there he bade us perform the usual ablutions. We then placed our money in his lap, and after he had breathed on it several times he put it with his own hands into our purses, wrapped them up in seven sheets of paper, and then strictly enjoined us not to open them till, on our arrival at Tcheran, we had performed our devotions three times in the mosque. It is now six weeks since we left Meshed; and imagine our fright, when yesterday, after the third prayer, we opened our purses and found in them, instead of our dear ducats, nothing but heavy reddish sand. The poor fellows uttered bitter complaints and seemed almost to have lost their wits. The cunning rogue from Cashmere had, while pronouncing the blessing, changed the money without being perceived by the simple Tartars, who continued their journey to Teheran in the perfect persuasion of the efficacy of the ceremony,—a persuasion which they now found had cost them dear.

It is the same with dervishism as with all the other oriental institutions, customs and manners; the more we penetrate towards the East, the greater is the purity with which they have been preserved. In Persia the dervishes play a much more important part than in Turkey; and in Central Asia, isolated as it has been from the rest of the world for centuries, this fraternity is still in full vigour, and exercises a great influence upon society. In my "Travels," I have frequently alluded to the position occupied by the *Ishan* or secular priests in Central Asia. Their influence may be called a fortunate one, contrasted with the fearful tyranny existing in those countries. This is the reason why every one occupies himself with religion; every one tries to pass himself off as a worker of miracles (Ehli Keramet); or, if he fails in that, he endeavours to be recognised as a saint (veli ullah . . .) Those who make the interpretation of the sacred writings their business are great rivals of the *Ishans*, who, by the mysticism by which they surround themselves, enjoy a large share of popular esteem. The native of Central Asia, like the wildest child of Arabia, is more easily imposed upon by magic formulas and similar hocus-pocus than by books. He may dispense with the services of a Mollah, but he cannot do without a *Ishan*, whose blessing (*fatiha*) or breath (*nefes*) is required when he sets out on one of his predatory expeditions, and upon which he looks as a talismanic power, when moving about his herds, his tent, or the wilds of the desert.

After the Ishans, the most interesting class are the mendicant dervishes (*Kalenter*),* which the Kirguese

---

* Kalentor is a corruption of the old Persian Kelanter=the greater. In eastern Persia the title is still given to the judges of villages.

and Turkomans call Kuddush* or Divani (insane). In the whole of the great deserts which stretch from the eastern boundaries of China to the Caspian Sea, it is only these people, in their ragged dress, who are able to move unmolested. They do not take any notice of the differences of tribe or family, and the mighty words, *Yaghi* or *Il* (friend or enemy) have to them no meaning. In travelling along they join whomsoever they meet, be it a peaceful caravan or band of *robbers*. The dervishes who travel through Kirguese or Turkoman steppes are generally this class of people, who form a strong inclination to do nothing, follow a trade which throughout the East is considered respectable, viz., that of a mendicant. All they have to acquire is a few prayers and a certain power of mimicry, with which the chiromantic feats are performed; and I have never seen a nomad who has not been moved when he found himself in the close presence of one of those long-haired, bare-headed, and bare-footed dervishes, who, with his fiery eyes, stared hard at the son of the desert, and whilst shaking his Keshkul † howled a wild "*Ja hu!*"

The arrival of one of these fakirs in a lonely group of tents is regarded as a joyful event, or almost a festi-

* Kuddus is derived from Kud, to become mad. Thus, the Arabs call the dervishes Medjnun, *i.e.*, insane.

† Keshkul is a vessel formed of half a cocoa nut,—the *vade mecum* of the dervishes,—in which he plunges all the food he has collected by begging, whether dry or fluid, sweet or sour. Such a dish of *tutti frutti* would but ill suit our gastronomers; and yet how delicious it tasted to me after a long day's march.

val; it is of especial importance in the eyes of the women; and the time of his arrival is differently interpreted. Early in the morning signifies the happy birth of a camel or a horse; at noon a quarrel between husband and wife; and in the evening a good prospect of marriage to the marriageable daughters. The dervish is generally taken in hand by the women, and is well supplied with the best things the tent contains, in hopes that he may be tempted to produce from beneath his battered dress some glass beads, or other talisman. Alms, which amongst the nomads seldom consist of money, are rarely denied him; and he often receives an old carpet, a few handfuls of camel hair or wool, or an old garment. He may also stop with the family for days, and move about with it without his presence becoming a burden. If the dervish possesses musical talent, *i.e.*, able to sing a few songs and accompany himself on the two stringed instrument called dutara, he is made much of, and has the greatest difficulty in getting away from the hospitable host.

It is very seldom that dervishes are insulted or ill-treated; this, however, is said to be the case amongst the Turkomans, whose rapacity knows no bounds, and prompts them to commit incredible acts of cruelty. A dervish from Bokhara, of robust figure and dark curly hair, whom I met at Maymene, told me that a Tekke-Turkoman, prompted by the thirty ducats which his athletic figure promised to fetch in the slave market, made him a prisoner to sell him a few days afterwards.

"I pretended," my colleague continued, "to be quite unconcerned, and repeated the *Zikr* whilst shaking my iron chains. The time was fast approaching when I was to be taken to the market, when suddenly the wife of the robber of my liberty and person was taken ill, and prevented him from starting. He seemed to see in this the finger of God, and began to be pensive, when his favourite horse, refusing to eat his food, showed signs of illness." This was enough. The robber was so frightened that he removed the chains of his prisoner, and returned to him the things he had robbed him of, begging him to leave his tent as soon as possible. Whilst a Turkoman impatiently awaited the departure of the ominous beggar, the latter fumbled about his dress, and pretended that he had lost a comb which his chief had given him as a talisman on the road, and without which he could not go a single step. The nomad returned in great haste to the place where the plunder had been kept, and as the comb did not turn up he became still more frightened, and promised the dervish the price of twenty combs if he would only take a single step beyond the boundary of his tent. The cunning bush-rite saw he was master of the situation; he pretended to be inconsolable about the lost property, and declared that he now would have to remain for years in the tent. Imagine the confusion of the deceived and superstitious robber! Like a madman he ran about asking his neighbour for advice. Formal negotiations were now commenced with the dervish, to whom, finally, a horse, a dress, and ten ducats were presented, to make up for the loss of the comb, and on condition that he should leave a tent whose proprietor will probably think twice before he ventures again upon molesting a travelling dervish.

Besides the dervishes who, as physicians, miracle-working saints, or harmless vagabonds, are wandering about in Central Asia, there is a class called " *Khanka neshin,*" or convent dwellers, who always wish to appear as the poorest, and are without doubt the most contemptible fellows in the world. Generally speaking they are opium eaters, who by their excessive filth, skeleton-like body, and frightfully distorted features, present a most repulsive appearance. The worst is that they do not confine themselves to practising this fearful vice themselves, but with a singular persistency endeavour to make converts amongst all classes; and, supported by the want of spirituous drinks, they succeed but too frequently in their wicked attempts. What surprised me most was that these wretched people were regarded as eminently religious, of whom it was thought that from their love to God and the Prophet they had become mad, and stupefied themselves in order that in their excited state they might be nearer the Beings whom they loved so well.

Speaking of dervishes we may mention a class of hypocrites who, under the pretence of carrying out sacred vows, indulge in their desire to travel, and after their return assume, under the title of Hadji (Pilgrims) authority and a good social position. The Koran says, "*Hidji ala beiti min isti Itaatun sebila*"—Wander to my house (*Kaaba*) if circumstances permit. These "circumstances" are reduced to the following seven conditions by the commentators. The pilgrimage must be undertaken, 1st,—With sufficient money for travelling expenses; 2nd,—In bodily health; 3rd,—In an unmarried state; 4th,—Without leaving debts behind; 5th,—In times of peace; 6th,—Overland and without danger; and, 7th,—By persons who have reached the age of puberty. That our good Tartars ill-observe these conditions will be evident to all who have some idea about the countries situated between Oxus and Yaxartes. In Persia people go to Kerbela, Meshed or Mekka, only when sufficient funds enable them to do it comfortably. In Central Asia, on the contrary, it is always the poorest class who undertakes pilgrimages. A certain taste for adventure, coupled with religious enthusiasm, are the two motives which prompt the inhabitants of Central Asia to start from the remote east for the tomb of their Prophet. True, they do not suffer any material losses, for a beggar's bag is a money bag; but they frequently lose what is most precious to them—their life; as every year at least one-third of the pilgrims from Turkestan die from exposure to the climate.

This sacred or profane desire to travel braves all danger; this vague thought of tearing himself away from his family, and friends, and countrymen, to see the wide world, surrounds the Hadji with a certain poetry. I have lived weeks with my companions, and yet it always interested me to behold them, palm staff in hand, as a sacred memento of Arabia, vigorously making their way through the deep sand or mud. They were returning happily to their homes; but how many did I meet who only commenced their long and tedious journey? and yet they were equally happy. On my road from Samarkand to Teheran I had as a companion a native of Chinese Tartary, who, in total ignorance of the route he had to take, asked me every evening, even when we were yet at Meshed, whether we should see to-morrow, or at the farthest after tomorrow, the minarets of Mekka. The poor fellow had no idea how much he would have to endure before he reached his destination. However, this should not surprise us when we remember that during the time of the crusades so many honest Teutons undertook a pilgrimage to the Holy Land, and after two or three days' journey hoped to behold the walls of Jerusalem.*

The routes to Arabia adopted by the pious Tartars are the following, viz.:—1. Yarkend, Kilian, Tibet, Kashmir.† 2. Through Southern Siberia, Kazan and

---

* See Nœsselt's "Geschichte für Tochter schulen," who also states that many pilgrims, ignorant of the road, allowed themselves to be led by a frightened goose which ran before them.

† From Yarkend to Kilian on the boundary line are three days' journey, from there, by way of Tagarma and Kadun, to Tibet, twenty days, and thence to Kashmir fifteen days.

Constantinople. 3. Through Afghanistan and India to Djedda. 4. Through Persia, Bagdad, and Damascus. None of these routes is a comfortable one, and the amount of danger to be incurred is very much dependent upon the season of the year and the political state of the countries through which they pass. The travellers form themselves in larger or smaller companies, and elect a chief (*Tchaush*) from amongst themselves, who also fills amongst them the office of *Imam*, (the person who first says the prayers to be repeated by the rest,) and who enjoys a considerable superiority over his companions. A visit to the Kaaba and the tomb of the Prophet (which may be paid at any season) is not so much the culminating point of the whole pilgrimage as the ascent of Mount Arafat. This can be made only once a year, viz., on the Kurban festival, (10th Zil Hidje,) which is nothing more or less than the sacrifice of Abraham and Isaac dramatized. All those who have taken part in this festival and have joined in the cry, "Lebeïk Allah!"— Command, Oh God," (in allusion to Abraham's implicit obedience,) are regarded as genuine Hadjis. This cry of "Lebeïk! Lebeïk!" uttered at the most solemn moment of the whole pilgrimage, seems also to have the deepest impression upon the pilgrim himself. My travelling companions, whenever they became excited or were in a happy mood of mind, always alluded to it; and the stillness of the Tartar deserts was often broken by this *memento* of the stony districts of Arabia.

However painful and heartrending separation from home may be when so long and dangerous a journey has to be undertaken, the joy which the Hadjis experienced on their return fully counterbalances it. Friends and relations, informed of his near arrival, go out to meet them several days in advance. Hymns are sung, and tears of joy are shed when the Hadji makes his entry into his native place. Every one wants to embrace him, to touch him, for the atmosphere of holy places still surrounds him, the dust of Mekka and Medina still covers his garments. In Central Asia the Hadji is held in much greater esteem than in any other Mohammedan country. It has cost him much to obtain his dignity, but he is amply repaid. Respected and supported by his fellow citizens he is better protected against the tyranny of the Government than any other citizen. The title of a "Hadji" is a patent of nobility, which, during his lifetime, he parades on his seal, after death on his tombstone.

The Hadjis, of course such as are not mere beggars, often transact, during their pious pilgrimage, a little commercial business. "*Hem tidjared hem ziaret.*"— "Commerce and pilgrimage together" are not allowed by their religion; but nobody seems to suffer any pricks of conscience in taking to his co-religionist in

Arabia a few articles from distant Turkomania. The products of Bokhara and other holy places of Central Asia are in high esteem amongst the people of Arabia; besides, every one wishes to show a Hadji some favour, and is easily induced to pay double the value for any article offered. This small trade is carried on between the easternmost point of Islamitic Asia to the Galata bridge of Constantinople. Amongst the crowd of that famous capital one often sees a Tartar, whose features contrast as strangely with the rest of the population as the colours of the thin silk kerchief differ from those of our European manufacture. Fine ladies seldom become purchasers of such articles, but old matrons are frequently seen, inspired by feelings of piety, paying a good price for them, pressing them repeatedly to their faces and forehead while repeating a loud "*Allahum u Sella,*" and continuing their walk.

That the successful sale of the exported articles leads to the importation of similar merchandize needs no confirmation. No Hadji leaves the holy places without making some purchases. At Mekka he lays in a stock of scents, dates, rosaries and combs, but especially water from the sacred well called Zemzem.* In Jamba and Djedda are bought European goods; these go by the name of Mali Istambul—"Stamboul

---

* Zemzem is the name of a famous well on the road, of miraculous power, the water of which is exported in small vessels to all Islamite countries, as a single drop of it taken just at the moment of death frees from 500 years of purgatory. The origin of the well is ascribed to Ismail, who, after being left behind by Hagar, stamped his little foot and made the well spring up.

Goods;" as the unbelieving Franks must not obtain credit for anything, and they consist of penknives, scissors, needles, thimbles, &c. Aleppo and Damascus enjoy the reputation of supplying the best misvak, a fibrous root, used as tooth brushes by all pious Moslems. In Bagdad are bought a hirka, made of camel's hair, and of superior quality at this place, as it is this kind of garment which the Prophet is said to have worn next his skin. Finally, in Persia, ink, powder and pens made of canes are purchased. In Central Asia all these articles are great curiosities, and they are paid for handsomely, partly from necessity, partly from religious motives.

Generally speaking a caravan of Hadjis, I mean one whose character has been well inquired into, are the best travelling companions one can have in Central Asia, or rather in the whole of the east, provided one can manage to agree with them. With regard to the travelling necessaries the Hadji is well supplied, and it was always surprising to me to see how a man who had only one poor donkey he could call his own, could make a display of a separate tea-service* (à la Tartar,) Pilou-apparatus, and carpet when arrived at the station at which we halted. Nobody is more clever than a Hadji in negotiating, be the people he has to deal with believers or unbelievers, nomads or agricultural tribes.

---

* The tea service consists of a can-like vessel made of copper, and is, next to the Koran, the most indispensable *vade mecum* of every travelling Tartar. Even the poorest beggar carries it, suspended by the handle, about with him.

A Hadji may be converted into anything, he being thoroughly penetrated by the principle "*Si fueris Romae.*" Instead of being cast down and gloomy, as his ragged exterior would lead us to suppose, he is of a merry disposition, and during the long marches the greatest saint and miracle-worker occasionally indulges in a profane joke. The comicality of these generally serious faces has often made me forget the privations which I was myself undergoing.

CHAPTER II.

RECOLLECTIONS OF MY DERVISH LIFE.

On the evening of the 27th of March, 1863, my excellent friend, the Turkish ambassador in Teheran, gave me a farewell supper, at which all declared—to inspire me, of course with fear, and divert me from my adventurous undertaking,—that I was for the last time in my life to enjoy European food in the European manner. The handsome dining room at the residence of the ambassador was brilliantly lighted, the choicest viands were served, and the choicest wines handed round; for the intention was clear,—to give me a strong dose of reminiscences of European comforts on the difficult expedition before me. My friends were for ever scrutinizing my features, to discover whether my outward appearance might not betray some trace of inward excitement. But they were very much mistaken. I had ensconced myself comfortably in the velvet arm chair, which had been brought thither from the distant land of the Franks; the wine had tinged my face with the same colour as the fez which covered my head. A pious dervish and wine—what a frightful antithesis! To-night, however, I must transgress, the penance will be a long one, whether or no. . . . .

Twenty-four hours later, in the evening of the 28th of March, I was in the midst of my company of beggars on the road to Lar, in a half-dilapidated mud hut, called Dagaru. The rain was pouring in torrents. We had been pretty well wetted through during our day's march, so that all were anxious for shelter and a dry roof; and, the space being narrow, fate brought me the very first evening into the closest contact with my travelling companions. Their tattered garments, never very sweet-scented, and now thoroughly soaked with the rain, gave out the strangest evaporations; and no wonder if, under such circumstances, I had no great desire to take my share out of the large wooden bowl, from which the starved Hadjis, splashing about with their fists, were eating their supper. Moreover, hunger tormented me less than fatigue and my wet, ragged garments, to which I was as yet unaccustomed. Rolled up like a ball, I tried to get to sleep; but this also was impossible, packed together as we were in such close quarters. Now I felt the hand, now the head of one of my neighbours, falling upon me; then my opposite companion stretched out his foot, to scratch me behind the ears. It required the patience of Job to defend myself against these unpleasant civilities; and yet I might have had some sleep, but for the loud snoring of the Tartars, and above all the loud moaning of a

Persian muleteer, who was sadly troubled with the gout.

Finding that all endeavours to close my eyes remained unsuccessful, I rose and sat upright in the midst of this mass of people, who were lying about in the most utter confusion. The rain kept falling, and, as I looked out into the dark and gloomy night, my thoughts returned to the difference in my position only twenty-four hours before, and the sumptuous farewell supper at the splendid Turkish embassy. The whole scene appeared to me not unlike a dramatic representation of "King and Beggar," in which I acted the chief part. The bitter feeling of reality, however, made little impression. I myself was the author of this sudden metamorphosis, and I had prepared my fate for myself.

The hard task of self-control lasted but a few days. As far as all outward peculiarities were concerned, I soon became familiar with the habitual as well as physical attributes of dervishism, such as dirt, &c. I gave my better garments, which I had brought with me from Teheran, to a weak and sickly Hadji, an act of kindness which gained all hearts. My new uniform consisted of a felt jacket, which I wore next my skin without any shirt, and of a *djubbe* (upper garment),[*]

---

[*] It is called *Hirkai dervishan* (the dervish cloak), which even those dervishes that are most comfortably off are obliged to wear over their otherwise good garments. It is the symbol of poverty, and is often composed of countless small pieces of new patchwork, cut round the edge in points of unequal length; and, while it is sewn together on the outside with thick packing thread

composed of innumerable pieces of stuff, and fastened with a cord round the loins. My feet were enveloped in rags, and an immense turban covered my head, serving as a parasol by day and pillow by night. I had also, in conformity with the rest of the Hadjis, hung round me a voluminous Koran in a bag, which resembled a cartridge pouch; and, viewing myself thus, "*en pleine parade*," I had reason proudly to exclaim: " Yes, indeed, I am born a beggar!"

The outer or material part of the *incognito* was thus easily assumed, but the moral part presented more serious difficulties than I expected. Although I had had the opportunity, for some years past, of studying the contrast between European and Asiatic modes of life, and the critical position in which I found myself made it incumbent upon me ever to be strictly on my guard, nevertheless, I could not avoid committing many glaring mistakes. The difference between Eastern and Western society does not consist merely in language, physiognomy, and dress. We Europeans eat, drink, sleep, sit, and stand, nay, I feel inclined to say, laugh, weep, sigh, and gesticulate otherwise than Eastern people. These things are visible trifles, but in reality difficult ones, and yet they are as nothing when compared with the effort required to disguise one's feelings. When travelling, people are naturally of a more eager

and large stitches, the lining often consists of silk or some other valuable material. It is the *ne plus ultra* of hypocrisy; but long before the Romans the wise men of the East have said, *Mundus vult decipi—ergo decipiatur.*

and excitable temperament than in everyday life, and therefore it costs the European an unspeakable effort to conceal his curiosity, admiration, or any kind of emotion, when brought into intercourse with the indolent orientals, who are for ever indifferent to all and everything around them. Besides, the object of my travelling was merely to travel, whilst that of my friends was to reach their distant homes. My individual person excited their interest only during the first moments of our acquaintance, while to me they were each a continual study; and it certainly can never have entered the head of any one of them that, whenever we laughed and joked most intimately together my mind would just then be doubly occupied. No one but he who is practically acquainted with the East, can have any idea of the difficulty of entering into all these marked differences. I had been pretty well schooled by a four years' residence at Constantinople; yet there I played merely the part of an amateur, whilst here I dared not deviate even a hair's breadth from reality. Nay, I will make no secret of the fact, that during the first few days the struggle, though short, was severe, and that repentance and remorse seized me at every fresh difficulty. However, my mind, being stimulated by vanity, was in that state of excitement when everything had to give way before the irresistible impulse of its ardour; and, supported in its triumph by a sound constitution, it was enabled to bear easily whatever might happen.

I shudder even now when I think back of the fatigue I underwent during the first few days, and how much I suffered from the wet and cold, the uncleanliness—which makes one's hair stand on end—and the never-ending, harassing worry with the fanatic Shiites, during our long and tedious day-marches in Mazendran, a part of the world of historical reputation for its bad roads. Sometimes it rained from early in the morning until late in the evening, and, whilst not a thread of my tattered garments remained dry, I was moreover obliged to wade for hours knee-deep in mud. The narrow mountain-path has become hollow by the wear of centuries, and in many places it resembles a muddy brook, winding along between huge fragments of pointed rock that have fallen from the heights above. It is a sheer impossibility to remain in the saddle; and, in order to avoid danger, the best course is to tread slowly and cautiously, sounding the hollows with one's foot. No one will doubt that, under such circumstances, we arrived at the station at nightfall thoroughly exhausted and fatigued. Fire and shelter are the chief objects of desire, for which the eye looks longingly around. They both exist in Mazendran; but we, the Sunnitic beggars, had preferred, for the sake of quiet, to pass the night undisturbed and far from any human dwelling. A fire was kindled, to dry ourselves and our clothes, when the elder of our Tartar fellow-travellers observed, that such a proceeding would be prejudicial to health; and, indeed, they always preferred to dry themselves in another and more singular fashion. It is well known that, throughout the East, horse dung is dried and then ground into powder, to serve as stabling for the horses by night. During the day it is exposed to the sun, either spread out or made into conical-shaped heaps; and I was not a little astonished to see how my companions, divesting themselves entirely of their apparel, buried their soaked bodies up to the neck in such like *poudre de santé*. I need not add, that contact with this *poudre*, so well known as strong and stinging, cannot be very agreeable; but its effects are only felt during the first quarter of an hour, and I can assert, from my subsequent personal experience, that such a bed induces a most sweet and refreshing sleep, however it may offend the European eye and sense of refinement.

In spite of the drawbacks, I should have felt quite contented with my lot had it not been that, besides these fatigues common to all, an extra share was allotted to me, being a stranger in the company. As such, it was my duty to affect the qualities of modesty and devotion, to show myself not only friendly, but submissive, to all; and to endeavour to conciliate the affection of old and young, by professing an obliging disposition, and a readiness to perform any kind of small service. At first these offers were declined by most of them, since they did not wish to offend in me the character of "efendi," having made my acquaintance as such. However, it was my duty in no case to yield, but on the contrary, to strive continually to make myself useful to one or the other. Besides the minor services I performed on the march, I had to try to be helpful to every one at the station, either by preparing tea and baking bread, or by looking after the riding horses, or by packing and unpacking. Some of my companions were obliging to me in return for my attention, but others, who soon had forgotten my former position, treated me like an old fellow-traveller. Services were demanded and performed without the smallest ceremony; and I could not help laughing heartily, when a Hadji from Khokand once coolly handed me his shirt for me to free it from the many "uninvited guests," he being fully occupied in like manner on another part of his costume.

It was to be foreseen that in this way an *entente cordiale* would speedily ripen between us. The more I accommodated myself to my present position, forgetting the past, the quicker also disappeared the barrier between me and the other Hadjis. The society of others exercises a powerful influence upon us, uniting as it does the most opposite elements; and after I had lived for a whole month as dervish, all appeared to me not only natural and endurable, but the charm of novelty in the life around me had actually effaced Teheran, Stamboul, and Europe, from my memory; and the continual excitement in which I lived had produced in me a state of mind which was extraordinary, it is true, but never disagreeable.

One feeling alone disquieted me: this was the fear of discovery, or, rather, of its consequences,—the terrible death of torture which Tartar cruelty and offended Mahometan fanaticism would have invented for my punishment. Already during the first days of my residence with the Turkomans I became aware that, in assuming my incognito, I was playing a dangerous game; and, but for the unlimited confidence I placed in the fidelity of my companions, and my own preparations, this spectre would have haunted me every moment of my existence. During the greater part of the day, society, occupation, and events of various interest prevented the intrusion of these suspicions; but at night, when everything around was hushed in silence, and I sat alone in a solitary corner of my tent, or in the waste and barren desert, I became absorbed in thought. Fear appeared before me in its blackest guise and most terrible aspect; nor would it leave me for a long, long time, however much I attempted to dispel it by sophistry or light-heartedness. Oh, this terrible Megæra! How she tormented me, how she tortured me, at those very moments when, seeking repose, I was about to lose myself in contemplation on the grandeur of nature and the wonderful constitution of man. In the long struggle between us, fear was finally subdued; but it is this very struggle, which I now blush to remember; for it is marvellous what efforts are required to grow familiar with the constant and visible prospect of death, and how great the anxiety in seeing only a doubtful foundation for the hope of one's further existence.

No one, I am sure, will blame me for acting with precaution, nay, at first, with scrupulous precaution; but often it degenerated into ridiculous extremes. I was, for instance, conscious of my habit of gesticulating with the hands when speaking,—a habit peculiar to many Europeans, but strictly forbidden in Central Asia;—and, fearing lest I might commit this mistake, I adopted a coercive remedy. I pretended to suffer from pains in the arms, and strapping them down to the body, they soon lost the habit of involuntary movement. In like manner I seldom ventured to make a hearty meal late in the evening, for fear of being troubled with heavy dreams, which might cause me to speak some foreign, European language. I laugh now at my pusillanimity, for I might have remembered that the Tartars, being unacquainted with European languages, would not have noticed it; and yet I rather bore in mind the words of my companions, who observed one morning with great *naïveté*, that my snoring sounded differently from that of the Turkestanis, whereupon another interrupted and informed him: "Yes; thus people snore in Constantinople."

It may be objected, that as so many of my actions might cause remark or offence when in company with others, I must at all events have shaken off this restraint when alone. But alas! Even then I was the slave of precaution; and is it not striking, or rather ridiculous, that at night, when in the boundless desert and at a considerable distance from the caravan, I did not venture to eat the unleavened bread, mixed up with ashes and sand, or take a draught of stinking water without accompanying it with the customary Mahometan formula of blessing! I might have thought to myself, no one sees you, all around are asleep; but no! the distant sand hills appeared to me like so many spies, who were watching whether I was saying the Bismillah, and whether I had broken the bread in the proper ritualistic manner. Thus it happened when in Khiva, that, when sleeping alone in a dark cell, bolted and barred, I started up from my couch at the call to prayer, and began the troublesome labour of the thirteen Rikaat. When at the sixth or eighth, I had a great mind to leave off, thinking I was safely out of sight. But no! it struck me, that perhaps the eyes of a spy might be watching me through the crevice in the door, and conscientiously I performed my unpleasant duty.

Only time, the universal panacæa, could remedy this evil. Although my moral sufferings were considerably more painful than the physical ones, time and habit came to my aid, and gained me here also the victory, and after having lived happily through four months, my mind had grown as hardened to any fear or terror as my body to dirt and uncleanliness. The epoch of indifference succeeded, and with it I began to feel the true charms of my adventure. I was attracted above all by the unlimited freedom of our life as vagrants, the total absence of trouble as to food and clothing, the gratuitous manner in which the dervish had everything provided for him, and, in addition, the mental superiority which he exercises over the people at large. No wonder, then, that I lost no opportunity in amply profiting by the advantages of my position. My companions admitted that I possessed eminent talents for the life of a dervish, and whenever the question rose how to get money from hard-hearted villagers, or to beg and collect a larger store of victuals, I was always entrusted with that part of the business. I one day brilliantly justified the confidence thus placed in me, in an encampment of Tchandor Turkomans. These, the wildest of all nomad people, had the reputation of being exceedingly wicked, and Hadjis, Tshans and Dervishes habitually avoided going near their tents. Having been told of this I set out on my way, accompanied by three companions who were known as famous singers, and taking with me a goodly store of holy dust, Zemzem water, tooth-picks, combs and the like gifts, presented by pilgrims. Some received me rather coldly, but yet the son of the desert, however wild he may be, cannot resist the words or the mimics of a dervish's strategy, and not only did I receive ample presents in the shape of wheat, rice, cheese and pieces of felt, but I succeeded in persuading one of the men to load his own ass with this harvest, and take it to our astonished caravan.

Success leads to boldness. No wonder, then, that after several successful expeditions, I assumed a demeanour in which many will trace a certain degree of impudence. And, indeed, I can hardly refute this accusation entirely, but how was I to have done otherwise? No European can realize to himself what it is to stand, a disguised Frenghi, (this word of terror to orientals,) face to face with such a tyrant as the Khan of Khiva, and to have to bestow upon him the customary benediction. If this man were to discover the dangerous trick, this man with the sallow face and sinister look, as he sits there surrounded by his satellites—such an idea is only endurable to a mind steeled to the highest pitch of resolution. At my first audience I appeared really with a step so firm and gesture so bold, as if my presence were to bestow felicity upon the Khan. All looked at me with astonishment, for submissiveness is befitting to the pious and saints. However, they thought such was the custom in Turkey, and I heard no remark made about it.

Such bold measures, however, were seldom necessary, and, in its ordinary routine, the life of a dervish has often given me moments of the greatest happiness. Without feeling any inclination to imitate the Russian Count D——, who, wearied of the artificial life of Europeans, withdrew into one of the valleys of Kashmir, turning beggar-dervish, I must confess that a peculiar feeling of enjoyment came over me when, basking in the warm rays of the autumnal sun, either in some ruin or other solitary spot, I could, in true oriental manner, absorb myself in vacant reflection. It is inexpressibly pleasurable to be rocked in the soft cradle of oriental repose and indifference, when one is without money or profession, free from care and excitement. To us Europeans such an enjoyment of course can only be of very short duration, for if our thoughts turn at such moments toward the distant, ever-active, and stirring west, the great contrast between these two worlds must at once strike the eye, and instinctively we feel attracted towards the latter. European activity and Asiatic repose are the two great subjects which occupy the mind, but we have only to cast our look upon the ruins scattered around us to see which of the two follows the right philosophy of life. Here everything is on the road to ruin and servitude, there everything leads to prosperity and the sovereignty of the world.

These varied scenes of life, in which I moved during my incognito, were far from being devoid of attractions, as many a prejudiced European might imagine, although they naturally could fascinate but for a time. I was truly frightened one day, when the Khan of Khiva proposed to me seriously to marry and settle in Khiva, since persons of such extensive travelling as myself were far from disagreeable to him. The idea of spending my whole life in Turkestan, with an Œzbeg wife for my partner, was horrible, and I should certainly have thrown up my plans if I had been obliged to accept the offer; but, as it is, I shall certainly never repent having spent a few months in an adventure which ended happily. I say never, for even the remembrance of all I experienced is indescribably sweet, and even now, when already more than three years have elapsed since my return, I find every circumstance as fresh in my memory, the whole scene as near and vivid, as if I had arrived with my caravan only last night, and were obliged to start off again on the morrow, and load my ass for the journey; as often as I think back on my fellow-travellers, the most pleasant feelings are re-awakened in remembrance of that intimate and hearty friendship which existed between us. We chatted, laughed, and bantered with each other on our long day's march, as if we could not wish for a more enjoyable existence; it was above all my merry humour which greatly pleased them, and my jokes and puns afforded to them an endless source of amusement when we were alone, for in public we all of us wore the long, stony faces suited to the gravity of our character as holy men. What would they say if they could see me now in the midst of so many unbelievers, and dressed in a garment so ridiculous in their eyes, the forked garment, as they designate European trousers?—*me*, in whom they and the rest of the world believed to see a true specimen of a western Mahometan Mollah! I must confess that although the pleasant episodes of my incognito are even now frequently the cause of cheerful moments of recollection, the sad hours of suffering and extremity of danger loom like black clouds on the horizon of the present. Their gloomy shadows remind me vividly of past terrors, and even now, whenever I start up in my sleep, haunted by oppressive dreams, it was very often His Majesty, the Khan of Bokhara, or the frightful tortures of thirst, or a fanatic group of Mollahs, who, hastening hither from Central Asia on the wings of Morpheus, honoured me with a visit. How happy do I feel on awaking, to find myself in Europe, in my dear native country, in my peaceful home!

I have often been in critical, nay, extremely critical situations, but on the whole only a few episodes have left behind on me such an impression as never will be effaced, and which, from being associated with the most imminent danger to my life, will never be forgotten by me as long as I live.

I.

The evening in the Khalata desert, when, after having endured for two days the torments of thirst, I felt, with the last drop of water, my vital energies gradually ebbing away. Around me were lying many of my fellow-travellers, suffering, probably, as acutely as myself, to judge from their wild, haggard looks, and rigid features. Raising my heavy head with the greatest effort, I met the glance of those near me. They all seemed to be looking at me with expressions of bitter resentment, for during the afternoon I had heard the old ascetic, Kari Messud, repeat several times, "We are, alas! the propitiatory victims for some great evil-doer who is amongst us in our caravan." Possibly not one of them referred to me, but I felt, nevertheless, full of anxiety. Meanwhile the hour of evening prayer was approaching. Only a few could join in it. The sun was fast setting, and, as the last rays lit up the unhappy group of sufferers in that vast desert, I could not help casting a look towards the spot, where from the horizon he sent his last beams towards me,—that spot, which we call the west, the beloved west, which I had little hope to live to see the next morning again; and with unspeakable sadness I clung to the word 'west;' my half-exhausted senses revived anew, for with the word returned the thought of Europe, of my beloved home, my early departure from this world, the hard struggles of my past life, the wreck of all my aspirations, of all my pleasant hopes. My heart nearly broke with the burden of this great sorrow; I longed to weep, but could not. This moment is one of imperishable memory; the terror of that scene has impressed itself indelibly on my mind, and whenever my thoughts turn towards the Khalata desert it will rise and haunt me like a phantom.

II.

The next occasion was during my audience with the emir of Bokhara, in the palace of Samarkand. This prince, who had been represented to me as a person of doubtful character, had been severely examining my countenance as I sat by his side, in order to discover in me a Frenghi in disguise. The readers of my travels are already acquainted with a part of the conversation that took place between us. I hoped to gain him over to our interests, but it cost me a giant's effort not to betray by my countenance, and especially my eyes, the excitement within me; and, although I shook and trembled in every nerve, I was obliged to suppress even the slightest symptom of fear. An old adept in the part I played, I effectually succeeded in preventing a blush, or any change of colour, but I did not feel confident about the result. Let the reader realise my position, when the emir, after an audience of a quarter of an hour, called to him one of his servants, cautiously whispered something in his ear, and, motioning to me with a serious expression of countenance, ordered me to follow his attendant.

I rose quickly from my seat. The servant led me through room after room, and court after court, whilst the uncertainty of my fate filled me with alarm; and, as oppression of heart breeds none other but images of terror, I fancied that this ominous walk was leading me to the torture-chamber, and to that dreadful death which so often had presented itself to my imagination. After some time we came to a dark room, where my guide ordered me to sit down and wait for his return. I remained standing, but in what state of mind my

readers may readily imagine. Perhaps I should have felt less terror could I only have known what my death was to be, but this uncertainty was like the torture of hell, and I shall never forget it as long as I live. With a feverish impatience I counted the minutes, until the door should open again. . . . .
A few more seconds of torture and the servant appeared. I fixed my eyes upon him, and perceived by the light that entered through the doorway that he did not bring with him the dreaded instruments of the executioner, but carried under his arm, instead, a carefully folded-up bundle. This contained a dress of honour, presented to me by the emir, as well as the 'viaticum' for my long pilgrim road.

III.

The third instance occurred to me when waiting for the arrival of the Herat caravan on the banks of the Oxus, during the hot days of August, in the company of the Lebab Turkomans. I dwelt in the court of a deserted mosque, and in the evenings the Turkomans usually brought with them one of their collections of songs or ballads, from which I had to read to them aloud, and it gave me especial pleasure to witness the undivided attention with which they listened to the deeds of some popular hero, while the silence of the night air around us was only broken by the hollow murmur of the rolling waters of the Oxus. One evening our reading lasted till near midnight. I felt rather tired, and, unmindful of the advice I had often received, not to sleep in the immediate proximity of ruined buildings, I stretched myself out beside a wall, and soon fell sound asleep. After about an hour I was suddenly awakened by an indescribably violent pain in my foot, and jumping up and screaming aloud, I felt as if hundreds of poisoned needles were shooting through my leg, and concentrating in one small point near the big toe of my right foot. My screams awakened the eldest of the Turkomans, who slept near me, and without questioning me, he exclaimed, "Poor Hadji, a scorpion has bitten thee, and that during the unlucky period of the Saratan (the dog days!) May God help thee!" With these words he seized my foot, and bound it up round the ancle with such violence as if he were going to cut it in two, then searching in all haste with his lips for the wounded spot, he sucked with such force that I felt it all through my body. Another soon took his place, and two more bandages having been applied they left me with these words of comfort, that, if it be the will of Allah, between now and the hour of the next morning prayer, it would be seen whether I should be released from pain, or freed from the follies of this world of vanity.

Although I felt completely maddened by the itching, pricking and burning, which kept increasing more and more in violence, yet I remembered the legend of the scorpions of Belkh, well known for their venomous nature even in ancient times. The reasonable apprehension of death rendered the pain still more unbearable, and that, after many hours of suffering, I really did surrender all hopes of recovery, was shown by the fact that, forgetting my incognito, I began to pour out my lament in expressions and sounds which, as the Tartars afterwards told me, appeared to them extremely droll, since they are in the habit of using them when shouting for joy. It is remarkable that the pain spread in a few minutes from the toe to the top of the head, but only on the right side, and kept flowing up and down me like a stream of fire. No words can describe the torment I had to undergo the hour after midnight. Loathing any longer to live, I was about to dash my head to pieces by beating it upon the ground, but my companions observed my intention and tied me fast to a tree. Thus I lay for hours, half fainting, whilst the cold sweat of death was running down me, and my eyes turned fixedly towards the stars. The Pleiades were gradually sinking in the west, and whilst awaiting in perfect consciousness the voice that calls to prayer, or rather the break of morning, a gentle sleep fell upon me, from which I was soon roused by the monotonous la illah il Allah.

No sooner was I fully awake when I was sensible of a faint diminution of the pain. The pricking and burning disappeared more and more, in the same way as it had come, and the sun had not yet risen a lance's height over the horizon when I was able, though weak and exhausted, to rise to my feet. My companions assured me that the devil, having entered my body through the bite of the scorpion, had been scared away by the morning prayer, a fact I dared not of course discredit. But that terrible night will for ever remain engraven on my memory.

It is these three events which were the critical moments in my adventures in Central Asia. As to the rest, the many curious eyes that scrutinised me, the various suspicions I laboured under, as well as the unspeakable fatigues of travelling in the guise of a beggar, all these privations and obstacles have left behind but few sad remembrances. The fascinations in seeing those strange countries, for which my eyes were longing from the earliest days of my youth, possessed in itself a charm at once animating and invigorating, for, except in the few cases just mentioned, I felt always particularly cheerful and happy. This much is certain, that I often miss, in my present civilised European life, the bodily and mental activity of those days, and who knows but that I may, in after years, wish that time to return, when, enveloped in tatters and without shelter, but vigorous and high in spirits, I wandered through the steppes of Central Asia.

CHAPTER III.

FROM MY JOURNAL.

AMONGST THE TURKOMANS.

13th April.

STRUCK with astonishment and surprise at the strange, social relations, amongst which I was to-day living for the first time, I was sitting in the early morning hours upon one and the same carpet with Khandjan, my hospitable host, listening with eager attention to his descriptions of Turkoman life and manners. He was one of the most influential chiefs amongst the nomads, by nature an upright man, and anxious to make me acquainted with the faults as well as the merits of his countrymen; for being firmly convinced of my Turkish and semi-official character, he hoped to gain, through my position with the Sultan, on whom the whole Sunnitish world relies, assistance against Russians and Persians. He spoke with zeal, without betraying it outwardly; and after having given me his first lesson he rose, to show me, as he said, his house and court-yard, or in our phraseology, to make me acquainted with the ladies of the family. This is a very especial mark of distinction among Asiatic nations; however, a man supposed to be an agent of the Sultan, well deserves such an attention; and accordingly I endeavoured, by my attitude in sitting, my whole mien and carriage, to show myself worthy of it.

After a few minutes I heard a strange clattering and clinking, the curtain of the tent was raised, and there entered a whole crowd of women, girls and children, who, headed by a corpulent and tolerably old matron, walked towards the place where I was sitting. They were evidently as much struck as myself by the scene; looking timidly around, the young women cast down their eyes, whilst the children clung with evident signs of fear to the clothes of their parents. Khandjan introduced the matron to me as his mother. She was about sixty years old, in the primitive costume of a long, red silk garment, and wearing across her chest, to the right and left, several large as well as small silver sheaths, in which as many talismans of great virtue were preserved; some even were inlaid with precious stones, as were also a considerable number of armlets, necklaces and anklets,—the heirlooms of the family through several generations, and, to judge from their appearance, bearing the traces of high antiquity. The other women and children were likewise arrayed in ornaments of a similar kind, varying, however, with the wearer's rank and position in the favour of their lord and master. The clothes themselves are often torn and dirty, and are looked upon as quite a matter of secondary importance; but a Turkoman lady is not fashionably dressed, unless she carries about her person one or two pounds of silver in ornaments.

The old lady was the first to extend her wrinkled hands for the customary greeting, the others followed, and, after the young girls and children had embraced me,—for such is the rule of the *bon ton*,—all squatted down around me in a semicircle and began to question me about my health, welfare, and happy arrival. Each one addressed me three or four times on the same subject. I had to return just as many answers; and not in Europe alone does it happen that a circle of ladies may perplex and embarrass an inexperienced Solomon: even in the desert of Central Asia the like may occur. Everywhere among the nomad people of the Mahomedan East the women lose more and more their moral and physical attributes, the older they grow. During my first interview I was obliged to reply to the most delicate questions of the younger portion; whilst the elder ones conversed on religion, politics, and the domestic relations of the neighbouring tribes. I had to guard against exhibiting surprise at the manner of either of them; the younger women I succeeded in inspiring with awe for my strict virtue as a Mollah, and the elderly ones received an ample share of blessings. Several men, neighbours and relatives, arrived during this visit, but they caused no disturbance or discomposure among the ladies, who enjoy, as I have often had the opportunity of observing, a certain respect, although they are exclusively the working class of the community. And indeed the Turkoman women deserve such, for nowhere in the East have I met with their equals in exemplary virtue, devotion to their families, and indefatigable industry.

This visit lasted nearly an hour, and towards the end of it I had to write several talismans, in return for which the women presented me with sundry small gifts, their own handwork. The old lady came several times afterwards to visit me; once I even accompanied her to the tumulus which is raised over the remains of her husband, in order to pray for the soul of the departed. The good understanding between us two struck even the nomads: however, at present the reason for it is sufficiently clear to me. In the first instance a certain foreign look in my appearance, as well as the halo of piety which surrounded me, had attracted her, at the same time that I was ever ready to lend a patient ear to her conversations; listening attentively to her discourses on the short-comings of the Persian female slaves in her household, on the want of skill in the women of the present day, in weaving carpets, preparing felt, &c., interspersing now and then an observation of my own, as if I had been accustomed to these subjects from my youth and took an especial interest in all the details of a nomad household.

And, after all, this is the philosophy of life that should guide a traveller everywhere, if he wishes to learn anything. Here, for instance, a pliant demeanour proved of considerable use, since the affection of the old matron towards me contributed in a great measure to render my residence amongst the Turkomans agreeable,—a people, amongst whom not even an Asiatic stranger can move freely, still less an European.

16th April.

I entered the tent of Khandjan after the morning prayer and found here a whole company, listening with the greatest attention to the narrative of a young Turkoman, who was covered with dust and dirt, and whose face bore evident traces of excitement and severe hardships. He was describing in a low voice, but in lively colours, a maurading excursion against the Persians of the evening before, in which he had taken part. Whilst he was speaking, the women, servants and slaves (what must have been the thoughts of these latter), squatted down around the circle of listeners, and many a curse was hurled at the slaves, the clanking of the chains on their feet interrupting for a time the general quiet. It struck me as remarkable, that, in proportion as the speaker warmed in describing the obstinate resistance of the unfortunate people, who were fallen on unawares, the indignation of the audience increased at the audacity of the Persians, not to have at once quietly submitted to being plundered.

No sooner was the narration of this great feat of arms at an end when all rose to their feet to have a look at the spoils, the sight of which excites in the

Turkoman's breast a mixed feeling of envy and pleasure. I followed them likewise, and a terrible picture presented itself to my eyes. Lying down in the middle of the tent were two Persians, looking deadly pale and covered with clotted blood, dirt and dust. A man was busily engaged in putting their broken limbs into fetters, when one of them gave a loud, wild shriek, the rings of the chains being too small for him. The cruel Turkoman was about to fasten them forcibly round his ancles. In a corner sat two young children on the ground, pale and trembling; and looking with sorrowful eyes towards the tortured Persian. The unhappy man was their father; they longed to weep, but dared not;—one look of the robber, at whom they stole a glance now and then, with their teeth chattering, was sufficient to suppress their tears. In another corner a girl, from fifteen to sixteen years old, was crouching, her hair dishevelled and in confusion, her garments torn and almost entirely covered with blood. She groaned and sobbed, covering her face with her hands. Some Turkoman woman, moved either by compassion or curiosity, asked her what ailed her, and where she was wounded. "I am not wounded," she exclaimed, in a plaintive voice, deeply touching. "This blood is the blood of my mother, my only one, and the best and kindest of mothers. Oh! ana djan, ana djan (dear mother)!" Thus she lamented, striking her head against the trellised woodwork of the tent, so that it almost tumbled down. They offered her a draught of water, and her tongue became loosened, and she told them how she (of course a valuable prize) had been lifted into the saddle beside the robber, but that her mother, tied to the stirrups, had been obliged to run along on foot. After an hour's running in this manner, she grew so tired that she sank down exhausted every moment. The Turkoman tried to increase her strength by lashing her with his whip, but this was of no avail; and as he did not want to remain behind from his troop he grew in a rage, drew his sword, and in a second struck off her head. The blood spirting up, had covered the daughter, horseman and horse; and, looking at the red spots upon her clothes, the poor girl wept loud and bitterly.

Whilst this was going on in the interior of the tent, outside the various members of the robbers' family were busy inspecting the booty he had brought home. The elder women seized greedily upon one or another utensil for domestic use, whilst the children, who were jumping about merrily, were trying on the different garments,—now one, now another, and producing shouts of laughter.

Here all was triumph and merriment; not far from it a picture of the deepest grief and misery. And yet no one is struck by the contrast; every one thinks it very natural that the Turkoman should enrich himself with robbery and pillage.

And these terrible social relations exist within scarcely a fortnight's distance from Europe, travelling by St. Petersburg, Nishnei Novogorod, and Astrakhan!

18th April.

Eliaskuli, who dwelt in the fourth tent from mine on the banks of the Görgen, was a "retired" Turkoman, who, up to his thirtieth year, had carried on the usual profession of kidnapping and pillaging, and had now retired from business, in order, as he said, to spend the rest of this futile, ridiculous life (fani dünya) here below in the pious exercise of the law; as far as I know, however, it is because several shot wounds of the "hellish" weapons at Ashurada prevented him from carrying on any longer his infamous trade. He was in hopes I might invoke upon his wicked head every blessing of heaven by my prayers, and to this effect he narrated to me, with many details, how the Russians, after having declared a religious war, had once landed here, and attacked and set fire to all the tents that stood on the banks of the Görgen. This religious war was in fact nothing else than that the Russians wanted to release some countrymen of theirs, whom these robbers had carried off prisoners, but the fight lasted more than a whole day. He added, that although the Russians, being too cowardly to come near, shot only from a distance, yet the valiant Gazis (religious combatants) could not resist their devilish arts, that he too received at that time some death wounds, and was a whole day without giving a sign of life, until at last his Pir (spiritual chief) called him back into existence.

This same Eliaskuli offered to accompany me to-day to the Ova of the Ana Khan, who is the chief of the Yarali tribe, and dwells on the upper Görgen, close to the Persian frontier. From curiosity, perhaps, or some other motive, he wished to make my acquaintance. Our road lay for some time along the left bank of the river, but soon we were obliged to make a considerable circuit, in order to avoid the large marshes and morasses. Unacquainted as the people around me were with my motives for travelling, I laid myself open to suspicion, no doubt; but the experience of a few days calmed my fears for the security of my position, and indeed all misgivings vanished, when I saw how the people, whenever we were passing some tent on our route, came towards me with milk, cheese and other presents, asking for my blessing. Thus I rode on in high spirits, troubled at nothing but the heavy Turkoman felt cap, on the top of which in addition several yards of linen were folded round in the shape of a turban, and the heavy musket on my back, which for propriety's sake I was obliged to carry, in spite of my character as Mollah. Eliaskuli sometimes remained behind for full half an hour, but I continued my way alone, meeting now and then a few marauding stragglers, who, returning home empty from some unsuccessful foray, measured me with sinister looks from head to foot. Some saluted me, others only asked, "Whose guest art thou, Mollah?" in order to judge from my personality whether it was feasible to plunder me or not; but no sooner did I reply "Kelte Khandjan Bay," when they rode on in evident displeasure, muttering in their beard an abrupt "Aman bol," (farewell.)

Towards evening we arrived at the tents, together with Khandjan, who, having taken a different road, had joined us on the way. Ana Khan, the patriarchal chief, a man about sixty years of age, was seated on the green slope of a hill, surrounded by his grandchildren and little children, (it is only in the east that one meets with people, thus related to one another, of the same age,) watching them with looks of pleasure, as also the flocks of sheep and herds of camels who were returning home from their rich pasturage. Our reception was short, but friendly. Walking before us, he conducted us into the ready prepared tent, where I was appointed to the seat of honour; the proper conversation, however, not beginning until the very last remnants of the sheep, killed expressly for the occasion, had disappeared from the table. Ana Khan spoke little, but he listened attentively to my description of Turkish life and Russo Turkish relations. The next morning, however, he grew rather more talkative, and he began by treating us with the narrative of an act of hospitality on his part towards an English iltshi (ambassador) on his way to Khiva. I guessed at once that this must have been the mission of Mr. William T. Thomson, who was sent thither by his government to adjust the differences between Persia and the Khan of Khiva. Ana Khan, in describing the arms, trinkets and person of the Frenghi ambassador, laid such particular stress upon the resemblance of his features to mine, that the cause of his curiosity was at once evident, as well as his reason for wishing me to visit him. Looking significantly and with glowing eyes at his countrymen, as if to persuade them of the keenness of his perceptions, he came close up to me, and gently tapping me on the shoulder, said, "Efendi! the Tura (rule) of the Sultan of Rum is held in high honour amongst us; first, he is the prince of all the Sunnites; secondly, Turkomans and Osmanlis are blood-relations, and thou art our honoured guest, although thou hast brought us no presents." In this remark I read much, but inferred still more from it. My incognito, then, as dervish, did not always meet with implicit belief. The majority, however, especially the Mollahs, trusted in me, and single sceptics did not by any means cause me disquiet.

I observed, moreover, that Khandjan did not share the views of Ana Khan, the subject was never again broached, and I enjoyed the full hospitality of the suspicious chieftain.

20th April.

In distant Mergolan, in the Khanat of Khokand, religious zeal recommends the frequent collection of money among the people, to support the high schools at Medina, which town possesses a large number of such institutions. Here, at the fountain-head of Islamism, ardent students crowd together, eager interpreters of the Koran, who, under the protecting Ægis of their pious occupation, are supported in luxurious idleness by all the Mahometan countries far and near. Stipends arrive here from distant Fez and Morocco; the chiefs of the Algerine tribes send their annual gifts; Tunis, Tripolis and Egypt as well as other smaller Mahommedan states, send hither their tribute. Turkey vies with Persia in the support of these pupils. The Tartar, living under Russian protection, the native of India, subject to English dominion, all give freely to the high schools of Medina. And yet all this is not deemed sufficient; even the poor inhabitants of the oasis in Turkestan are asked to contribute their mite.

It was at the time of my travels in Central Asia, that Khodja Buzurk, the much-revered saint in those parts, had collected, no doubt by dint of immense assiduity, 400 ducats for Medina. Mollah Esad, the confidential friend of His Holiness, was commissioned to take the sum to its destination. Although in Central Asia the possession of money, the great source of danger for its possessor, is always kept secret, yet the above-mentioned Mollah made no mystery of the object of his journey, in the hope of enlarging his fund. Bokhara, Khiva and other towns he visited had contributed to increase it, and in the belief of meeting with equal success among the Turkomans, he entered upon his journey through the desert, relying upon his letters of recommendation to several of the nomad learned men.

He reached Gömüshtepe without any mishap, but with the news of his arrival there spread simultaneously that of the contents of his travelling bag. The Turkomans were told at the same time that the money was destined for a pious object, but this did not trouble them. Each man endeavoured to catch him before he became the guest of any one, for until a traveller enjoys the rights of hospitality he is completely unprotected among the nomads; he may be plundered, killed, sold into captivity,—there is no one to call the offender to account. The host alone it is, whose vengeance is dreaded; whosoever is taken under his protection is looked upon as a member of his family, and is tolerably secure from attack.

With these facts our Khokand Mollah must have been acquainted, and nevertheless he trusted to the mere lustre of his religious zeal. One morning, having gone a short distance from the caravan, he was fallen upon by two Turkoman men, and plundered of all his money. No entreaties on his part, no appeal to the holiness of his mission, no threats of terrible and condign punishment, nothing was of any avail; they stripped him even of his clothes, and left him nothing but his old books and papers. Thus he returned to the caravan, stunned and half naked. This happened about a fortnight before my arrival, during which time the delinquents were found out and summoned before the religious tribunal. In my position, as Mollah from Constantinople, I had the good luck to be honoured with a seat in court, and the scene at which I was present, and in which I took an active part, will long remain vivid in my recollection. We, that is to say, the learned men, had assembled in a field, where we were sitting in the open air, forming a semi-circle, and holding large volumes in our hands, surrounded by a great crowd, who were eager with curiosity. The robbers made their appearance accompanied by their families and the chief of their tribe, without betraying the least embarrassment, just as if they had come for the settlement of some honest transaction. When questioned, who has taken the money? the culprit answered in the haughtiest tone, "I have taken it." I felt sure from the very beginning that a restitution of money would never be made. Most of the council having exhausted their talents of rhetoric by endless quotations from the Koran, it was my turn to try and impress the hero, and I did so by pointing out to him the wickedness of his deed. "What wickedness!" the Turkoman exclaimed, "is robbery punished in thy country? This is strange indeed! I should have thought that the Sultan, the Lord of the Universe, was a man of more sense. If robbery is not permitted amongst you, how do thy people live?"

Another Mollah threatened him with the Sheriat (religious precepts,) and depicted in glowing colours the punishments of hell, which the Turkoman had to expect in another world. " What Sheriat? " he replied, " each man his own! Thou, Mollah, possessest laws and precepts in thy tongue, which thou twistest as thou likest, I possess my Sheriat in my good sword, which I brandish whenever my arm commands! " After long and fruitless exhortations, and equally long consultations amongst the grey-beards, our sitting was closed without any success on our part. The Turkoman went away with his money, which he spent in furnishing himself with new weapons, instead of its being sent to Medina towards the support of her students. Mollah Esad returned with a sad heart to Khokand, having learnt from bitter experience that the Turkomans, although calling themselves orthodox, are the blackest Kafirs on the face of the earth.

6th May.

Oraz Djan, a young, daring and wild looking Turkoman, of about eighteen years old, who had taken part in marauding excursions ever since he was twelve, was a daily guest in our tent at Etrek, in order to listen to the Pir (spiritual chief) of the kidnapping robbers, in his discourses on religion and moral philosophy. It happened one day, that Omer Akhond, a Mollah from the neighbourhood, was present, a man celebrated for his great knowledge, and still better known as the owner of a particularly excellent horse. The animal was spoken of, and every one was loud in the praise of its high qualities, when young Oraz, catching fire on hearing this, called out half in earnest, half in joke, " Akhond, I will give thee three asses and a Persian for thy horse. It is a pity that it should rest in the stable, whilst the Persians so freely wander in their fields. But, if thou dost not consent, then mark my words, in a few days it will be stolen from thee!" The Mollah and Pir rebuked him severely, but he laughed aloud wildly, and the conversation continued as before.

Scarcely four days had passed when the Mollah entered our tent one morning with tears in his eyes, and looking very sad. "My horse has been stolen from me," he exclaimed with a sigh, "thou alone, Kulkhan, canst restore it to me. Let me entreat thee, by the love of the Tshiharyar (the four first chiefs,) do thy utmost!" "This is the work of the Haramzade (Bastard) Oraz," muttered Kulkhan, "you will see, I shall tear his black soul from out of his dirty body."

At the time of evening prayer our amiable Oraz was, as usual, among the rest of our orthodox friends, who assembled on the terrace-like height, where stands the mosque of the desert, and certainly no one would have guessed, from his devotional expression at his prayers, that this very day he had been robbing a father of the church. When after the Namaz all formed the customary circle (Khalka,) Oraz did not fail-to come. Kulkhan at once addressed him with, "Young fellow! The horse of the Mollah has been stolen, thou knowest where it is; to-morrow morning he must be again in his stable, do you hear me?" This address caused the young robber not the least embarrassment. Playing with one hand in the sand, and with the other pushing on one side his heavy fur hat, he replied, "I have the horse, but I shall not return it; he who wants it must fetch it." These words, I thought, would have roused the indignation of every one present, but not a trace of it was seen in the features of one of the company. Kulkhan went on speaking to him in his former quiet tone of voice, but the robber insisted on refusing to restore the horse, and when some of the grey-beards began to use threats, he, too, caught fire, and having turned to his spiritual chief with "Hast thou done better with the mare of the Hadji?" rose and left the company; and for some time was heard singing aloud the refrain of the poem Körogli, in the still evening air, thus proving sufficiently his joy at the victory he had gained.

A considerable time was spent in consultation after he was gone. No one ventured to attack him, since his tribe, according to custom, would have taken him under their protection, in spite of his abominable conduct, and they were too powerful to risk an attack. Spiritual aid, therefore, had to be called in, and that it should have taken immediate effect is not to be marvelled at.

According to the *Deb* no greater punishment can befal a living man, than to be accused before the shade of his departed father or ancestor. This is done by planting a lance upon the top of the grave, and fastening to it a couple of blood-stained rags, if murder has been committed, and for any other crime a broken bow. Such an appeal unites the Turkomans as one man against the offender and his tribe, and how deep an effect it has on the mind of the culprit, I saw on this occasion, for no sooner did Oraz perceive the lance fixed upon the high Yoska of his grandfather, when in the silence of the following night he led the horse back to the tent of the Mollah, and tied it to its former place. This act of restitution, as he himself told me, will pain him for a long time to come. But it is better to lie in the black earth than to have disturbed the repose of one's ancestors.

CHAPTER IV.

THE CARAVAN IN THE DESERT.

"THE *Chil menzili Turkestan*, or the Forty Stations across the desert of Turkestan," I often heard my friends say, "are far more troublesome and much more difficult to get over than the *Chil menzili Arabistan*, or the Forty Stations on the Pilgrims' route from Damascus to Mecca. On this last one finds every day fresh cisterns, which furnish drinkable water for thousands; the pilgrim is sure to get fresh bread, a good dish of pilaw or meat, cool shade, and all the comforts he longs for after the exhausting day's march. But on the former route, man has done nothing for the support of the poor traveller. He is in constant danger of dying from thirst, of being murdered, of being sold as a slave, of being robbed, or of being buried alive under the burning sand-storm. Well-filled water-skins and flour sacks, the best horses and arms, often become useless, and there is nothing left to one but to strive to get forward as fast as possible, while invoking the name of Allah."

The readers of my "Travels in Central Asia," may be supposed to have some idea of the awfully imposing journey from Persia to the oasis-lands of Turkestan. I may here furnish a few additional particulars about the experience of our caravan. I have several times been blamed for being too concise to be graphic, and this charge, I confess, is not altogether undeserved. I propose here to make up for my faults of omission.

During the first three days' march, the impressive, endless silence of the desert—a silence as of the grave —cast a most powerful spell over my soul. Often did I stare vacantly for hours, my eyes fixed on the distance before me, and as my companions believed me to be sunk in religious meditations, I was very seldom disturbed. I only half observed how, during the march, certain members of our caravan nodded in sleep on the backs of their camels, and by their ludicrous movements and sudden starts afforded our company exquisite amusement. Any one overcome with sleep would lay hold of the high pummel of the saddle with both his hands, but this did not prevent him from either, with a forward lurch, knocking his chin with such force that all his teeth chattered, or, by a backward one, threatening to fall with a summersault to the ground. Indeed this last often happened, arousing the hearty laughter of the whole party. The fallen became the hero of the day, and had to support the most galling fire of jokes on his awkwardness.

The most inexhaustible fountain of cheerfulness was a young Turkoman, named Niyazbirdi, who possessed no less liveliness of spirits than agility of body, and by every word and movement contrived to draw laughter from the most venerable of the Mollahs. Although he was owner of several laden camels, he was, nevertheless, for the most part, accustomed to go on foot; and running now right, now left, he alarmed by cries or gestures any group of wild asses that showed themselves along our route. Once, indeed, he succeeded in getting hold of a young wild ass, which, through fatigue, had loitered behind the rest. The young shy creature was led along by a rope, and was the occasion of really droll scenes, when its lucky captor gave a prize of three spoonfuls of sheeps-tail fat to any one who dared to mount it. Three spoonfuls of mutton fat is a tempting prize for Hadjis in the desert, so that many were seduced by the prospect of gaining it. Nevertheless, they could make nothing of this uncivilized brother of Balaam's charger, for the unfortunate Hadjis had no sooner seated themselves on its back than they were stretched sprawling in the sand.

Only after a march of several hours is general weariness to be remarked. All eyes are then turned towards the *Kervan bashi*, whose gaze at such a time wanders in every direction to spy out a suitable halting place, that is to say, one which will afford most plentiful fodder for the camels. No sooner has he found such, than he himself hastens towards it, while the younger members of the caravan disperse themselves to right and left to collect dried roots, or scrub, or other fuel. Dismounting, unpacking, and settling down, is the work of a few moments. The hope of much-desired rest restores the exhausted strength. With speed the ropes are slackened, with speed the heaviest bales of merchandize are piled up in little heaps, in whose shade the wearied traveller is accustomed to stretch himself. Scarcely have the hungry camels betaken themselves to their pasture-ground when a solemn stillness fills the caravan. This stillness is, I may say, a sort of intoxication, for every one revels in the enjoyment of rest and refreshment.

The picture of a newly-encamped caravan in the summer months, and on the steppes of Central Asia, is a truly interesting one. While the camels, in the distance but still in sight, graze greedily, or crush the juicy thistles, the travellers, even the poorest among them, sit with their tea-cups in their hands and eagerly sip the costly beverage. It is nothing more than a greenish warm water, innocent of sugar, and often decidedly turbid; still human art has discovered no food, has invented no nectar, which is so grateful, so refreshing in the desert, as this unpretending drink. I have still a vivid recollection of its wonder-working effects. As I sipped the first drops a soft fire filled my veins, a fire which enlivened without intoxicating. The later draughts affected both heart and head; the eye became peculiarly bright and began to gleam. In such moments I felt an indescribable rapture and sense of comfort. My companions sank in sleep; I could keep myself awake and dream with open eyes.

5

After the tea has restored their strength the caravan becomes gradually busier and noisier. They eat in groups or circles which are here called *kosh*, which represent the several houses of the wandering town. Everywhere there is something to be done, and everywhere it is the younger men who are doing it, while their elders are smoking. Here they are baking bread. A Hadji in rags is actively kneading the black dough with dirty hands. He has been so engaged for half an hour, and still his hands are not clean, for *one* mass of dough cannot absorb the accumulations of several days. There they are cooking. In order to know what is being cooked, it is not necessary to look round The smell of mutton-fat, but especially the aroma, somewhat too piquant, of camel or horse-cutlets, tells its own tale. Nor have the dishes when cooked anything inviting to the eye. But in the desert a man does not disturb himself about such trifles. An enormous appetite covers a multitude of faults, and hunger is notoriously the best of sauces.

Nor are amusements wanting in the caravan-camp when the halt is somewhat prolonged. The most popular recreation is shooting at a mark, in which the prize is always a certain quantity of powder and shot. This sort of diversion was very seldom possible in our caravan, as on account of our small numbers we were in continual danger, and had therefore to make ourselves heard as little as possible. My comrades were accustomed to pass their leisure time in reading the

Koran, in performance of other religious exercise, in sleeping, or in attending to their toilet. I say "toilet," but it is to be hoped that no one will here understand the word to imply a boudoir, delicate perfumes, or artistical aids. The Turkomans are accustomed to pluck out the hair of the beard with small pincers. As to the toilet of the Hadjis, and, indeed, my own, it is so simple and so prosaic as to be scarcely worth alluding to. The necessary requisites were sand, fire, and ants. The manner of application I leave as a riddle for the reader to solve.

Certainly, of all the nations of Asia, the Tartar seems to fit in most appropriately with the bizarre picture of desert life. Full of superstition, and a blind fatalist, he can easily support the constant dread of danger. Dirt, poverty and privations, he is accustomed to, even at home. No wonder, then, that he sits content in clothes which have not been changed for months, and with a crust of dirt on his face. This inner peace of mind could never become a matter of indifference to me. At evening prayers, in which the whole company took part, this peace of mind struck me most forcibly. They thanked God for the benefits they enjoyed. On such occasions the whole caravan formed itself into a single line, at whose head stood an imâm, who turned towards the setting sun and led the prayers. The solemnity of the moment was increased by the stillness which prevailed far and wide; and if the rays of the sinking sun lit up the faces of my companions, so wild yet withal so well satisfied, they seemed to be in the possession of all earthly good, and had nothing left them to wish. Often I could not help thinking what would these people feel if they found themselves leaning against the comfortable cushions of a first-class railway carriage, or amid the luxuries of a well-appointed hotel. How distant, how far distant are the blessings of civilization from these countries!

So much for the life of the caravan by day. By night the desert is more romantic, but at the same time more dangerous. As the power of sight is now limited, the circle of safety is contracted to the most immediate neighbourhood; and both during the march and in the encampment every one tries to keep as close as possible to his fellows. By day the caravan consisted of but one long chain; by night this is broken up into six or eight smaller ones, which, marching close together, form a compact square, of which the outmost lines are occupied by the stoutest and boldest. By moonlight the shadow of the camels as they stalk along produces a curious and impressive effect. During the dark starless night everything is full of horror, and to go one step distant from the side of the caravan is equivalent to leaving the home circle to plunge into a desolate solitude. In the halt by day each one occupies whichever place may please him best. At night, on the contrary, a compact camp is formed under the direction of the *Kervan bashi*. The bales of goods are heaped up in the middle; around them lie the men;

while without, as a wall of defence, the camels are laid, tightly packed together, in a circle. I say laid, for these wonderful animals squat down at the word of command, remain the whole night motionless in their place, and, like children, do not get up the next morning until they are told to do so. They are placed with their heads pointing outward and their tails inward, for they perceive the presence of any enemy from far, and give the alarm by a dull rattle in the throat, so that even in their hours of repose they do duty as sentinels. Those who sleep within the *rayon* find themselves in immediate contact with these beasts, and, as is well known, they have not the pleasantest smell. It often happens that the saline fodder and water which these animals feed upon produce palpable consequences for such as sleep in their immediate neighbourhood. I myself often woke up with such frescoes. But no one takes any notice of such things, for who could be angry with these animals, who, although ugly in appearance, are so patient, so temperate, so good-tempered, and so useful?

It is no wonder that the wanderers over the desert praise the camel as surpassing all other beasts of the field, and even love it with an almost adoring affection. Nourished on a few thorns and thistles, which other quadrupeds reject, it traverses the wastes for weeks, nay, often for months together. In these dreary, desolate regions, the existence of man depends upon that of the camel. It is, besides, so patient and so obedient that a child can with one "*tshukh*" make a whole herd of these tall strong beasts kneel down, and with a "*berrr*" get up again. How much could I not read in their large dark blue eyes! When the march is too long or the sand too deep, they are accustomed to express their discomfort and weariness. This is especially when they are being laden, if too heavy bales are piled upon their backs. Bending under the burden, they turn their heads round towards their master; in their eyes gleam tears, and their groans, so deep, so piteous, seem to say, " Man, have compassion upon us!"

Except during a particular season of the year, when through the operation of the laws of nature it is in a half-intoxicated, half-stupefied condition, the camel has always a striking impression of seriousness. It is impossible not to recognise in its features the Chaldee-aramæan type, and in whatever portions of the earth he may be found at the present day, his original home is unquestionably Mesopotamia and the Arabian desert. The Turkomans disturb this serious expression of countenance by the barbarous manner in which they arrange the leading-rope through the bored nose. With the string hanging down to the chest, the camel resembles an European dandy armed with his lorgnon. Both of them hold their heads high in the air, and both are alike led by the nose.

As the word of command to encamp is enlivening and acceptable, so grievous, so disturbing, is the signal for getting ready to start. The *Kervan bashi* is the first to rouse himself. At his call or sign all prepare for the journey, Even the poor camels in the pastures understand it, and often hasten without being driven to the caravan; nay, what is more extraordinary, they place themselves close to the bales of merchandize with which they were before laden, or the persons who were mounted on them. In a quarter of an hour everybody has found his place in the line of march. At the halting-place there remains nothing but a few bones, gnawed clean, and the charred traces of the improvised hearths. These marks of human life in the desert often disappear as quickly as they were produced; sometimes, however, they are preserved through climatic accidents for a long time; and succeeding travellers are cheered by falling in with these abandoned fireplaces. The black charred spot seems to their eyes like a splendid *caravanserai*, and the thought that here human beings have been, that here life once was active, makes even the vast solitude of the desert more like home.

Speaking of these spots where a fire has been kindled, I am reminded of those vast burnt plains, often many days' march in extent, which I met with in the desert between Persia and Khiva, and of which I heard so many wonderful tales from the mouths of the nomads. During the hot season of the year, when the scorching sun has dried shrubs and grass till they have become like tinder, it often happens that a spark, carelessly dropped, and fanned by the wind, will set the steppe on fire. The flame, finding ever fresh fuel, spreads with such fearful rapidity that a man on horseback can with difficulty escape. It rolls over the scanty herbage like an overflowing stream, and, when it meets with thicket and shrubs, it flares up with wild wrath. Thus traversing large tracts of country in a short time, its raging course can only be checked by a river or a lake. At night such conflagrations must present a terrible appearance, when far and wide the horizon is lit up with a sea of flame. Even the bravest heart loses its courage at the appalling sight. The cowardly and hesitating are soon destroyed, but one who has sufficient presence of mind can save himself, if, while the flames are yet a great way off, he kindle the grass in his neighbourhood. He thus lays waste a space in which the approaching fire can find no sustenance, and in this he himself takes refuge. Thus only with fire can man contend against fire with success.

This weapon is often used by one tribe against another, and the desolation thus caused is terrible. It is often used by a runaway couple to secure themselves against pursuit. As long as no wind blows they can easily fly before the slowly-advancing fire; but it often happens that the flames are hurried forward by the least breath of wind, and the fugitives find a united death in the very means they had taken to secure their safety.

It is remarkable that the imposing aspects and most frequent natural phenomena of the desert do not fail to impress even the nomads who habitually witness them. As we were crossing the high plateau of Kaflan

Kir, which forms part of Ustyort, running towards the north-east, the horizon was often adorned with the most beautiful Fata Morgana. This phenomenon is undoubtedly to be seen in the greatest perfection in the hot, but dry, atmosphere of the deserts of Central Asia, and affords the most splendid optical illusions which one can imagine. I was always enchanted with these pictures of cities, towers, and castles dancing in the air, of vast caravans, horsemen engaged in combat, and individual gigantic forms which continually disappeared from one place to reappear in another. As for my nomad companions, they regarded the neighbourhoods where these phenomena are observed with no little awe. According to their opinion these are ghosts of men and cities which formerly existed there, and now at certain times roll about in the air. Nay, our *Kervan bashi* asserted that he also saw the same figures in the same places, and that we ourselves, if we should be lost in the desert, would after a term of years begin to hop about and dance in the air over the spot where we had perished.

These legends, which are continually to be heard among the nomads, and relate to a supposed lost civilization in the desert, are not far removed from the new European theory, which maintains that such tracts of country have sunk into their present desolation, not so much through the operation of natural laws as through changes in their social state. As examples are cited the great Sahara of Africa and the desert of central Arabia, where cultivable land is not so much wanting as industrious hands. As regards these last countries, the assertion is probably not without some truth, but it certainly cannot be extended to the deserts of Central Asia. On certain spots, as Mero, Mangishlak, Ghergen, and Otrar, there was in the last century more cultivation than at present; but, taken as the whole, these Asiatic steppes were always, as far back as the memory of man goes, howling wildernesses. The vast tracts which stretch for many days' journeys without one drop of drinkable water, the expanses—many hundred miles in extent—of deep loose sand, the extreme violence of the climate, and such like obstacles, defy even modern art and science to cope with them. " God," said a central Asiatic to me, " created Turkestan and its inhabitants in his wrath; for as long as the bitter, saline taste of their springs exist, so long will the hearts of the Turkomans be full of anger and malice."

CHAPTER V.

THE TENT AND ITS INHABITANTS.

An able critic of my "Travels in Central Asia" wrote —"Mr. Vambéry wandered because he has the wild spirit of dervishism strong within him." On first reading this it struck me as a little too strong, and I shall ever protest against such attribution of the title of vagabond, however refined may be the terms in which it is couched. Still I must candidly confess that the tent, the snail shell of the nomad, if I may be allowed so to call it, has left on my memory an ineffaceable impression. It certainly is a very curious feeling which comes over one when he compares the light tent with such seas of stone buildings as make up our European cities. The vice of dervishism is, to be sure, contagious, but happily not for everybody, so that there is no danger in accompanying me for a little while to Central Asia, and glancing at the contrast there presented to our fixed, stable mode of life.

It is almost noonday. A Kirghiz family, which has packed house and household furniture on the backs of a few camels, moves slowly over the desert towards a spot indicated to them by the raised lance of a distant horseman. The caravan rests, according to nomad notions of rest, while thus on the march, to become lively and busy when they settle themselves down to repose according to our ideas. Nevertheless, the elder women seated on the bunches of camels (for the younger ones travel on foot), grudge themselves repose even then, and occupy their time in spinning a sort of yarn for sacks out of the coarser camels' hair. Only the marriageable daughter of the family enjoys the privilege of being completely at leisure on her shambling beast. She is polishing her necklace of coins, Russian, Ancient Bactrian, Mongolian, or Chinese, which hangs down to her waist. So engrossed is she in her employment, that an European numismatist might take her for a fellow connoisseur; nevertheless not a movement of the young Kirghizes, who seek to distinguish themselves by all manner of equestrian gymnastics, as they caracole around the caravan, escapes her notice.

At last the spot fixed on by the guide is reached. An inhabitant of cities might imagine that now the greatest confusion would arise. But no—everybody has his appointed office, everybody knows what he has to do, everything has its fixed place. While the paterfamilias unsaddles his cooled horse and lets him loose on the pasture, the younger lads collect, with frightful clamour, the sheep and the camels, which are only too disposed to wander. They must stay to be milked. Meanwhile the tent has been taken down. The old matron seizes on the latticed framework and fixes it in its place, spitting wildly right and left as she does so. Another makes fast the bent rods which form the vaulting of the roof. A third sets on the top of all a sort of round cover or lid, which serves the double purpose of chimney and window. While they are covering the woodwork with curtains of felt, the children inside have already hung up the provision-sacks, and placed the enormous tripod on the crackling fire. This is all done in a few moments. Magical is the erection, and as magical is the disappearance of the nomad's habitation. Still, however, the noise of the sheep and camels, of screaming women and crying children, resounds about the tent. They form, indeed, a strange chorus in the midst of the noonday silence of the desert. Milking-time, the daily harvest of these pastoral tribes is, however, the busiest time in the twenty-four hours. Especial trouble is given by the greedy children, whose swollen bellies are the result and evidence of an unlimited appetite for milk. The poor women have much to suffer from the vicious or impatient disposition of the beasts; but, although the men are standing by, the smallest help is rigorously refused, as it would be held the greatest disgrace for a man to take any part in work appointed to women.

Once, when I had, in Ettrek, obtained by begging a small sack of wheat, and was about to grind it in a handmill, the Turkomans around me burst out into shouts of laughter. Shocked and surprised, I asked the reason of their scornful mirth, when one approached me in a friendly manner and said: "It is a shame for you to take in hand woman's work. But Mollahs and Hadjis are of course deficient in secular *savoir faire*, and one pardons them a great many such mistakes."

After the supply of milk has been collected, and all the bags of skins (for vessels of wood or of earthenware are purely articles of luxury) have been filled, the cattle, small and great, disperse themselves over the wide plain. The noise gradually dies away. The nomad retires into his tent, raises the lower end of the felt curtain, and while the west wind, rustling through the fretted wood-work, lulls him to sleep, the women outside set to work on a half-finished piece of felt. It is certainly an interesting sight to see how six, often more, of the daughters of the desert, in rank and file, roll out under their firm footsteps the felt which is wrapped up between two rush mats. An elderly lady leads this industrial dance and gives the time. It is she who can always tell in what place the stuff will be loose or uneven. The preparation of the felt, without question the simplest fabric which the mind of man has invented, is still in the same stage among these wandering tribes as when first discovered. The most common colour is grey. Particoloured felt is an article of luxury, and snowy white is only used on the most solemn occasions. Carpets are only to be found among the richer tribes, such as the Turkomans and the Œzbegs, as they require more skill in their manufacture and a closer contact with more advanced civilization.

The inwoven patterns are for the most part taken from European pocket-handkerchiefs and chintzes; and I was always surprised at the skill with which the women copied them, or, what is still more surprising, imitated them from memory after having once seen them.

While the poor women are fatiguing themselves with their laborious occupation, their lord and master is accustomed to snore through his noonday siesta. Soon the cattle return from their pasture ground and collect around the tent. Scarcely does the afternoon begin to grow cooler, than the migrating house is in a trice broken up, everything replaced on the backs of the camels, and the whole party in full march. This is already the second day of their journey, and yet all, men and beasts, are as lively as if they had dwelt for years on the spot, and, at length released from the talons of ennui, were delighted at the prospects of a change.

Long after sunset, while the endless waste of the desert is gradually being over-canopied by the clear starry heaven, the caravan still plods steadily, in order to rest during the colder hours of the night under the shelter of their warm felts. Quickly is their colossal *batterie de cuisine* placed on the fire; still more quickly is it emptied. No European can have any idea of the voracious appetite of a nomad.

The caravan has been scarcely an hour encamped before everybody has supped and retired to rest; the older members of the family within the tent, the younger ones in the open air, their flocks around them. Only where a marriageable maiden lives is there any movement to be found. Among the nomad tribes of Central Asia, Islamism has not succeeded in carrying into effect its rigorous restrictions on the social intercourse of the sexes. The harem is here entirely unknown. The young nomad always knows by what star to direct his course in order to find the tent of his adored on the trackless desert. His appearance is seldom unexpected. The nomad young lady has already divined from what quarter the hoof-tramp will sound through the nightly stillness, and has already taken up an advanced post in that direction. It is scarcely necessary to observe that the conversation of the two children of the desert, in this their tender rendezvous, is not quite in unison with our ideas of æsthetical propriety; but poetry is to be found everywhere, nay, I might say, is more at home in the desert than in these western countries. Sometimes a whole company of loving couples come together, and on such occasions the dialogue, which must be in rhyme and adorned with the richest flowers of Tartar metaphor, seems as if it would never come to an end. I was at first enchanted with listening to such conversation; but how irritated I was when I had to pass the night in the same tent with such amorous society, and in spite of all the fatigue of the day could not find quiet slumbers to refresh me!

The above is but a faint picture of the life of the

nomads during the more agreeable portion of the year. In winter, especially in the more elevated regions, where severe cold prevails, this wandering life loses everything which can give it the least tinge of poetry in our eyes. Even the inhabitants of the cities of Central Asia marvel that the nomads can support life in the bleak open country, amid fearful storms and long weeks of snow. Indeed, with a cold of 30° Réaumur, it cannot be very pleasant to live in a tent; still even this occasions no serious inconvenience to the hardy child of Nature. Himself wrapped up in a double suit of clothes, he doubles the felt hangings of his tent, which is pitched in a valley or some other sheltered spot. Besides this the number of its inhabitants is increased, and when the *saksaul* (the root of a tree hard as stone and covered with knobs) begins to give out its heat, which lasts for hours, the want of a settled home is quite forgotten. The family circle is drawn closer round the hearth. The daughter of the house must continually hand round the skin of *kimis*. This favourite beverage opens the heart and looses the tongue. When, furthermore, a *bakhshi* (troubadour) is present to enliven the winter evenings with his lays, then even the howling of the tempest without serves as music.

When no extraordinary natural accidents, such as sand-storms or snow-storms, break in upon his regular course of life, the nomad is happy; indeed, I may say, as happy as any civilization in the world could make him. As the nations of Central Asia have but very few wants, poverty is rare among them, and where it occurs, is by no means so depressing as with us. The lives of the inhabitants of the desert would glide peacefully away, were it not for the tendency to indulge in feuds and forays—a leading feature in their character. War, everywhere a curse, there draws after it the most terrible consequences which can be conceived. Without the smallest pretext for such violence, a tribe which feels itself stronger often falls upon the weaker ones. All who are able to bear arms conquer or die; the women, children, and herds of the fallen are divided as booty among their conquerors. Often does it happen that a family, which in the evening lay down to rest in all the blessedness of security, find themselves in the morning despoiled of parents, of freedom, and of property, and dragged into captivity far apart from one another!

Among the Turkomans near Khiva I saw many Kirghiz prisoners, who had formerly belonged to well-to-do families. The unfortunate creatures, who had been but a short time before rich and independent, and cherished by parents, accommodated themselves to the change of their fortunes as to some ordinary dispensation of nature. With what honesty and diligence did they attach themselves to their masters' interests! How they loved and caressed their masters' children! Yet these same masters were they who had robbed them of their whole property, murdered their father, and branded them for ever with the opprobrious title of " Kul " (slave.)

Buddhism, Christianity, Mohammedanism, have one after the other attempted to force their way into the steppes of upper Asia. The first and the last have succeeded to some extent in making good their footing, but the nomads have, nevertheless, remained the same as they were at the time of the conquests of the Arabs, or of the campaigns of Alexander—the same as they were described by Herodotus. I shall never forget the conversations about the state of the world which I had with elderly Turkomans and Kirghizes. It is true that one can picture to oneself beforehand a specimen of ancient simplicity, but that is still something quite different from seeing before you one of these still standing columns of a civilization several millenniums old.

The Central Asiatic still speaks of Rome (Rum, modern Turkey) as he spoke in the days of the Cæsars; and when one listens to a grey-beard as he depicts the might and the greatness of this land, one might imagine that the invincible legions had only yesterday combated the Parthians and that he was present as an auxiliary. That his Rum (Turkey) is a state of but miserable proportions in comparison with old Rome, is what he cannot believe. He has learned to associate with that name glory and power. At the most, China may be sometimes compared to Rome for might and resources; although the legends that are told of this latter empire dwell rather on the arts and the beauty than on the valour of the Chinese people. Russia is regarded as the quintessence of all fraud and cunning; by which means alone she has of late years contrived to effect her conquests. As for England, it is well known that the late emir of Bokhara, on the first occasion in which he came into contact with the British, was quite indignant "that the Ingiliz, whose name had only risen to notice within a few years, should dare to call themselves *Dowlet* (government) when addressing him."

Extremely surprising to the stranger is the hospitality which is to be found among the nomads of Central Asia. It is more abounding than perhaps in any other portion of the east. Amongst the Turks, Persians, and Arabs, there still linger faint memories of this old duty, but our European tourists have had, I believe, ample opportunity of satisfying themselves that all the washing of feet, slaughter of sheep, and other good offices, are often only performed in the hope of a rich *Bakhshish*, or *Pishkesh*, (as they say in Persian.) It is true that the *Koran* says, "Honour a guest, even though he be an infidel;" but this doing honour is generally the echo of orders issued from some consulate or embassy. Quite otherwise in Central Asia. There hospitality is, I may say, almost instinctive; for a nomad may be cruel, fierce, perfidious, but never inhospitable.

One of my fellow-beggars went, during my sojourn

among the Turkomans, on a round of begging visits, having first dressed himself in his worst suit of rags. Having wandered about the whole day he came at evening to a lonely tent, for the purpose of lodging there for the night. On entering he was saluted in the customary friendly manner; nevertheless he soon observed that the master of the poverty-stricken establishment seemed to be in great embarrassment, and moved hither and thither as if looking for something. The beggar began to feel very uncomfortable when at last his host approached him, and, deeply blushing, begged him to lend him a few *krans*, in order that he might be able to provide the necessary supper, inasmuch as he himself had nothing but dried fish, and he wished to set something better before his guest. Of course it was impossible to refuse such a request. My comrade opened the purse which he carried under his rags, and when he had given his host five *krans*, everything seemed to be satisfactorily arranged. The meal was eaten amidst the most friendly conversation, and when it was ended, the softest felt carpet was assigned to the stranger as his couch, and in the morning he was dismissed with the customary honours.

" I was scarcely gone half an hour from the tent," so my friend related his adventure subsequently to me, " when a Turkoman came running towards me, and with violent threats demanded my purse. How great was my astonishment when I recognised in the person of the robber no other than my host of the previous night! I thought he was joking, and began to address him in a friendly manner; but he grew only more and more serious. So, in order to avoid unpleasant consequences, there remained nothing for me but to hand over my purse, a few leaves of tea, my comb, and my knife, in one word, my whole property. Having so done, I was about to proceed on my way, when he held me back, and opening my—that is to say now his—purse, and taking out five *krans*, gave them to me with these words:—'Take my debt of yesterday evening. We are now quits, and you can go on your way.'"

CHAPTER VI.

THE COURT OF KHIVA.

The courts of oriental princes have been frequently and variously described. Beginning with the shore of the Bosphorus, where Dolma Bagtsche, Beshiktash and Serayburun furnish the first pictures in the panorama, and ranging as far as the palaces of Pekin and Yedo, we have read again and again of the love for ostentation and empty splendour, the glitter of gold and diamonds of oriental life. But to complete the series, a few sketches of life at the court of Turkestan sovereigns are wanting, and the description of such may not, therefore, be deemed superfluous.

My readers must not expect either to be dazzled, or to have their amazement and admiration excited, and yet it will repay the trouble to accompany me through the tortuous streets of Khiva and the bazaar with its vaulted roof to the Ark (the Royal Castle.) Like all the residences of sovereigns in Central Asia, this castle is strangely fortified and surrounded by a double wall. Through a narrow gate we enter into the first court, which is crowded with the royal body-guard and other soldiers and servants. Near the entrance two cannons are planted, brought thither by the mighty Nadir, and left behind on his hasty retreat. They are decorated with pretty symmetrical ornaments, and seem to have been made at Delhi. After having passed the second gate, we enter a more spacious court, with a mean looking building on one side, not unlike an open coach-house; it is here that the high officials pass the hours of office, the Mehter (Minister of the Interior) presiding. To the left of this building is a kind of guard-house, in which divers servants, policemen and executioners live during the day time, awaiting the commands of their royal master. A small gate leads between these two buildings, to the residence of His Majesty of Khiva. On the outside it resembles a poor mud-hut, like all the other houses in the town, and is of course without windows, nor is any particular luxury to be met with inside, except several large and valuable carpets, a few sofas and round cushions, together with a considerable number of chests—the entire furniture of this place—which serve in some degree to remind us of the princely rank of the master. The number of apartments is very small, and as every where the case, is divided into the Harem, (the rooms set apart for the women,) and the Selamdjay, (the reception hall.)

Nowhere are any signs of splendour perceptible; the large train of followers alone mark the distinction, the lacqueys are the sole insignia of the ruler. Let us pass them in review before us. At the head of the household is the Desturkhandji, (literally, the man who spreads the table cloth,) whose peculiar office is to superintend the royal table. He is present during dinner, clothed in full armour and state dress, and on him devolves the inspection and control of the entire number of servants. Next to him follows the Mehrem, a kind of valet de chambre *in officio*, but in reality rather a privy councillor, who shares in the business of the state besides his immediate domestic affairs, and, conjointly with the former, exercises the most powerful influence upon his royal master. Then follows the rest of the servants, of whom each has his distinct office. The Ashpez, or cook, prepares the food, whilst the Ashmehter serves it. The Sherbetshi prepares tea, sherbet, and other drinks, but he is expected to be skilled besides in the decoction of wonder-working elixirs. The Payeke is entrusted with the tchilim (pipe,) which at court is made of gold or silver, and must be replenished with fresh water every time it is filled with tobacco. This office does not exist in any other court in Central Asia, tobacco being strictly forbidden by law. His Tartar Majesty has no dressing room, it is true, but, nevertheless, several servants are appointed to assist at the toilet. Whilst the Shilaptshi kneeling holds the wash-hand basin, the Kumgandshi (the man who holds the can or jug) pours the water from a silver or golden vessel, and the Rumaldshi is ready, as soon as the two former have withdrawn, to throw the towel to the prince, holding it with the tips of his fingers. The Khan has an especial Sertarash (who shaves the head,) who is expected to have nimble fingers and at the same time a skilful hand for squeezing the skull, a favourite operation throughout the east. Then the prince possesses a Ternaktshi, or nail cutter, a Khadimdshi, whose duty it is to knead and pummel his back, also to kneel upon him and make his limbs crack, whenever the Khan, after long fatigue, wishes to refresh himself. Lastly, there is a Töshektshi, or bed maker, whose office it is to spread out at night the soft pieces of felt or the mattresses. The magnificent harness, saddles and weapons are in charge of the Khaznadshi (treasurer,) who, whenever the sovereign rides out in public, walks beside him. The Djigadj, or keeper of the plumes, walks at the head of the train of servants.

In dress and food, the prince's household is little distinguished from that of rich merchants or officials of rank. The king wears the same heavy cap of sheepskin, the same clumsy boots, stuffed out with several yards of linen rags, the same thickly-wadded coats of print or silk as his subjects, and, like them, endures in this Siberian costume, under the oppressive heat of July, a state of fearful perspiration. On the whole, the position of the Prince of Kharezm is one little to be envied, nay, I feel inclined to say, it is far more wretched than that of other Eastern princes. In a country, where pillage and murder, anarchy and lawlessness, are the rule, and not the exception, a sovereign has to maintain his authority by inspiring his subjects with the utmost dread and almost superstitious terror for his person; never with affection. Even those nearest to him fear him for his unlimited power; and wife and children, as well as relations, not unfrequently attempt his life. At the same time, the sovereign is expected to be the model of Islamitic virtue and Œzbeg manners and customs; every most trifling, insignificant error of his Majesty, becomes the talk of the town; and although nobody would venture to blame him for very considerable offences, yet in the former case it is the influential Mollahs who would feel affronted,— a result entirely opposed to the interests of the sovereign.

The Khan, like every orthodox Mussulman, is obliged to leave his bed before sun-rise, and to be present at the morning prayer in full assembly. It lasts rather more than half an hour, after which he partakes of several dishes of tea, seasoned with fat and salt. Not unfrequently some of the learned Mollahs are invited, in order to enliven the breakfast, by explaining some sacred precept or arguing upon some religious question, of which his highness rarely of course understands anything. Profound discussions generally invite sleep, and no sooner does his Majesty begin to snore aloud, when the learned men take it as a signal to withdraw. This sleep is called the morning doze, and lasts from two to three hours. When it is over, the selam (reception) of the ministers and other high dignitaries commences, and the Khan enters in full earnest upon his duties as sovereign. Consultations are held as to the marauding expeditions to be undertaken, politics are discussed in reference to the neighbouring state of Bokhara, the Yomut- and Tchaudor-Turkomans, the Kasaks, and at present probably the Russians, who are pushing their advances nearer and nearer;—or the governors of the provinces and the tax-gatherers, who had been sent out over the country, have to submit to the Khan and his ministers their several accounts. Every farthing has to be paid over with the most scrupulous accuracy, and woe to that man in whose account the smallest error is detected; it may happen that he is dismissed, leaving his head behind. And now, after having transacted for several hours the ordinary business of the state, breakfast is served, consisting for the greater part of rather light food, that is to say, "light" for an Œzbeg digestion—the déjeuner à la fourchette of his Majesty of Khiva sufficing in all probability for several of our active working men at home. During this meal all present have to stand round respectfully and look on, and after having finished, he invites one or the other of his favourites to sit down and play with him at chess,—an amusement which is continued until the time for mid-day prayer. This lasts about an hour. When it is over, his Majesty proceeds to the outer court, and taking his seat on a kind of terrace, the arz (public audience) takes place, to which every rank, every class is admitted,—men, women, and children, either in the greatest négligé or even half naked. All crowd round the entrance, where amidst noise and shouting they wait for audience. Each in turn is admitted, but only one person at a time, who is allowed to approach quite close to his sovereign; to speak out freely and without reserve, to make entreaty or complaint, nay, to engage even in the most violent altercation with the Khan, the smallest sign from whom would suffice to deliver his subject, without any reason whatever, into the hands of the executioner. Thus the East is, and ever was from times immemorial, the land of the most striking contradictions. The inexperienced may interpret this as love of strict justice. I, however, see in it nothing but a whimsical habit of demeanour, permitting one person to defy the royal authority in the coarsest terms of speech, while another forfeits his life for the smallest offence against the rules of propriety.

At the arz not only all great and important lawsuits are settled, and sentences of death pronounced and executed; but even trifling differences are not unfrequently adjusted, as for instance, a quarrel between a husband and wife, or between one man and his neighbour on account of some few pence or the stealing of a hen. No complainant whatever can be refused a hearing; and although the Khan may send him to the Kadi, yet he must first listen to whatever he has to say. The afternoon prayer alone puts an end to this wearisome occupation. Later in the day the prince takes his customary ride on horseback outside the town, and usually returns just before sunset.

Evening prayers again are said in full assembly, and these ended, the prince retires to take his supper. The servants, and all those who do not live in the palace, withdraw, and the king remains alone with his confidants. Supper is a luxurious meal, and lasts longer than any other. Spirituous drinks are seldom taken by the sovereigns of Khiva and Bokhara, although the other members of the royal family and the grandees frequently transgress on this point, and indulge in the practice to excess. After the supper, singers and musicians make their appearance, or jugglers, with their various performances. Singing is very popular in Khiva, and the native singers of this place are the most renowned in Turkestan, and indeed throughout the whole Mahomedan East of Asia. The instrument upon which they excel is called girdshek, and bears a general resemblance to our violin. It has a longer neck and three strings, one of wire and two of silk; the bow, too, is like our bow. Then there are the tambur and dutara, on which instruments the Bakhshi plays the accompaniment to his songs, improvised in praise of some popular hero of the day.; whereas at the royal court they select for the most part ghaseles from Nevai and the Persian poets. The young princes are instructed in music, and it often happens that the Khan invites them to perform either alone or with the troubadours at court. Particular merriment and good humour, such as presides at the drinking-bouts at Teheran, or at the banquets in the palaces on the Bosphorus, is not to be met with at the court of Œzbeg princes; it is unknown here, or at least such is not the custom. The national character of the Tartar is chiefly marked by seriousness and firmness; to dance, jump, or show high spirits, is in his eyes only worthy of women or children. I have never seen an Œzbeg person of good manners indulge in immoderate laughter.

About two hours after sunset the Khan retires to the harem, or to his sleeping apartment, and with it his daily labours as sovereign are ended. The harem is here very different from those of the Turkish or Persian court. The number of women is limited, the fairy-like luxuriousness of life in a harem is entirely wanting, strict chastity and modesty pervade it; and in this respect the court of Khiva is eminently superior to all Eastern courts. The present Khan has only two lawful wives, although the Koran allows four. These are always chosen from among the royal family; and it is an extremely rare thing for the daughter of a dignitary, who does not belong to the family, to be raised to this rank. The Khan, although possessing the same unlimited power over his wife as over any of his subjects, treats her without severity, and on the whole with tenderness, unless she be found guilty of any particular offence. She possesses no titles or prerogatives whatever; her court is distinguished in nothing from the other harems, but that she has more female servants and slaves about her; the former consisting of the wives or daughters of officials, the latter for the most part of Persian and a few dark Arab women. The daughters of Iran are far inferior to the Œzbeg women in personal beauty, and their mistress has no cause to fear from either of them any rivalry. As regards their intercourse with the outer world, the princesses of Khiva are far more restricted than the wives of other Eastern potentates. The rules of modesty require that they should pass the greater part of the day in the harem, where comparatively little time is lavished upon the embellishments of the toilet. And in fact, the ladies of the harem have very little leisure for idleness, since in accordance with the custom of the country it is desirable that the greater part of the clothes, carpets, and other stuffs, for the use of the prince, should be prepared by the hand of his wife. This custom reminds one strongly of the patriarchal mode of life of which Turkestan, in spite of its roughness, has preserved many remnants of simple refinement.

The princess of Khiva is permitted occasionally to visit the neighbouring royal summer palaces and chateaux, never on horseback, as is the general custom in Persia, but in a large carriage, painted with gaudy colours, and completely covered and shut in with red carpets and shawls. Before and behind the vehicle trot a couple of horsemen, furnished with white staves. On her progress all rise respectfully from their seats and salute her with a profound bow. Nobody thinks of daring to cast a look of curiosity into the interior of the carriage; not only would this be useless, so closely is it covered, but such temerity would have to be atoned for by death, whether the object be the wife of

THE COURT OF KHIVA.

the sovereign or any subordinate official. Whenever the Queen of Persia takes a ride on horseback, the numerous ferrash (servants) who head the cavalcade cut right and left with their sabres at the crowd, who disperse in terror and confusion, in spite of their eager curiosity. Such a proceeding, however, is not necessary with the grave Œzbegs; for here life in the harem is not regulated with the same severity, and it is well known that the less strictly its laws are administered, the less frequently they are transgressed.

During the summer the royal family inhabit the castles of Rafenek and Tashhauz, near Khiva. Both were erected in the Persian style by former princes, and are distinguished by possessing some window-panes and small looking-glasses—the latter, especially, being considered articles of great luxury in the eyes of the people of Khiva. Tashhauz has not been built without taste. The chateau stands in a large garden; it has several reservoirs, and resembles the castle of Nigaristan, near the town gate, Shimran at Teheran. The winter is spent in the town, but when here his Œzbeg highness occupies a light tent which is pitched inside the walls; and herein he shows no bad taste, for the round-shaped dwelling, made of snow-white felt, with a cheerful fire burning brightly in the middle, is not only quite as warm as any building of stone, but there is something pleasant about it, and it makes a far less gloomy impression than the windowless mud-huts of Turkestan.

CHAPTER VII

JOY AND SORROW.

Joy and sorrow are undoubtedly the mirror, in which not only is the character of a people clearly reflected, but which likewise offers the most faithful image of their manners and customs. In joy and sorrow every sign of dissimulation vanishes, man shows himself in his true colours, and the lights and shades of his temperament become at once apparent; for, in any matter of real feeling, it is vain to try to speak and act differently to the dictates of this potent voice within us. And nowhere is a better opportunity offered for studying the various features of joy and sorrow, than at a birth, marriage, and death,—those three stages in the great family of mankind. The main outlines are no doubt everywhere the same, but in the colouring and composition a variety is produced, not found even among civilized nations. Ethnography has frequently thrown light on this subject in different parts of the world; but we must confess that Central Asia in this respect is wrapt in considerable obscurity. To attempt to dispel this darkness may therefore not be deemed superfluous; and, the savage Polynesian and Central

African having resisted vainly the spirit of inquiry, we will in like manner raise the veil from the rude and suspicious Œzbeg. It is a first attempt, and consequently a feeble one.

1. Birth.

As soon as a woman in Central Asia (I refer to a settled family), about to become a mother, feels the first pangs of childbirth, she sends for her neighbour, her nearest relations, a midwife, and a nurse for the child. A new felt or carpet is spread out in the tent or room, and upon this the woman is placed, with her legs doubled under her. As the pains increase, her nearest relations squat round her; and she, flinging both her arms round the neck of two of her most intimate friends, the midwife seizes her by the thighs, and moves her about, until she has been delivered of the child. She is now placed upon a bed, the relations taking the mother under their care, and the midwife having charge of the child. The former is restored to strength by friction on the temples and pulse, whilst the midwife sets about cutting out swaddling-clothes from a new piece of linen, in which she wraps the infant, strictly observing the various superstitious customs. Then taking the remainder of the linen to the mother, she informs her of the sex and appearance of her child; she also is the bearer of the happy tidings to the father, from whom she receives a present on this occasion. In fact, the kindik kesen (swaddling-clothes maker) plays a very important part in the whole affair For three days the child is invisible to every one, during which time it is frequently smeared over with butter, and, to prevent any redness in them, which is considered extremely objectionable, the eyes are washed with salt water. It is then clothed in a little shirt, and finally it is laid upon a pillow of camel's hair, and exhibited. Now all the friends and acquaintances pay their visits, and the husband offers a present to his wife, who is anxious to hear from her guests their prognostications as to the future of her child, which experienced matrons draw from the limbs and movements of its little body. Thus for instance, it is a bad sign, if it has entered the world with the left foot or hand first; a small apple of the eye augurs that her offspring will be a thief; a broad forehead denotes valour; a restless kicking of the feet future wealth, and so forth. Every one scrutinizes the infant with insignificant gestures; and well might the fear of the evil eye make the mother uneasy, but that she herself has tied the white magic-stone on the left arm of her child.

After the chille (forty days) have elapsed, festivities begin. In the case of a girl, not much is done; but if the child be a boy, even the poorest make every effort to gather round them a considerable number of guests, and to feast them as sumptuously as possible. Grand banquets, horse-racing, wrestling and music, are the order of the day; and finally, a special celebration in honour of the birth, the so-called Altin Kabak, takes place, which consists in hanging up a golden or silver ball on the top of a high tree, and whosoever brings it down at the first shot, with either ball or arrow, gains this prize, together with a certain number of sheep, and often even camels and horses.

During the first year the greatest care is taken to guard the child against cats, evil spirits, and other dangerous influences, after which time the above-mentioned white stone is replaced by a round-shaped bone, and on his little cap are hung the argushtek (a piece of wood, carved and dyed mysteriously), a nusha (amulet), which must be written by the hand of some learned man, several corals, the tooth of an hyæna, and, if circumstances permit, a small bag with holy earth from the grave of Mohamed. All these things, together, often make up a considerable weight, which presses very heavily on the head of the poor little creature; but this is not taken into consideration. On the contrary; the mother examines with jealous care to see that not a single thing be found wanting, each being looked upon as a certain means of protection against so many dangers.

In Central Asia, as throughout the whole East, children are allowed but a very few years to devote merely to play. Girls are early taught to spin, weave, sew, to make cheese, &c.; and boys are put on horseback, and learn to ride as early as their fifth year, and are employed as horsemen in sham fights, and as jockeys in horse races in, and even before, their tenth year.

It is only the more wealthy parents who give their children in charge of a Mollah. When they have learned to read, the Korantoy, or the festival of the Koran, is celebrated, which is of the same nature as the Chatem-düyünü of the Osmanlis, with this difference: that the latter takes place when the lad has, for the first time, read through the sacred book of Mohamed, and here, when he begins reading.

2. Marriage.

Although childhood is of short duration among the Œzbegs, yet a youth does not receive the name of yighid (a mature youth) until his eighteenth year, nor the girl that of kïz (virgin) before she is sixteen years old. In the country the intercourse between the two sexes is not in the least degree influenced by the Koran. Here, as in Western countries, we see the "rosy play of love" represented with all its joys and sorrows, all its fascination and enthusiasm. At first I felt amazed that the tenderest of feelings should find room in the heart of a man in Central Asia, accustomed as he is from his earliest youth to robbery and murder, and hardened to the tears of widows, orphans and slaves. But I had the opportunity of convincing myself, that love is here more frequently the cause of the most extraordinary adventures than in other Mahomedan countries. The Œzbeg is passionately devoted to music and poetry, and hence it is but natural that his heart should be susceptible to the emotions of love.

JOY AND SORROW.

When two young people have formed a mutual attachment the secret is entrusted to their parents, and if these make no objections, the young man opens the transaction by despatching two female ambassadors, Soutchi Khatin, to ask them formally for the hand of their daughter. The parents, for the most part, have been previously informed of the demand, and receiving the embassy with honour and distinction, they express their satisfaction at the offer, but refrain from giving any decisive answer. To pronounce a regular straightforward "yes," is contrary to the rules of propriety, and the young man has to interpret, from trivial allusions, whether his suit will be granted or not. The next thing is to talk over the kalim (marriage portion) which the man is ready or able to give for his future wife. The question is always, how many times nine, *i.e.*, how many times nine sheep, cows, camels or horses, or how many times nine ducats, as is the custom in a town, the father is to receive for giving up his daughter. The less wealthy give twice nine, the wealthier six times nine, and the Khan alone has to pay nine times nine, for the purchase of his bride. The kalim having been settled, the next question to be considered is one of great importance, the eginbash (present in ornaments) to be presented by the future husband. It consists of eight rings, yüzük, a semi-tiara (sheghendjin), a tiara (shekergül), a bracelet (bilezik), ear-rings (isirga), nose-rings (arabek), and ornaments for the neck (öngülük). This whole set of ornaments must be presented complete, and not a single article wanting; it is also previously settled, whether it is to consist of gold or silver. No doubt a man in Central Asia has to pay dearly for his wife. The negotiations are generally a protracted business; and finally, when every thing is definitely settled, neighbours and relations are invited to the fatiha toy (feast of promise), which is celebrated for two days in the home of the future bride, and two more in that of the future husband. The Mollah, or some grey-beard, announces the new arrangement to the guests. He tells them the exact purchase-price for the girl, and when the wedding is to take place, and concludes his short address with a fatiha, after which the festivities begin and are continued for four days. In entertainments of this kind, called toy, all the guests are assembled in one and the same apartment, but form different groups. The upper part of the room is occupied by the elderly people; the women range themselves along the right side of the wall and the girls and lads sit down in some corner, generally near the musicians and singers. The toy consists not merely in eating and drinking, but there is also music and singing, and above all, horse-racing, which latter forms the chief part of all festivities in Central Asia. Prizes of considerable value are given, and young and old take the most lively interest in the sport. The race-course varies from one to three fersakh in length; on the former only two year olds are admitted, on the latter full-grown strong horses. Two villages are chosen, lying at this distance apart, and whilst the crowd are assembling in one of them, a toy emini, steward, is appointed in the other. It is his duty to see that a fair start is effected, and that horse is proclaimed the winner, who first passes the goal which is fixed at the entrance of the opposite village. The horses are trained for several weeks for the race, and are ridden by young boys, who wear on this occasion short and tight-fitting clothes, very similar to those worn by jockeys in England.

The interval between the fatiha toy and the marriage is fixed according to the age of the "promessa." A week before the wedding, the toyluk (food for the wedding) is sent by the man to the house of his future wife; and consists of meat, flour, rice, fat, sugar and fruit. Soon after, his mother and nearest female relations arrive, who have been invited as guests for several weeks. Two days before the beginning of the festival the future husband mounts his horse, and, surrounded by his friends, all of whom, as well as their horses, are decked out in the gayest colours, goes also to the home of her parents, his father alone remaining behind, not for the sake of taking care of the house, but in order to make all necessary preparations for the due reception of the newly-married couple on their return.

Meanwhile, in the house of the future wife, where the first days of the marriage-feast are celebrated, the greatest bustle and activity prevails. The young girls have to do the cooking, and are fully employed with their gigantic cauldrons. The quantity of food brought together for an Œzbeg wedding is as enormous as the appetite of the numerous guests. Whilst the young girls are busy at cooking and baking, the young swains carry on a lively flirtation with them. The galant homme, who is lucky enough to obtain from his beloved a bone or some tit-bit out of the cauldron, regards the gift as a signal sign of favour, but still more lucky is he who gets a few sharp raps with the cooking ladle, the highest of all favours, and appreciated far above the daintiest morsels. Men and women gather round the fire-place in groups, laughing, talking, joking and shrieking, whilst musicians play and sing, and children shout and yell. These noises are mingled with the bleating of sheep, barking of dogs, neighing of horses and braying of donkeys, while loud above the general hubbub is heard the clown's stentorian voice in coarse sallies of Œzbeg wit and humour. He is the very life of the whole party. His gesticulations, the grimaces with which he accompanies his jests, give rise to continual bursts of laughter. Now he mimics this person or that, now he tells of some droll prank or merry adventure, or whistles like a bird and mews like a cat, and thus he has to continue without interruption, although from sheer exertion the perspiration runs down his face in streams.

It is a strange custom that, for the last few days before his wedding, the young man is not allowed to leave his tent, the young girl and her companions watching it, meanwhile, with looks of the utmost curiosity. It is said that friends and relations sometimes assist in bringing about a secret *tête-à-tête*, but not until after the marriage ceremony is he permitted to mix with the company. This ceremony takes place at the end of the second day, in the presence of the whole assembly. Each party is represented by two witnesses, to whom the Mollah puts the question, whether the two young people mutually agree as to the marriage. He then proceeds at once to perform the ceremony, when the witnesses of the young girl put in their veto. They declare (with a feigned reluctance) their unwillingness to give up the treasure entrusted to them, unless the young man should present them with a certain sum of money, or some other present. He finds the demand exorbitant, and now begins a bargaining and haggling, which continues until both parties are satisfied, when the solemn ceremony is at last performed. The Mollah reads aloud the permission of the reis (religious chief,) the witnesses attest on oath, and with significant gestures, the marriage compact, a short prayer is read, and the ceremony is over.

The bride now hands round fruit and a rich cake, and distributes white kerchiefs, garments, or other presents among the Mollahs, grey-beards, and above all, the young men who have acted as witnesses.

The bridegroom now makes his appearance, but is not permitted to approach the company nearer than a few steps from the door! and all having partaken of an enormous repast, the festivities in the bride's home terminate.

The elderly, as well as the married folk, now take their departure, but the young people remain, and pack the bride and her marriage portion on a sort of carriage, and thus accompanied by her female companions and friends, she sets out for the home of her husband. The journey, called bolush, is protracted as much as possible, and often when the distance is short, one or two long circuits are made, in order to have the opportunity of continuing the amusements on the road. The bride sits in the first carriage with her future sister-in-law, the young men accompany the procession on horseback, and he who can manage to force his way first to the front, riding full gallop, receives from her a handkerchief as the prize. The others try to snatch it from him, he flies and is pursued, and the chase does not cease till he has reached the carriage again. The handkerchiefs thus gained are tied to the horse's head, and preserved a long time as valuable trophies.* Whenever the procession passes a village on the route, they are generally stopped, and a toll is demanded. The sister-in-law sitting next the bride distributes cake, and the passage is again free. Amidst continued sport and chaff the bride arrives at the home of her husband, and no sooner does she draw near it, than

---

* In Hungary we find the same practice prevailing at the present day, for the custom of tying coloured handkerchiefs to the heads of the horses at marriage feasts most probably has its origin in this ancient usage.

she wraps her veil around her, changing her merry expression of face to one of the utmost gravity. Her father-in-law lifts her from the carriage, conducts her into the room, and leads her to a tent improvised with curtains and carpets in a corner of the apartment. The husband soon follows her, and for the second time raises her veil in the presence of his father, who compliments his daughter-in-law on her charming appearance, the first sight of which he has to requite with presents. The young couple are left alone, but have to endure for some time the jokes of the noisy crowd assembled outside the tent, who are eager to exhibit on these occasions their slender store of wit and humour. They disperse late at night, and at last all is quiet.

Among the Turkomans and Kirghis it is customary for newly-married people to be separated for a whole year, after they have lived together for a few days, and although the husband is allowed to make his appearance in the house of his wife, it must be only at night and in the most clandestine manner. In the opinion of the nomads, married life, in its beginning, is made all the more pleasant by acting up to the proverb, "stolen kisses taste the sweetest," and hence also the belief, that the first born child must always be handsome and vigorous.

The great national festival, called noruz (new year), of the Œzbegs, has been transmitted to them by the Persians, and is celebrated in Central Asia with the same pomp which distinguishes it in Persia, with this only difference, that the Œzbegs have an old and a new noruz. The latter, however, is of no especial importance. There is no lack of amusing games, but it is very remarkable that some have degenerated into the most pernicious gambling. Playing cards (sokti) are introduced from Russia (without the court cards), but have not yet come into general use. The favourite game is the Ashik-game (Ahsik—the anklebones of sheep), which is played in the manner of European dice with the four anklebones of a sheep, and with a degree of passionate excitement of which one can form no idea. The upper part of the bone is called tava, the lower altchi, and the two sides yantarap. The player takes these four little bones into the palm of his hand, throws them up and receives half of the stake, if two tava or two altchi, and the whole of the stake, if all four tava or altchi turn up. The advantage to be gained arises entirely from dexterity in throwing; trickery is impossible, since the bones are frequently changed. This game is equally popular with the dweller in settlements as with the nomad; and although apparently a trivial amusement, it not unfrequently happens that the Ashik player, in the heat of his passion, stakes the whole of his possessions, nay, even his wife. Mankind, in fact, are everywhere the same. The refined European makes his offerings at rouge et noir upon the green table; the Œzbeg on the sandy ground with four anklebones.

3. Death.

Whenever a member of a family is on the point of death, his nearest relations usually leave the house or tent. The Mollah, or the elderly among the neighbours, surround the dying man, watching for the last breath and repeating the customary prayers, while outside the air is filled with wailing and lamentations. If he should have been lying speechless for some time, some wool is moistened by his friends, and water dropped into his mouth, for fear lest, deprived of his speech, he might die of thirst. The rolling of the eyes and the contraction of the nose are regarded as symptoms of death; and no sooner has the dying man drawn his last breath than his jaws are tied up, and the body is stripped and then covered over. The clothes are destroyed, for even the poorest Œzbeg could not be persuaded to put on anything worn by a dying man.

The corpse is not allowed to be kept longer than twelve or fifteen hours, in accordance with the custom among all Mahomedan nations. It is not washed upon a board, but on a mat (buria), which is immediately after burnt; and the relations and neighbours, nay, often the whole population of the place, having wept and wailed their fill, the body is taken to be buried. The settled inhabitants of Central Asia possess cemeteries for their dead, but among the nomads each dead body is buried singly in the desert; and if he has been a man of influence and consideration, a large mound (tumulus) is generally raised over his grave, in the construction of which all the male members of the tribe are expected to take part. The more honoured the person, the higher and larger the mound (yoska). The surviving relations look upon it with pride; on certain festivals, and on the anniversary of the death, food or other presents are placed upon it for the benefit of the poor; and no sooner does the nomad come in sight of it, however great the distance may be, than he mutters a short prayer for the repose of the dead.

Men that fall in battle are neither undressed nor washed. The blood of a brave soldier being regarded as his greatest adornment, is consequently not removed.

The funeral feast begins immediately after the burial with a simple repast, at which the iyis (bread baked in fat) is distributed among rich and poor, and must be eaten by everybody. The feast is repeated on the third, seventh, and fortieth day after the death took place, besides which the anniversary is celebrated in like manner,—a duty which even the poorest would not omit to perform, for fear lest, by neglecting it, the departed might appear to them at night, and, exhorting the survivors, complain that they had forgotten to invite those of this world who are to pray for the welfare of his soul.

Among the nomads, the funeral feast occupies a more important part. Once every week, throughout the first year, a repast is prepared on the day of the death, and daily, as mentioned already in our "Travels among the Turkomans," the women sing the song of lamentation at the hour in which the member of the family breathed his last. With the latter, moreover, the memory of a dead person is held in the highest regard, and peculiar respect is paid to his grave for a long time after, if he has fallen in battle, or on some marauding expedition. The shaft of his lance is planted upon it, and decked with various-coloured pieces of stuff, ram's horns, a horse's tail, or like mementos,— friends and members of the same tribe contributing, as a matter of course, every time they pass it. The "yoskas" are called by the name of those that repose beneath; children play around, but, however playfully inclined, are careful not to climb upon them. It is even said, that horses go to visit the yoskas of their former masters, and are seen standing before them, with heads bent downward in mourning; and young warriors habitually look with veneration on these mounds, and draw from them the inspiration to their greatest deeds of valour.

Whenever we happened to meet one of these graves in our travels in the steppes of Central Asia, each member of our caravan was obliged to tear off a little piece of his clothes and fasten it to the shaft, or to a bench, or all joined in a hymn sung in his praise, Karavan bashi saying every time: "He who does not honour the dead will never receive honour from the living."

CHAPTER VIII.

HOUSE, FOOD, AND DRESS.

THE house, or fixed dwelling, has never, up to the present day, gained a firm footing among the nations in Central Asia, not even in those parts where regular settlements have existed for several hundred years. Part of the population build houses for themselves, but they are generally looked upon as gloomy places, producing feelings of melancholy, and the light, airy tent is in all cases preferred. It is principally the Œzbeg people who build houses, an art they have learnt from the original Persian settlers, and, as they resemble in many points the inhabitants of Iran, the architecture in Central Asia is in the early Iranic style, and at the same time very similar to the new Persian.

The first thing before building a *house*, is to level and prepare the ground by stamping it down with a heavy pounder. Foundations are only made to large buildings. The common-sized houses are made with a mud flooring, two feet high, and upon this, after it has dried hard, the walls are raised with a layer of rushes or wood underneath, in order to keep them from the damp rising from the ground. The walls are either "tam," *i.e.*, of clay or stone, or "akchub," *i.e.*, of wooden laths, laid crossways, and the interstices filled up with clay and unbaked tiles. The ceiling consists of planks, closely fitting together; in the houses of the poor these are left bare, and in those of the rich they have a coating of plaster and lime. Small holes serve as windows; they are open in summer, and in winter are pasted over with oiled paper. The roof, similar to those in Persia, is like a terrace, and serves as a sleeping place during the heat of the summer. Regular bricklayers are seldom met with. Every man is his own architect, convinced of possessing sufficient knowledge to build for himself a house suitable to his wants; and the plumb-line being still unknown, it is not to be wondered at that the walls are crooked and uneven, bulging either in or out, and soon become dilapidated.

The interior arrangement of a house is as follows: you enter by a wide gate, which forms the chief entrance, into a covered passage, called dalar. To the right of the gate are one or two rather large apartments (mihmankhane), which serve as reception-rooms for guests, and contain weapons as well as useful domestic utensils. Next to these are two small rooms, used as store-rooms. To the left are the stable and the shed for the carts and trucks, whilst a small door at the back of the dalar, opposite the entrance, leads to the inner apartments or harem. These are for the most part ayvans, that is, rooms which are open on one or two sides, and generally look out upon a garden. In towns they are used as favourite summer apartments, and it is really pleasant to live in them, especially during the night, with a peshekhane, a square tent made of gauze, like mosquito-nets, over one's bed, as a protection against catching cold, which is as dangerous in Central Asia as it is in Persia. In the country the dwellings are scattered. The farmstead (havli), which consists of several different parts, is always surrounded with a high wall for protection, and looks like a small fortress. The interior is very roomy; on one side are the buildings, always lower than the wall, on the other the tents, the fixed dwellings being set apart here also exclusively for animals and store-rooms. Sometimes the inner space is so large that a small kitchen-garden has found room within it. Outside, but near the walls, is a large reservoir, the edges of which are bordered with plantains, and afford a most agreeable resting-place. These trees flourish admirably in this part of Asia, where they are found of an astonishing height and breadth, and reach the great age of from 300 to 400 years. On hot summer days they afford the most refreshing shade, and for hours the Œzbeg is seen sleeping beneath the spreading branches. Not only does the thick foliage protect him from the burning rays, but the breeze, which always blows under the plantains, drives away tormenting insects.

The furnitures of a house are the same as in Persia, and consist of carpets, coverlets of felt, large chests, painted red, for keeping clothes, some cauldrons and other vessels for cooking, and holding water. Splendour or luxury are entirely wanting, and even the modern improvements in windows and doors, met with sometimes, come from Persia, from whence some clever and expert slave has introduced them into Central Asia. Nothing can find its way here from Europe, it has always to pass through the channel of Turkish and Persian civilization, And everything travels its customary snail's pace; the Persian imitates European institutions second hand from the Turks, and the nations in Central Asia adopt nothing but what reaches them through the medium of Persia.

The *food* of the Tartars consists principally of meat. Bread, in many parts of the country, although not unknown, is yet a rare luxury. Mutton is the favourite meat; next to this goat's flesh, beef, and horse flesh; camel's flesh is least valued. Occasionally, the horse is declared to be "mekruh" by the religious, and is not eaten, but in the country little notice is taken of it; and the *Torama*, horse flesh boiled soft and mixed up with onions, carrots and dumplings, is a very popular dish. It is worthy of remark, that the water first used in boiling the horse flesh is poured away, as far too strong and heavy for even Tartar digestion, and that only the second infusion can be eaten as broth. In some parts of Central Asia sausages are made of the entrails, and considered a dainty dish; but I have nowhere found, that the delicate parts of this animal are held in such high favour among the Œzbegs as is asserted throughout Persia. Camel's flesh is hard and tough; it is cut in small pieces, covered with paste, boiled, and then fried in lard. This dish, called *Somsa*, is not quite tasteless, but to our digestions like a weight of lead.

The favourite national dish is the *Palau*, also called ash, which, though related to the pilau of the Persians and the pilaf of the Turks, by far surpasses both these in savour. I have lived on it for a long time, and willingly impart to Europeans my knowledge of how it is prepared. A few spoonfuls of fat are melted (in Central Asia the fat of the tail is usually taken) in a vessel, and as soon as it is quite hot, the meat, cut up into small pieces, is thrown in. When these are in part fried, water is poured upon it to the depth of about three fingers, and it is left slowly boiling until the meat is soft; pepper and thinly-sliced carrots are then added, and on the top of these ingredients is put a layer of rice, after it has been freed from its mucilaginous parts. Some more water is added, and as soon as it has been absorbed by the rice the fire is lessened, and the pot, well-closed, is left over the red-hot coals, until the rice, meat and carrots, are thoroughly cooked in the steam.

After half an hour the lid is opened, and the food served in such a way that the different layers lie separately in the dish, first the rice, floating in fat, then the carrots and the meat at the top, with which the meal is begun. This dish is excellent, and indispensable alike on the royal table and in the hut of the poorest. From here it was introduced among the Afghans; by them to the Persians, who call it kabuli (kabul). The pilau, if I am not mistaken, has its origin in Central Asia, and spread from thence far and wide over Western Asia.

Another national dish of the Tartars is *Tchörek*, a soup with small dumplings in it, which are filled with spice and minced meat. I say "a soup," and yet this dish alone suffices for a whole dinner, since it is partaken of in such quantities that any other dish can be easily dispensed with. It is known among the Osmanlis by the name of tatar börek. Thirdly, *Sheöle*, a porridge of rice mixed up with meat and dried meat. Fourthly, bulamuk, a dish consisting simply of flour, water and fat. Fifthly, *Mestava*, rice boiled in sour milk, a dish exclusively for the summer, as the former is for the winter. Besides these dishes there are the *Yarma*, corn bruised and boiled in milk; *Godje*, a kind of porridge, made of the molcussorghum; and *Mashava*, likewise a porridge of grits, eaten with fat, and sometimes with oil. Heavy, strong and piquant dishes are generally preferred, few sweets are eaten, sugar and honey being unknown, and the many syrups (shires) prepared of grapes, melons, and other fruits, are rarely used in cooking. Of bread only enough for the day's consumption is baked, as is the custom everywhere in Asia. The dough is not made into thin cakes, as in

Persia, but into round thick loaves, such as are used in the neighbourhood of Erzerum, and are called lavash. There is also a sort of biscuit baked in fat, eaten when travelling.

Among the settled nations of Central Asia, tea is the favourite drink, and among the nomads, especially the Kirghis tribe, it is the *Kümis*. In summer they drink green tea, which thins the blood and promotes digestion; but in winter a black tea (brick tea) of a very harsh taste and an extraordinary stimulant; its effects are for a long time unbearable, and must be very dangerous. Cooling drinks are the *Airan*, sour milk mixed with water, and various decoctions made of dried fruit. Coffee is entirely unknown; even in Persia it is only met with in the southern province of Fars, and in Irak among the higher classes. Wine and brandy are sometimes sold secretly in the capitals, by Jews who manufacture both, but the number of consumers is very small. The Islamitic laws are severe on this point, and forbid, under pain of death, the use of spirituous liquors, but they do not prevent the vice of intoxication. Those who wish for stimulants use opium, teriak, or other narcotic poisons, and thus, in order to obviate a small evil, the door is opened to a much larger one, the gratification of which costs health and life.

The wretched poverty among the inhabitants of Central Asia is shown in nothing more strongly than in their *dress*, and the eye is with difficulty accustomed to the simple cotton stuff, or silks of glaring colours, in which every one is clothed, man and woman, young and old. Cloth or other European manufactures are only exhibited on extraordinary festive occasions, and are worn by wealthy or great dignitaries, as a *ne plus ultra* of luxury. At any other time, whether winter or summer, a garment, the so-called *Aladja*, is worn, and the only difference made in the various seasons is, that they put in a thicker lining, of either linen, wool, or fur. The cut of it is, perhaps, the most primitive among all the settled nations of Asia. No one has any idea of dressing tastefully and yet conveniently, or of setting off their figure to advantage, the only object is to cover or rather envelope it, and the Persian is perfectly right when he satirically says of his rude neighbours, that the whole nation moves about wrapt up in bed clothes. The *Tchapan* (upper coat) is the chief article of a man's wardrobe; it is not unlike our European dressing gowns, and cut out in Khiva so as to fit the body pretty well; in Bokhara it is already so large that two people can envelop themselves in it, and in Khokand it is widest of all. It is a highly ludicrous sight to see a man trot along in this smock-frock-like garment, full of folds, and puffing out at every part, and though I can well understand the many folds round the chest, forming as they do a receptacle for a whole set of cooking utensils, and all the necessaries for travelling, and food to last at least for two days, yet it will always be a mystery to me why the sleeves are twice as long as the arms, and what is the advantage of tucking them up and making an enormous roll or puff on the top of the arm. Under the tchapan is worn in summer a *Yektey* (a thin under dress), and under this the shirt, which reaches down to the ankles, and is distinguished from other shirts, worn in Asia, by being open on the left shoulder instead of in front, very much like a sack. At night the Turkestans have the strange habit, before going to sleep, of drawing their arms out of their shirt sleeves, and doubling themselves up. In winter an extra garment, *Tchekmen*, of ample dimensions and made of coarse stuff, is added to this costume. In some parts of the country, especially in Khiva, where the cold is greater, thickly-wadded, clumsy trousers are worn. As a covering for the head they wear in Khiva the telpek, a broad, conical-shaped hat of fur, which is very heavy; throughout Bokhara the turban is worn. It has a very picturesque appearance, with its long loops hanging down on the left side, and the trim natty way in which it is put on. In Khokand a small light cap used to be worn until twenty years ago, not unlike our clergyman's scapula (skull cap,) but since then it has yielded to Bokhariot civilisation, and has been supplanted by the turban. As to boots, those made in Bokhara and Khokand are the best. The leather is good, the shape rather handsome, but for the ludicrously long and thin heel, the end of which is scarcely broader than a nail's head. People of rank wear a kind of stocking made of morocco leather (mest), and over these, shoes, of which the best are made in Samarkand.

With respect to the dress of the women, it seems as if they were still more desirous than the men to avoid any approach to ostentation, luxury or smartness. When in undress, the women wear in summer a long shirt, reaching down to the ankles, the hind part of which is made of coarse linen, and the front mostly of a light coloured strong Russian print. The trousers are in like manner made of linen down to the knee, and the lower part, which fits close to the ankle, is made of print, or any other coloured stuff. The women wear in winter, over the shirt, one or two thickly-wadded jackets, fastened round the loins with a shawl. When abroad they put over all this a long garment, not unlike a man's coat, in which the woman muffles herself, holding it tightly together with both hands across her chest. The feet are covered with clumsy boots. It is a sorry sight to see a town woman of Central Asia walk about in this wretched costume, with her whole attention engrossed by the effort not to let the over-coat escape from her hands, since she would be regarded as an impudent woman indeed, if she allowed her under garments to be seen, and although the boldest stare cannot penetrate the coarse veil of horse-hair, yet she has to be for ever on the watch not to attract the looks of the passers by.

In the country, women are allowed to move with less restraint. Married women are seldom veiled, young girls never. The overcoat is shorter, and is merely thrown across the shoulder, and the broad shawl girded round the waist, with long ends fluttering to the breeze, gives a certain picturesqueness to their appearance. This indulgence, however, is only enjoyed in Khiva and Khokand; in Bokhara, even in the country, the tyrannical laws of Islamitic civilisation are executed with great severity, and it is rare to meet with an exception.

Among the men, various objects of ornament are seen, those which hang from the *Koshbag*, such as good knives with silver or other ornamented handles, gold-embroidered bags for tea, pepper and salt; further, rings for the fingers, tesbih (rosaries,) seals sometimes, but rarely, bracelets, gold and silver sheaths for amulets and watches, which latter are especial articles of luxury, and only to be found among the great. The objects of ornament among women I have already mentioned when speaking of the customs at weddings. It is useless to look for comfort or luxury either in the dwellings, food, or clothing of the natives of Central Asia, every thing here bears the impress of very ancient manners and customs, and every one conforms to them willingly, not wishing for anything better. The government, supported by the Mollahs, labours to keep up this status quo of things, by declaring all foreign productions contraband, and endeavouring to supplant them in the market, for fear the inhabitants of Turkestan might become aware of their poverty, and attribute it, not to the natural, but to the social circumstances of their country. And yet such an endeavour is fruitless, railroads and steam vessels bring their powerful veto, even in these rude countries, to bear upon a whole nation's backwardness. The ships which plough the Indian Ocean, the Black Sea, the Caspian Sea, the Lake of Aral, the Volga, and, at the present time, the Yaxartes likewise, have considerably lessened the distance between Central Asia and the west of Europe. The locomotives, which on the south run as far as Lahore, on the north to Nishnei-Novgorod, and astonish and perplex the eastern nations, are still, it is true, far from the inland waters of the Oxus and Yaxartes; yet, nevertheless, they exercise a considerable influence upon the communication of these countries. The Œzbeg trader need only go as far as Orenburg on the one, and Peshawur on the other side, and he has St. Petersburg, Bombay, and the whole of Europe before him. Inaccessible as Central Asia still is to all scientific, as well as commercial travellers, yet within the last twenty-five years an essential material advancement is apparent. We need only look over the custom-house list of the English and Russian frontier towns, and we should be surprised at the enormous increase of articles imported from Europe. From 1840 to 1850 goods were transported across the Russian frontier of nearly a million pounds sterling in value, and in the year 1860 they amounted already to the value of two millions. Cotton and silk stuffs have been more largely imported than any other goods, and in spite of the detestation and horror felt towards the producer, the productions of the west grow more and more in request, and are well paid for. Cottons, handkerchiefs and cambrics, as is well known, are the great forerunners of civilisation, the mute apostles of western culture, who spread blessings in their path, even though European arms and military tactics occasionally accompany their footsteps. And, however much the condition of half savage nations may be extolled for its happiness by foolish and weak-brained enthusiasts, yet a practical observer must feel convinced that our civilisation is preferable, and that it is a sacred duty on our part to transplant it to every clime and country.

CHAPTER IX.

FROM KHIVA TO KUNGRAT AND BACK.

THE young Mollah from Kungrat, who had joined our caravan in order to reach Samarkand, was planning to go and take leave of his native town and kindred whilst we were staying at Khiva; and great was his joy when he learned that I was desirous of accompanying him thither, partly from a wish to make a begging tour and collect all I could, and partly for the sake of escaping the uncomfortable crowding in hot, sultry Khiva. In his delight he promised me mountains of gold, describing everything in the most glowing colours, to sustain me in my resolve. I needed, however, no urging, too glad to meet with such an opportunity; and two days after I was actually on my way to Yengi Urgendj, from whence I hoped to reach the Oxus, where a half-laden vessel was ready to take us on board for a moderate fare.

The journey from Khiva to Kungrat is chiefly made by water in the summer, and down the river at high water it never lasts longer than five days; that is, during the very heat of summer, when the river has reached its greatest height, owing to the melting of the snow on the Hindukush and the tops of the Bedakhshan mountains. In the autumn and spring, at low water, the voyage lasts longer, and in winter it is entirely interrupted, the Oxus being in many parts, although not wholly, covered with ice.

The traveller can take ship, if so inclined, from the very walls of Khiva, that is, on the canal Hazreti Pehlivan, but not without making a great *détour*, since its mouth is to the south, near Hezaresp, instead of being to the north. The same objection applies to the second canal, Gazavat, which is at a considerable distance from the town, and flows rather eastward than northward. For this reason the traveller prefers to go to Yengi Urgendj, the first manufacturing and commercial city in the Khanat, and then on to Akhun Baba, the tomb of a saint, with a few scattered havlis (farmsteads) near it, which is situated on the banks of the Oxus, and is the first stage on the road. The distance is about eighteen English miles, in a well cultivated and tolerably populous district, the road leading through fields, gardens and meadows. Here are found the finest mulberry trees in the greatest abundance, and consequently the cultivation of silk is extremely flourishing; in fact, this part of the country justly deserves to be called one of the most beautiful in the whole Khanat.

The heat was so fierce and intolerable on the banks of the Oxus, that I could not help expressing some uneasiness to the boatmen, but they comforted me by saying, that down stream this evil would be remedied, by putting up a *Peshekhane* (mosquito net), which would not be in their way, the boat being steered only at either end. The mosquito net was at once put up; it had the shape of a canopy, and was to protect us in the day time from the sun, at night from the dangerous mosquitoes; and the necessary fatiha (blessings) on starting having been pronounced, we pushed off in company of four boatmen and two other passengers.

The voyage was at first very monotonous. The two men, one at the upper end and one at the lower end of the boat, kept steering it to those parts of the river where the water was yellowish and turbid, the current being here the strongest, as they explained to us. The rudders consisted of long poles, flattened at the end, and the two steersmen generally remained seated down at their work, unless special care and attention were required. They were relieved about every two hours, when, less fatigued by their labour than scorched by the sun, they would join us in our sheltered retreat, stretch themselves out at full length, to our great annoyance, and soon be heard snoring in chorus, until they had to return to their task. Of our two fellow-travellers, happily only one was very loquacious; and whenever my Tartar friend explained to me this or that point of interest, he would interrupt him with his copious emendations, and thus satisfy my curiosity by a full and detailed commentary.

The banks of the Oxus present few features especially worthy of interest, although far more than Boutenieff notices in his travels, who, in his mission in 1858, took the same route from Kungrat to Yengi Urgendj, up stream. On the right bank, opposite the place where we embarked, is seen the great ruin, Shahbaz Veli (the sacred hero), which is said to have been a strong fortress in ancient times, and which was destroyed by the Kalmucks. In the history of Khiva these people are regarded as the great destroyers of the Khanat; and although it is true that at the time of their invasion under Djengiz, the then flourishing Kharezm suffered terribly at their hands, yet it is an exaggeration to assert, as tradition does, that all the ruins are the sole work of their lust for devastation. Farther on I met with another extensive ruin with the remains of stone buildings, called Gaur Kaleszi (the fortress of the Gaurs). Under the term "Gaur," I first understood the Gebers or fire-worshippers, but soon I learned to my great astonishment, that by this name are designated, throughout Central Asia, the Armenians or rather the Nestorians, who possessed here large colonies, extending from the Sea of Aral far into China, in pre-Islamitic times down to the decline of the Mongol dominion.

On the right bank extends for more than three leagues, from the above-mentioned ruins down to the water's edge, a somewhat dense forest (togay), called Khitabegi. The trees are not particularly high, but the sun is nevertheless unable to penetrate and dry up the marshes fed by the Oxus. Only in very few places is the forest inhabited, and that by the Karakalpak tribe, who rear cattle. The left bank is the really inhabited part; here the chain of Havlis is scarcely interrupted, and here and there villages of some size are seen lying close to the water, such as the Œzbeg village Tashkale, which is situated on a high bank, and the smaller village of Vezir, near which the canal Kilidjbay discharges, or rather forms a basin, previous to losing itself beyond Yilali in the sand.

To make tea, prepare palau, and either listen to or tell sacred legends, was the alternate occupation of the day. Sometimes it happened that all my companions, the steersmen alone excepted, fell fast asleep, producing a pause, which was to me a most pleasant change; and as I fixed my eyes upon the yellow, turbid waters of the ancient Oxus, my imagination loved to revert to the clear mirror of many a European river, whose waters are ploughed by hundreds of ships, and whose verdant, smiling banks, are full of life and activity. What a gigantic contrast!

The Oxus is the typical representative of the country it traverses,—wild and unruly in its course, like the temperament of the Central Asiatics. Its shallows are as little marked as the good and bad qualities in the Turkoman; daily it makes for itself new channels similar to the nomad, whose restless spirit, wearied of staying long in one spot, is ever craving for novelty and change.

Early the second day we passed the town of Görlen at a short distance from the shore. The proper landing place is a village near, called Ishimdji, and opposite to it on the right bank is situated the fort Rehimberdi Beg, which I mention merely because here begins the mountain chain of Oveis Karayne, extending from south-east to north.* At first sight it bears much resemblance, as well in height as in its formation, to the Great Balkan in the desert, between Khiva and Astrabad; but on a nearer approach its larger circumference soon becomes apparent, and the luxuriant vegetation and the woods with which several of its heights are clothed, present a scene of agreeable surprise. On one of them is said to be the tomb of Oveis Karayne, a celebrated place of pilgrimage in Khiva, and in the distance we discovered several buildings, which Rehimberdi Beg had erected for the convenience of the devotees. Further on is the Munadjat daghi (mount of devotion), which is pointed out as the resting place of a holy lady, called Amberene (Mother Ambra). Holy women are not often met with in Sunnitic Islamism; there are, however, a few of them in Central Asia, which may be taken as a fresh proof that Islamism

---

* Oveis Karayne is the name of a faithful follower of Mohammed, who out of love to the Prophet had all his teeth knocked out, the latter having lost two of his front teeth in the battle at Ohud, through a blow from the enemy's weapon. After Mohammed's death he even intended to found an Order, with this self-mutilation as a condition of membership; but his efforts proved unsuccessful. The assertion, that he came to Khiva and died there, belongs rather to the region of fiction.

does not treat the fair sex with such unnatural harshness as people in Europe are apt to imagine. As to my lady Amberene, tradition tells us that, a Zuleikha in beauty, a Fatima in virtue, she was hated and afterwards expelled by her husband, solely because she professed the Mohammedan religion, of which he was an arch-enemy. Driven from her princely abode in Urgendj, she was obliged to take refuge in this wild spot, and would have died of starvation but for a hind which appeared daily at the entrance of her cave, waiting to be milked, and then again disappeared. Who, in hearing this tale, is not reminded of the story of Genoveva? The Parisians in those days were not better than the Œzbegs of to-day; nor can we fail to be struck with the identity that exists in fables of social and religious life, among nations living widely separated from each other.

After leaving Görlen we went on for about four hours down stream, and came to Yengï yap, an insignificant hamlet, surrounded by earth walls, and about one hour and a half distant from the river. Two hours later we reached the district of Khitayi, which begins where the Yumalak, a conical hill, rises close to the left bank. On the right the Oveis mountains approach nearer and nearer to the Oxus, and soon we passed the prominent peak Yampuk, crowned with the ruins of an old castle. Opposite Yumalak the mountain chain, Sheikh Djeli, which runs from east to west, forms a very narrow channel (here called kisnak), much narrower than the Iron Gates on the Danube, and often dangerous to navigation from the force and rapidity of the current. The waters here roar, as if the Oxus, that unruly son of the desert, were angry at being so imprisoned between the rocks. The narrowest part is, however, very short; on the left bank the mountains terminate abruptly, while on the right bank the high lands gradually slope, and after having passed Tama, which lies on the left, the country is everywhere flat. With the mountains disappeared every romantic feature along the banks of the Oxus. After a voyage of two days our eyes and imagination were fully satisfied, and although the morning and evening hours had their charms, yet the heat became intolerable in the day-time, and the mosquitoes and flies at night—insects, in comparison with which the Golumbacz on the Lower Danube are harmless and insignificant as butterflies. As soon as the sun began to set, every one crept carefully under the mosquito-net, made, of course, of linen, the air under which had become so thoroughly poisoned by my fellow-travellers, that I felt keenly not to be able to exchange it for the purer air outside. Towards evening we reached the district of Mangit, which has a town of the same name, about two hours' distance from the river, but not visible from the boat on account of a small wood which intervenes. Here we remained for some time moored along the bank, and having comfortably cooked our dinner in the open air, instead of on the narrow hearth in the boat, we continued our voyage. We reached Basuyap, after another hour's journey, at night, much to the regret of my friend, who had been anxious to pay a visit with me to a very celebrated *Nogaï Ishan*, who resided there, in order to ask his advice and blessing on the journey he had undertaken. These *Nogaï*, who fled hither to escape the Russian authorities or the conscription, are in Central Asia regarded as martyrs to freedom and Islamism, and revered as such; but I have frequently met among them the most consummate rascals, and thought that they had probably run away from a fully merited chastisement.

Early in the morning we passed Kiptchak, which is the second stage on the journey, and lies on both sides of the Oxus. At this place a rock rises from the water, which, extending across the river, narrows the channel by more than half its width, and renders the navigation so extremely dangerous, that it is never attempted, except at broad daylight. At low water some of the points are visible, and it is no uncommon thing to see children, a foot deep in water, clambering upon them.

Kiptchak itself is a place of considerable importance, inhabited by an Œzbeg tribe of the same name, and possesses several mosques and colleges. Of the latter, the college situated on the right bank of the river was founded by Khodja Niaz, and is deservedly celebrated for its rich endowments. Not far from this building, which stands separately, is seen the ruin Tchilpik, on a hill rising close to the water. Tradition asserts that in ancient times it was a strong castle, and the residence of a Princess, who, having fallen in love with one of her father's slaves, and dreading the anger of her offended parent, fled hither for refuge with her lover. In order to obtain water, they were obliged to pierce the hill downwards to the river, and the subterranean passage exists at the present day.

From Kiptshak up the stream begins the forest already mentioned, which extends with few interruptions along the right bank of the river to some distance beyond Kungrat. I could not see from the boat how far its breadth stretched eastward, but I have been assured that it is from eight to ten hours' journey. Its approach from the river is intercepted by bogs and morasses, which render it only in a few places accessible. In the less thickly-wooded parts graze numberless herds of cattle, the property of the Karakalpaks, who find abundance of game in the forest, but sometimes suffer greatly from the numerous wild beasts, especially panthers, tigers, and lions, which infest that district. From here to Görlen the stream has so many shallows, that we were incessantly striking aground. The left bank rises to an elevated plateau, which extends far in a north-westerly direction, and is called Yilankir (the field of serpents) by the natives. On the western frontier of the desert it forms a declivity as steep as the Kaflankir, or the whole table-land of Ustyurt. The population of this region consists of Jomut-Turkomans and Tchaudors; the former lead a nomadic life near the river, and in the country round Porsu and Yilali; the latter inhabit the skirts of the desert and the several oases of the Ustyurt. Both tribes, as may well be imagined, live in constant feud with each other,—a condition as much to their disadvantage, as it is to the advantage of the Œzbegs, the immediate neighbourhood of a strong and united nomad people proving always most dangerous to the dwellers in settled habitations.

On the evening of the third day we stopped at Khodja Ili,* a town about two hours' distance from the river. Most of the inhabitants derive their origin from Khodja, and they are not a little proud of comparing their ancestry with that of the other Œzbegs. The whole district is thickly populated, and the left bank forms as far as Nöks† an uninterrupted chain of wood and cultivated land. Here is one of the most dangerous places in the Oxus, a waterfall, which at the time of our voyage rushed down from the height of three feet with the swiftness of an arrow and with

---

* Khodja Ili.—The people of the Khodja, or descendants of the prophets, a considerable number of whom inhabit this part of the country. They have as much a purely Œzbeg physiognomy, as the numerous Seids in Persia bear the stamp of an Iranic origin. The former, however, enjoy considerably more privileges.

† In the map to my "Travels in Central Asia," Nöks has by mistake been confounded with Khodja Ili; the former also is full an hour farther from Kungrat than is there stated.

a tremendous noise, which is heard at the distance of more than a league. The natives call it Kazankitken, *i.e.*, the spot where the cauldrons went to the bottom, since a vessel laden with these utensils is said to have been lost here. Full fifteen minutes before reaching the waterfall the boats are brought close to the shore, and carefully towed along. From here down the stream the river has formed by inundations very considerable lakes, which communicate with one another by small natural canals, which seldom dry up entirely. The largest are: Kuyruklu Köl and Sari Tchöngül. The former is said to extend for several days' journey far towards the north-east; the latter is smaller in circumference, but much deeper.

We passed Nöks on the fourth day. Even on the left bank we saw cultivation gradually decreasing as we advanced; the river on both sides is bordered with forests, and forms half-way to Kungrat a broad and rather deep canal, called Ogüzkitken, which takes a south-westerly direction and falls into the lake Shorkatchi. Efforts have been made to cut off the latter from the large stream by raising dykes, but in vain, and the immense extent of water renders the navigation here exceedingly troublesome. The forest terminates at the tomb of a saint, called Afakkhodja, and the district of Kungrat begins, covered, as far as the eye can reach, with gardens, fields and "havlis." The town itself did not become visible until the evening of the fifth day, after we had passed the ruin of a fortress built by the rebel Törebeg at the time of Mehemmed Emin, and a whirlpool near it.

Our stay in this most northerly town of the Khanat of Khiva was of very short duration, since my young companion, having lost his parents a year before, was not long in taking leave of the relative who dwelt here, and himself urged a speedy return. The town has a far more miserable appearance than those in the south, and is chiefly known for its large fairs, to which the nomads of the neighbourhood resort, offering for sale large quantities of cattle, butter, carpets of felt, camels' hair and wool. A brisk trade is also carried on in fish, especially dried fish, which are brought from the sea of Aral, and sent afterwards from here all over the Khanat. I must mention as a very remarkable fact, that I met here with two Russians, who had turned Mahometans, and lived in the full enjoyment of a comfortable dwelling-house, a flourishing farmstead, and a numerous family. They were prisoners of the Perowsky Army, and received their liberty from Mehemmed Emin Khan, under the condition that they would adopt Islamism. One of them has been presented with a Persian slave: the dark-brown daughter of Iran and the fair-haired son of the north live very happily together, and although the latter has several times had the opportunity of returning to his native home, he has not been able to form the resolution of quittting his adopted fatherland on the banks of the Oxus.

In conclusion, I will state the scanty information I gathered here about the further course of the Oxus from Kungrat to its embouchure in the Sea of Aral. At two hours' distance from this town, going down stream, the river divides into two great arms, which are little distinguished from each other. The right one, which keeps the name of Amu Derya, reaches the lake first, but in consequence of its many ramifications it is too shallow, and at low water extremely difficult to navigate. The left arm, which bears the name of Tarlik (the strait)* is narrow, but of a certain depth throughout, and is little used, simply on account of the great circuit it makes on its way to the lake. The traffic on the Lower Oxus is inconsiderable, and not to be compared with that which enlivens the river between Tchihardjuy and Kungrat, where it forms the principal commercial highway between Bokhara and Khiva. In autumn it is chiefly fishing which takes the Œzbegs to the sea, and the trade in dried sea-fish is in all three Khanats an important one. It has

* Not Taldyk, as Admiral Butakoff called it in his treatise, read on the 11th of March, 1867, before the Geographical Society in London, nor can I agree with him about the two extreme arms of the Delta, of which he calls the eastern Yenghi, and the western Laudan. It is possible that it may have been so formerly, in consequence of the frequent changes of the water-course; but at present this is no longer the case. I learned from the most authentic source, that the name of Laudan is given only to the dry bed of the Oxus, which, beginning at Kiptchak, runs in a westerly direction past Köhne Urgendj. Butakoff designates the middle branch by the name of Ulkun, and here I must remark, that this word meaning "great," is always added to the name of the chief stream. Ulkun, more correctly Ulkèn, is consequently identical with my Amu Derya.

become an almost indispensable article to the inhabitants of the steppes, from their being too parsimonious to feed on meat, in spite of their wealth in cattle, and therefore preferring, as they do, dried fish as its substitute. In the spring, on the other hand, it is the wild geese, large numbers of which are found around the several mouths of the river, which tempt all those who are fond of shooting to the shores of the Sea of Aral. At this season of the year also most pilgrimages take place, undertaken by pious Œzbegs to the tomb of Tokmak Baba, which is situated upon an island of the same name, near these outlets. This saint is revered as the patron of fishermen, and rests under a small mausoleum, in the inner cell of which have been carefully preserved through remote ages his clothes and cooking utensils, among which a cauldron is an object of peculiar veneration. I was told, that even the Russians very rarely land on this island, although access to it has been greatly facilitated by steam-vessels, and that in case they do visit it, they never touch these relics,—as if moved by involuntary feelings of respect.

In surveying the whole course of this remarkable river, from its source on the Ser-i-kul (beginning of the sea) down to its embouchure, we perceive firstly, that it is not, as Burnes asserts, navigable throughout its entire length, but on the contrary, that only from Kerki, or rather from Tchihardjuy down stream can it be used for large and small craft. Upwards from these towns we meet nothing but rafts, carrying fuel and timber, in which the slopes of the Bedakhshan mountains abound, and supplying the scantily wooded plains, but seldom used by families emigrating to the Lower Oxus. Between Hezaresp and Eltchig, a part of the river which forms one stage on the way to Bokhara, larger boats already are used from and to Khiva, which carry goods and victuals; but the greatest traffic is undoubtedly on that part of the river, which flows in the Khanat of Khiva, where the river, with its many towns along its banks, affords a favourite and cheap means, up as well as down stream, for the transport of large freight, and is used among the poorer classes even for personal inter-communication. Secondly, it appears to me (I abstain from making any assertion, not possessing sufficient knowledge on the subject), that the Oxus has scarcely the capabilities of becoming the powerful artery for traffic and communication in Central Asia, which politicians, when speaking of the future of Turkestan, confidently expect. It never can become of the same importance as the Yaxartes, whose waters at this very moment are ploughed by Russian steamers, a conjecture sufficiently warranted by the fact, that the Russians entered Turkestan with their flotilla of the Sea of Aral, not by the Oxus, but by the Yaxartes, a river far less favourable to their plans of occupation. It has been urged, that the uninhabited shores of this last-named river are of greater importance to the

Court of St. Petersburg; but this is a worthless argument, and rests solely on our want of geographical knowledge with respect to Central Asia.

With steamers on the Oxus, the Russians would not only have been able to keep the Khanat of Khiva in check, to garrison the fortress of Kungrat, Kiptshak and Hezaresp, but they would have had the power of introducing with the greatest ease a strong *corps d'armée* by Karakul into Bokhara, and thus into the very heart of Central Asia, had not the extraordinary physical difficulties of this route rendered such a scheme impracticable. Moreover, of this the Russians themselves became sufficiently convinced, when making their very first appearance in Central Asia. Apart from the waterfall at Khodja Ili, the dangerous cliffs near Kiptchak and the Kisnak near Yampuk, the Oxus offers perhaps the greatest difficulties to navigation in its numerous sandbanks, which in some parts extend for many miles, and at the same time undergo such rapid changes in consequence of the large quantity of sand the stream carries along with it, that it is quite impossible to take observations, and even the most experienced steersman can do no more than guess the navigable channel by the colour, but can never indicate it with confidence or certainty. Thirdly, to regulate this stream, which at the beginning of the spring, and during the latter part of the autumn, is almost two-thirds smaller than in summer, would be of the greatest disadvantage to the inhabitants, since its numerous arms and canals not only are necessary for the cultivation of their fields, but supply with drinking water even the most distant parts of the country, to say nothing of the rapid current rendering such an undertaking extremely difficult. If the Khan of Khiva wanted to declare war against some rebellious part of his country, he would first of all cut off the canals and aqueducts, a stroke of policy which would be felt most severely; and a government, which were to shut the sluices in order to increase the water in the bed of the Oxus, would commit an act equivalent to a declaration of hostilities against the whole country at once.

Not only has the Oxus extremely rapid currents, but it continually deviates from its original channel. These deviations in the lower part of the river begin after its bend near Hezaresp, and are far more numerous than is generally supposed. Upon enquiring of the inhabitants about them, they reckoned up more than eight on each side, and although they may have included in this estimate former canals, nevertheless its irregularity must be admitted. Taking this view, there is very little difficulty in agreeing with Sir Henry Rawlinson, who founded his assertion on a very valuable Persian manuscript, that in former times the Sea of Aral had no existence whatever.

The journey from Kungrat to Khiva is generally made by land, since it requires from eighteen to twenty days up stream. The transport of freight is made by water. There are three roads by land ; 1, by Köhne Urgends, which is called the summer route, and avoids the lakes, outlets and arms of the Oxus, which at that season of the year are full to overflowing. This route is the longest, 56 farsakh* in length; 2, by Khodja Ili, a distance of 40 farsakh, which the traveller prefers in the winter, all the waters being frozen; and 3, the road on the right bank of the Oxus by Shurakhan, which makes several *détours*, and runs through a great many sand-steppes.

Our return journey had to be made with all possible speed, but nevertheless we were obliged to take the long road by Köhne Urgendj. We had the good fortune to join a party of travellers, of whom some were going to Köhne Urgendj, others to Khiva. All were capitally mounted, and even the horses placed at our disposal "lillah" (out of pious benevolence) were young, vigorous animals, and, as we carried no luggage except a few biscuits with a small store of provisions for our journey, we rode briskly along in spite of the heat, which even in the early morning made itself felt. Leaving the gate of the town behind us, we rode across the well-cultivated district of Kungrat, keeping always a north-westerly direction, and then crossing a barren tract of country, came to a large stagnant water, called *Atyolu*, which is marked out as the first stage, and is 7 farsakh long. A bridge leads over a narrow part of it, and here the road diverges

* Farsakh (*i.e.*, παρασάγγης), a Persian league, about 18,000 feet in length.

in two parts, the one of which skirts a low mountain, called Kazak Orge, and, crossing the great plateau of Ustyurt, goes to Orenburg; the other leads to Köhne Urgendj. We took the latter route, and passing through forests and sandy tracts, now and then came in sight of some ruin on either side of the road, of which two were pointed out as being worthy of notice;—Karagömbez (black dome), near which a salt is found as clear and white as crystal, and the finest in the Khanat, and Barsakilmez (he who goes does not return), a dangerous spot, inhabited even at the present day by evil spirits, and where many, who went there from curiosity, have lost their lives.

After a long ride of five hours we reached the second station, called *Kabilbeg Havli*. It is an isolated farmstead, but, in accordance with an old custom of the proprietors, we were received and treated with great hospitality, and remembering that we had the prospect of a long ride of eight hours from here to the next stage, *Kiziltchagalan*, our kind host had not forgotten to provide us at breakfast with meat and bread. It was still dark when we started. Our companions were examining their weapons with the utmost care, which made me fear that we might perhaps have to pass some hostile tribe of the Turkomans; but they removed my uneasiness on this point, cautioning me at the same time that we should have to travel the whole day long in a thick forest, in which there were many lions, panthers and wild boars, which sometimes have been known to attack the traveller. They added, that although they never reached the place of danger till broad daylight, yet they invariably moved forward with the greatest circumspection, and, above all, put great confidence in their horses, which no sooner prick up their ears, or begin to snort, than each and all seize their weapons. It is well known that lions and panthers in a climate like that of Central Asia are far less dangerous than their brethren in India and Africa, and therefore I did not share the fears of my young Tartar companion; on the contrary, I rather longed for adventure and the excitement of the chase. The Œzbeg, however, like a true Asiatic, possesses an excitable imagination; there was neither trace nor sound to indicate that we were near the abode of the king of animals, and we saw nothing but some herds of wild boars, who with a loud crash made their way through the thick underwood, and an immense, nay, fabulous number of Guinea-fowl and pheasants, of which we made rich spoil for our evening halt. These birds are in this part of the country of a much finer flavour than in Mazendran, the Œzbegs also understand far better than the Persians to dress and cook them. Emerging from the forest, we soon came in sight of the fortified place Kiziltshagalan, which is inhabited by Œzbegs. We arrived there in good time, and the following morning continued our road across a district inhabited by Yomuts.

Köhne Urgendj is considered the fourth station, although the journey thither does not occupy above three hours. This ancient metropolis of far-famed Kharezm, in Central Asia, is the poorest of all those cities in Asia which have shared the same fate, and however much its former splendour is extolled in word and writing, I could not help feeling at the sight of its still existing ruins, that it had been the centre of no higher than Tartar civilisation. The town of the present day is small, dirty and insignificant, although it must have been much larger in former times, to judge from the ruins that lie scattered outside the wall. These ruins are not older than the Islamitic era, and date from the reign of Shahi Kharezmian, an epoch of a higher culture. The most remarkable object here is the mosque of Törebeg Khanim (not Khan), of which I have already made mention in my "Travels," and which is larger and more splendid than Hazreti Pehlivan. The latter, nevertheless, has been considered hitherto the finest monument in Khiva, and it must be admitted that with its works in Kashi (glazed tiles), in which throughout the yellow colour predominates, it is not inferior to any architectural monument of the same kind in Turkestan. Further is seen the mausoleums of Sheikh Sheref with a high azure dome, of Piriyar, the father of the very celebrated Pehlivan, and of Sheikh Nedshm ed-din Kübera. The latter has of late been restored from decay by the liberality of Mehemmed Emin Khan. I was told that there are in the neighbourhood several towers and walls built of stone, such as Puldshoydu (money destroyed) which is distant three hours' journey. Whenever a storm ploughs up the sand-hills there, coins and vessels of gold and silver are discovered, and people who take the trouble of sifting the sand, find frequently their labour amply requited. There is also the Aysanem, or double kiosk of Aysanem and Shahsanem, the famous pair of lovers, whose romantic fate forms the subject of a collection of songs frequently sung by the native minstrels. The name appears to be a stereotyped name for any two isolated ruins, since there are Shahsanems to be found in other parts of Khiva and Bokhara, as well as in the neighbourhood of Herat, and everywhere the same legends are recorded of them with few variations.

At Köhne Urgendj the road divides, both branches running at a small distance from each other. The one less frequented runs by Porsu and Yilali, and is taken by people who travel in large parties; the proximity of the marauding tribes of the Tshaudors and Yomut Turkomans, rendering the road, at least as far as Tashhauz, very insecure. The second road, nearer the Oxus, runs with few interruptions along its banks, a tract of country strewn with farmsteads (Havlis), villages and hamlets. This road is generally taken in summer, although it is the longer of the two, and also more troublesome on account of the many ditches and canals for irrigation. Whereas, a caravan must keep together as far as Tashhauz on the former road, travellers on the latter may part company as early as at Kiptchak, and each continue his way separately.

CHAPTER X.

MY TARTAR.

I CANNOT conceive it possible to imagine a greater contrast than an Asiatic, and more particularly a Central Asiatic, who, as late as two years ago, wrapt in his national garb of ample width, hanging about him in loose folds, was feeding on the simple and primitive fare of a nomadic people, and who, at the present moment, booted and spurred, moves about in the closely-fitting costume of the Hungarians, and is already accustomed to the food and manners of the West; one, who, destined to lead the life of a Mollah, once spent his time in the lonely cell of the Medresse Mehemmed Emin at Khiva, absorbed either in prayer or in the doctrines of Islamism, and who is now seen turning over the large folios in the library of a European academy, acquainted with books on philosophy, or the history of the world and religion, Greek and Latin literature, and numberless authors besides; who scarcely ever had heard the name of Europe, or had heard it mentioned only in terms of the utmost abhorrence; who knew no other institutions, no other phases or aspects of men and things, but those in his own wild Eastern world, and recognised these alone as true and reasonable;—and who now is reading the leading articles of European newspapers, discussing the different politics of Western countries, and unhesitatingly making the boldest comparisons between the Eastern and Western hemispheres.

These are certainly clear and sharply-defined contrasts, and such contrasts my friend the Mollah exhibits "*in propriâ personâ*,"—the Hadji whom I brought with me from Central Asia, whom I met with whilst on his way to Mekka, who became my companion and associate, and who, instead of the holiest of holy cities, now lives with me in the metropolis of Hungary. How I succeeded in inducing him to form this resolution has been to many a matter of the liveliest curiosity to know; nor were their enquiries less eager as to the impression made upon him by my metamorphosis from the pious dervish into the European traveller. One fundamental error ran through all these enquiries,— namely, the strange belief that my change had been as sudden as that of the chrysalis to the butterfly. It was, on the contrary, extremely gradual, and its various phases are the more interesting, since they illustrate in a striking manner the difference between Eastern and Western life. The history of my transformation, in fact, deserves to be given in detail.

I first met my Tartar, as I mentioned before, in Khiva. A Mollah, young and animated with a desire for travelling, he was in search of a companion on his journey to Mekka, and in the full belief to find in me a Turk and a Mohamedan, the most suitable fellow-traveller, he at once attached himself to me with the utmost ardour and devotion. During the early part of our acquaintance he saw in me merely the learned Mollah, the wild zealot, whom he approached with the greatest veneration, listening most attentively to every word that fell from my lips. Such was the relation that existed between us throughout our journey to Bokhara, Samarkand, and Karshi, as far as the banks of the Oxus. Here I became more confidential towards him: occasionally I put off somewhat the disguise of my affected sanctity; we grew more and more intimate by degrees; our slender store of provisions was put into one common bag, and as he was thoroughly honest and true-hearted, his sincere and loyal friendship became a great support and comfort to me on my solitary and perilous journey. Only slowly, and with difficulty, could he accustom himself to a real and mutual intimacy; and on our begging expeditions he would take upon himself, as his own undisputed task, to collect the heavy contributions, such as wood, flour, &c., whilst he left to me the less onerous business of collecting the pence. In the evening he made it his duty to prepare the supper, and, after having served the rice on a piece of rag or a board, it was always a matter of conscience with him not to touch it until I had twice helped myself with my hands. I do not know whether veneration or conscience inspired him with this excessive respect, but, be the cause what it may, he invariably shrank from placing himself in a position of equality. Not wishing to spoil his pleasure, I therefore let him do exactly as he pleased.

On our journey from the Oxus to Herat, my feigned devoutness visibly decreased in exact proportion as the distance between me and fanatic Bokhara kept increasing. Prayers, ablutions, pious meditations—all became less frequent. My Tartar, no doubt, observed this, but it did not seem to trouble him, and he accommodated himself ungrudgingly to his master. His questions on religion were fewer, but he listened instead with more eager attention to my descriptions and narratives of the foreign land of the 'Frengi,' and the pictures I drew of those marvellous countries of the West. Such lectures as these were usually delivered during our night marches, when we were riding alone in intimate converse, and at some distance from the caravan. The pleasure I felt in being able to talk of my beloved West in a barbarous country, surrounded as I was with dangers in so doing, was not greater than my Tartar's astonishment when he heard that there were towns more beautiful than Bokhara, and countries where it was possible to travel without fear of robbers or of dying with thirst. He was especially struck when I assured him that the 'Frengis,' so far from being the savage, pitiless cannibals, such as they had been represented to him, possessed heart and feeling, and that they were infinitely superior to their reputed character in the East. Under different circumstances he might have doubted the truth of my assertions; but as I, the Efendi, his teacher and master, assured him of these facts, he placed implicit belief in all I told him. No wonder that I was pleased with his thirst for knowledge and his loyalty, and that I in return became greatly attached to my young Tartar. Moreover, he kept as much as possible aloof from the other Central Asiatics, his countrymen, uniting himself more closely to my society. As soon as I perceived—which I could not fail to do before long— that something could be made of the young man, I resolved not to let him leave me, but, if possible, to take him with me to Europe. If such was my determination long before we came to Herat, it was still further strengthened by the brilliant proofs of his attachment and fidelity which he showed to me during our residence in this town. Here, as is already known, my sufferings and privations reached their climax. Totally without means, I had not unfrequently to bear all the torments of hunger; and whenever, at this advanced season of the year, the cold prevented my sleeping during the night, it was my young Tartar who honestly shared with me his poor thin rags, in order to procure for me a warmer covering and a quiet sleep. During these six weeks that we spent in Herat we suffered, indeed, greatly; but I tried to strengthen the courage of my companion by assuring him that we should meet with certain help in Persia. The idea that a pious Sunnite should fare well in the heretical country of the Shiites, appeared to him sufficiently droll; but the child-like innocence of his heart, and his unaffected confidence in me, prevented his making any further conjectures. He looked, like myself, with intense longing to the frontiers of Iran, and the capital of Khorassan.

At last we arrived in Meshed. The hearty friendship of the English officer here, and his kindness towards me as well as my companion, were at first a great puzzle to my Tartar. He knew Dolmage was a Frengi ;—what strange thoughts must have crossed his mind, in his astonishment at seeing me, the pious Mohamedan, his "chef spirituel," sit for hours in the company of an unbeliever, talking with him in a foreign language, nay, eating with him out of one and the same dish. The servants of the English officer, and indeed every one in the town, repeatedly declared to him their opinion that his master was a Frengi in disguise. He shuddered at the thought, and although he heard these suspicions with feelings of anger and indignation, yet he never questioned me on this point, and his firm faith in me remained unshaken. Moreover, his attachment to me naturally increased, from finding in me at all times a friend and protector, especially on our journey to Teheran, when, on account of his Tartar costume, he had frequently to encounter the ill-will of the vindictive Shiites. On my part, again, it was, I consider, no small risk, to travel for a whole month alone with this man, to pass whole nights alone with him in desolate spots. Let one single evil thought arise in his heart, and it would have been an easy matter for him to kill me during my noon-day slumbers on the open road, and, carrying with him my horses, weapons and money, to escape into the desert northward to the Turkomans. But I never harboured any such suspicion. Fully confiding in him, I entrusted to his charge my musket, sword and horse; when tired and fatigued I stretched myself out upon the sand and slept soundly and securely, whilst he acted as sentinel; for at the very beginning of our acquaintance I had discovered that he had a true heart, and I cannot say that I have ever once been mistaken in this respect.

It was in Shahrud where he saw me for a second time embrace an unbeliever. He was struck by it, and said: "My master, thou art truly wise, in always associating with the Frengis; for these Persians, although they believe in the Koran and in Mohammed, are, by heaven! a hundred times worse than the unbelievers!" On this occasion he expressed to me also, after having met a second Englishman, his surprise at finding these Frengis, both "outwardly and inwardly, such agreeable persons;" and yet he found it difficult to approach them. He would stare at them and scrutinize them for hours, proving clearly that, although he had partly got rid of his deeply-rooted prejudices, a certain degree of shyness and reserve was still clinging to him.

During the latter part of our march towards the Persian capital, my joyous feelings occasionally woke within me some long-forgotten song or melody. I began first to whistle, and then to sing, popular airs of certain operas. Whistling is not practised in the East, and regarded as extremely frivolous and indecorous; nevertheless, he was greatly pleased with the charming melodies from the Troubadour, Lucia, and others. He asked me with great naïveté, whether in Mekka people recited the Koran with these accompaniments, and was greatly astonished when I replied in the negative.

It was at the post station of Ahuan for the first time he heard me called by my European name. This name touched the tenderest fibres of his heart, and no doubt he struggled long and painfully before he found the courage to question me. I replied, that I would give him an answer in Teheran, and this set him at rest for a time. On my arrival in Teheran, I lodged with my old friends in the Turkish embassy. The young Efendis, who represented the Sultan, were fashionable European diplomatists, bearing the signs of Frengiism in far stronger colours than myself. This lessened his suspicions; and when I enlightened him on the modern civilization of his Sunnitic brethren in the West, he gradually became aware of the immense gulf between Stamboul and Bokhara. He was told of the continuous efforts of the Osmanlis to assimilate themselves as much as possible to the Western countrics and their culture, and he could not help following this example himself. If we take into account, that he saw and heard nothing but what was good and excellent of the few Frengis whom he had hitherto had the opportunity of knowing, it was natural that his hatred and his prejudices should vanish day by day.

In Teheran he made the acquaintance of a countryman of mine, Mr. Szántó, who frequently came to see me, and with whom he was soon on terms of intimacy. Szántó told him with no small joy, that he and his master (he meant me) were the only Magyars in Persia. The Magyars, moreover, the philologizing tailor added, are the kindred of the Osmanlis,— a statement the Tartar felt surprised at, but which did not exactly disquiet him, our long intercourse and friendship reconciling him to all he saw and heard. And seeing in me more affection and kindness than in the genuine Turk, the trifling difference as to nationality troubled him very little. He roved about cheerfully in Teheran, making himself acquainted with the manners and language of the Persians, and was extremely glad, when, after a residence of several weeks, we were saddling our horses once more for our journey to Constantinople.

Hitherto no other plan had been talked of, but that he was to accompany me as far as Constantinople, and from thence go on to Mekka by Alexandria. But soon I perceived that this original plan no longer pleased him, and that he intended to do otherwise. Our life in the Turkish embassy in Teheran, where everything was arranged after the European manner, and our frequent intercourse with other embassies, had shown him a part of Western life in a very pleasant aspect, and awakened in him the desire to visit with me these wonderful countries. Nor is it difficult to understand how his original longing, to prostrate himself upon the grave of the holy Prophet, receded more and more into the background. His sound understanding was not long in penetrating this religious humbug; and, having naturally a great love for adventure, he soon resolved, instead of the illustrious Mekka, to go and visit Frengistan, a country formerly thought of with dread and detestation.

I pretended not to observe what was passing in his mind, and putting him on shore at Constantinople, I was about to take leave of him, after having amply provided him with money. The young Tartar looked at me fixedly with tears in his eyes, and in spite of the sight of the proud minaret, in spite of the crowd of orthodox worshippers who surrounded him here on every side, he felt constrained to say to me, in a voice trembling with emotion, and interrupted by frequent sobs: "Efendi, do not leave me here behind alone. Thou hast brought me from Turkestan into this strange land: I know here no one but thee. I follow thee, gladly, whithersoever thou goest!"—"What, wilt thou come with me to Frengistan?" I asked him; "from thence it is very far to Mekka; there are no mosques and public baths, no Mussulman food; how wilt thou live there?" For a moment he seemed perplexed; but after a brief silence he replied: "The Frengis are such good and kind people; I should like to see their country; and afterwards I will return to Stamboul." I required no more. Fully understanding the character of my Central Asiatic friend, I embarked with him once more on the shore of the Bosphorus, and in three days he was already upon a steamer on the Danube, surrounded by Europeans, and on his way to the not far distant capital of Hungary. On board the steamer I found him often absorbed in thought. Not yet venturing to taste European food, he gazed at everything around him with a shy timidity, but gradually he grew accustomed to the novelty of the scene, and a few days later he promenaded the streets of Pesth in Bokhara costume. During the first few days he could scarcely find words, so full was he of amazement. Everything, indeed, appeared to him like an enchantment. He admired all he saw, from the square-hewn paving stones in the streets to the lofty buildings and towers; and it can easily be imagined what singular, and at times comical, remarks he made;—he, the son of the desert, in the midst of one of the first cities in Europe. He was much struck with the quick walking of people in the streets, and the rapid movements of the vehicles; but, above all, the women arrested his attention; and he could not understand how the Frengi, clever and sensible people as they are, could allow their womenfolk to appear in public in such clumsy and uncouth attire, and without any protection. In the day time I often saw him standing by the telegraph wires, listening to the sounds that passed along them. At night he would stare at the gas lamps, full of curiosity to discover whether it was the iron that was burning. At the hotel, the luxury and magnificence that surrounded him filled him with astonishment. Judging of every person he met by his dress, he regarded every one as some mighty lord or potentate, and frequently exclaimed: "Oh! this is a happy country! Here seems to be not a single poor man!" He soon grew accustomed to the looks of curiosity that followed him wherever he went. His former dread of the Frengi had entirely disappeared; he had a pleasant face for every one, and frequently entered eagerly into conversation with the first person he met, forgetting, in his characteristic manner, that no one could understand him; and he would go on talking to his heart's content, without being in the least disturbed by the surprise exhibited by those he was thus addressing.

I should most gladly have taken him on with me to London, had I not deemed it better for him to leave him for the while behind in Hungary. A friend of mine, who lived in the country, received him kindly into his house; and when, after a year's absence, I returned from England, I was not a little surprised to find my young Tartar dressed in the Hungarian costume, and, instead of the turban, with his hair nicely curled and trimmed, with a rather droll air and demeanour, and a certain stiff gravity in his manner. He had learned the Hungarian language in a very short time; he was everywhere liked and heartily welcomed, and when, for the first time, I saw him smartly dressed, and with gloves on his hands, talking most courteously and earnestly to a lady in her drawing-room, I could scarcely refrain from laughter. Two years ago a Mollah of a Medresse, he is now grown into half a dandy:—in truth what cannot be made of an Oriental? Being able to write as well as speak Hungarian, my friends kindly procured him an appointment as assistant-librarian in the Academy, which position he fills at the present moment. When I question him about his new life, and talk to him of the difference between Eastern and Western manners and habits, I find that his past life floats like a dream across his mind, which he cherishes only as a distant reminiscence, but which he would not on any account exchange for his present existence. He rarely feels any longing for his native home, and he loves our Western civilisation for the following reasons. In the first place, he is particularly pleased with the perfect security that society affords to the individual, and the absence of any arbitrary tyranny on the part of the Government. In Central Asia a man's bare life is not safe on the roads from robbers; in the towns he is threatened with constant danger from the barbarous decrees of the authorities. The frequent cruel executions, the desolating civil wars in his country, have never struck him until now, when he has become aware how thousands of persons come in daily contact with each other, without quarrels, fighting, or bloodshed ensuing—all consequences of frequent occurrence in his native country. Secondly, the comfort which Europeans enjoy, at once benefits and captivates him. He finds the house of a simple citizen better appointed than the palace of his sovereign. The cleanliness in dress and food, the reciprocal offices of kindness and courtesies of society, are magnets which attract him and make him forget his rude and uncivilised home. Thirdly, it is a special delight to him to find that the various differences of religion and nationality are scarcely ever felt here, whilst in the East they form the strongest barriers between man and man. With him at home the mere notion of visiting the country of the Frengi would have been certain death, and now he lives in the very heart of their land, not only without encountering hostility, but actually received with cordiality and affection.

With regard to his feelings on Islamism, his own speculations had already in some degree enlightened him. He observed that the nearer he approached the West, the more Mahometan fanaticism decreased, and as he, in proportion with its decrease, drew nearer and nearer to humanity and order, he could not help suspecting very soon that Islamism, or at least the

Islamism he knew and confessed, was the declared enemy of civilisation and refinement of life, such as he met with in Europe. He has never yet uttered a word of aversion or reproach when referring to the doctrines of the Arabian prophet, but his subtle and speculative theories sufficiently indicate that a strong revolution has been wrought within him. Without wishing to assign the cause of this great contrast between the East and the West solely to the influence of Christianity, he has, nevertheless, arrived so far in his conclusions as to comprehend that our western culture and mode of life are incompatible with the teachings of Mahomet. He has never yet distinctly expressed to me his preference of either one or the other religion, and it will probably be long before he will venture to give expression to any thought of the kind. His allusions and fragmentary remarks, however, prove that his mind is occupied with questions of this nature, and that the great struggle with himself has begun.

Such, indeed, is the history of every Mussulman, whether Tartar, Arab, Persian, or Turk, as soon as he becomes thoroughly acquainted with our western civilisation—a complete transformation but seldom occurs. The highly important question, whether the civilisation of the East or West is the better—whether the teaching of Christ or of Mohammed is the true religion, will long remain undecided by the nations of Asia:—nay, so long, I feel inclined to say, as the rays of the sun produce with us a temperate, with them a burning, heat; so long as distance separates the east and the west. Were it possible to bring the doctrines of Christianity more into conformity with their views, by setting aside those of the Incarnation and the Trinity, and were these tenets, thus modified, put into the place of the Koran, an opportunity might be presented of making a small, but only a very small, step in advance. I say advisedly a small step, since Christianity, though sprung from an Eastern soil, has long ago proved to be a plant which can only flourish in the West. And who would deny that the Koran and Vedas, created as they are by an Eastern mind and in the spirit of Eastern nations, are prized and revered by them above everything besides? Their disappearance would bring new and similar productions into existence. I venture almost to assert that the Christian tenets would, after a time, become transformed, on Eastern soil, into a sort of Koran or Vedas, in order to be the typical embodiment of oriental sentiment, and be recognised by orientals as their real and peculiar property. Are not the Nestorians, Armenians, and other followers of the Eastern Church, all disciples of Christianity? but as great as the difference is between them and their co-religionists in Europe, so little do they differ in their mode of thought, their feelings, and views of life, from their Mohammedan fellow-countrymen in the East.

CHAPTER XI.

THE ROUND OF LIFE IN BOKHARA.

"HADJI! Thou hast, I am sure, seen many countries—tell me now, is there another city in the world in which it is so agreeable to reside as Bokhara?" Such was the inquiry with which I was frequently greeted in the Tartar capital, even by men who had already several times visited India, Persia, and Turkey. My answer upon these occasions it is not of course difficult to divine. Questions of a nature so delicate are an embarrassment to the traveller when he is in Paris, London, or St. Petersburg, just as much as when he is in Constantinople, Teheran, or Bokhara. One encounters egotism everywhere.

Bokhara, the focus of Tartar civilization, posesses beyond a doubt much to remind one of a capital, particularly when a man enters it as a traveller, coming immediately from a journey of many weeks through deserts and solitudes. As for the luxury of its dwellings, its dresses, and manner of living, that hardly merits attention at all when compared with what is to be seen in the cities of Western Asia. Still it has its peculiarities, which prevent one wondering so much that habit and partiality dispose the Bokhariot to be proud of his native city.

The houses, built of mud and wood, present, with their crooked paintless walls, a gloomier appearance than the dwellings of other Mohammedan cities. On entering the court through the low gateway, one fancies oneself in a fortress. On all the sides there are high walls, which serve as a protection, not so much against thieves as against the amatory oglings of intriguing neighbours. In Bokhara, the most shameless sink of iniquity that I know in the East, a glance even from a distance is regarded as dishonouring! The number of the separate apartments varies with the fortune of the proprietor. The more important part of them comprises the harem, styled here Enderun (the inner penetralia), the smaller room for guests, and the hall for receptions. This last is the most spacious, as well as the most ornamented apartment in the house, and, like the other rooms, has a double ceiling, with a space between used as a storeroom. The floor is paved with bricks and stones, and has only carpets round the sides near the walls. Rectangular stones, which have been hollowed out, are placed in a corner—a comfortable contrivance enabling the owner to perform the holy ablutions in the room itself. This custom is met with in no other Mohammedan country. The walls have no particular decorations; those, however, which are nearest to Mekka are painted with flowers, vases, and arabesques of different kinds. The windows are mere openings, each with a pair of shutters. Glass is seen nowhere, and few take the trouble to use paper smeared with fat as a substitute. Articles of furniture, still rarities throughout the East, are here scarcely known by name; but this need not excite surprise, for often have I heard Orientals who have visited Europe exclaim: "Is not that a stupid custom among the Frengi, that they so crowd their handsome, spacious rooms with such a heap of tables, sofas, chairs, and other things, that they have hardly place left to seat themselves in any comfort!" Of course meaning on the ground.

The expenditure upon the wardrobe is on a footing with the style of each house and its arrangement. Cloth is rarely met with: it serves for presents from the Khan to his officials of high rank. Different qualities of the Aladja (cotton) are employed by all classes, from king to dervish, for winter and summer. Although the Bokhariot over-garment has the form of a night-dress extending down to the ankles, still it is subject from time to time to little innovations as to cut, sleeve, collar, and trimming, in accordance with the fashion of the moment, which is as much respected in Bokhara as in Paris. A dandy in the former city takes especial care to have his turban folded according to the idea in force at the moment, as an evidence of good taste. He sees particularly to his shawl, by which he binds his trousers round the loins, and to his koshbag suspended to that shawl. The koshbag is a piece of leather consisting of several tongues, to which are fastened a knife or two, a small tea-bag, a miswak (toothpick), and a leathern bag for copper money. These articles constitute the indispensables of a Central Asiatic, and by the quality and value of each is a judgment formed of the character and breeding of the man.

Whoever may wish to see the *haute volée*, the fashionable world of Bokhara, should post himself on a Friday, between ten and twelve o'clock in the forenoon, in the street leading from Deri Rigistan to the Mesdjidi Kelan, or great mosque. At this time the Ameer, followed by his grandees, in great state, betakes himself to his Friday's devotions. All are in their best attire, upon their best horses; for these, with their splendid housings, serve as substitutes for carriages. The large, stiff, silken garments of staring colours are in striking contrast with the high and spurred boots. But what produces a particularly comic effect is the loose and waddling gait which all pedestrians studiously put on. Reftari khiraman (the waddling or trotting step), which Oriental poets find so graceful, comparing it to the swaying movement of the cypress when agitated by the zephyrs, and whose attainment is the subject of careful study in Persia as well as Bokhara, to us Europeans seems like the gait of a fatted goose floundering on his way home. But this is no subject for me to jest upon, for our stiff, rapid pace is just as displeasing to an Oriental eye, and it would not be very polite to mention the comparison they make use of with repect to us.

It does not excite less wonder on our part when we see the men in Bokhara clad in wide garments of brilliant colour, whereas the women wear only a dress that is tight to the shape, and of a dark hue. For in this city, where the civilization has retained with the greatest fidelity its antique stamp of Oriental Islamism, women, ever the martyrs of Eastern legislation, come in for the worst share.

In Turkey the contact with Christian elements has already introduced many innovations, and the Yaschmak (veil) is rather treated as part of the toilette than as the ensign of slavery. In Persia the women are tolerably well muffled up, still they wear the Tchakshur (pantaloons and stockings in one piece) of brilliant colouring and silken texture, and the Rubend (a linen veil with network for the eyes) is ornamented with a clasp of gold. In Bokhara, on the other hand, there is not a trace of tolerance. The women wear nothing that deserves to be named full dress or ornament. When in the streets, they draw a covering over their heads, and are seen clad in dark gowns of deep blue, with the empty sleeves hanging suspended to their backs, so that observed from behind, the fair ones of Bokhara may be mistaken for clothes wandering about. From the head down to the bosom they wear a veil made of horsehair, of a texture which we in Europe would regard as too bad and coarse for a sieve, and the friction of which upon cheek or nose must be anything but agreeable. Their *chaussures* consist of coarse heavy boots, in which their little feet are fixed, enveloped in a mass of leather. Such a costume is not in itself attractive; but even so attired, they dare not be seen too often in the streets. Ladies of rank and good character never venture to show themselves in any public place or bazaar. Shopping is left to the men; and whenever any extraordinary emergency obliges a lady to leave the house and to pay visits, it is regarded as *bon ton* for her to assume every possible appearance of decrepitude, poverty, and age.

To send forth a young lady in her eighteenth or twentieth year, in all the superabundant energy of youth, supported upon a stick, and thus muffled up, in the sole view that the assumption of the characteristics of advanced life may spare her certain glances, may be justly deemed the *ne plus ultra* of tyranny and hypocrisy. These erroneous notions of morality are to be met with, more or less, everywhere in the East; but nowhere does one find such striking examples of Oriental exaggeration as in that seat of ancient Islamite civilization, Bokhara. In Constantinople, as well as other cities of Turkey, there are certain Seir-yeri (promenades), where ladies appear in public. In Teheran, Ispahan, and Shiraz, it is the custom for the Hanims, *en grande toilette*, and mounted on magnificent horses, to make excursions to the places of pilgrimage situate in the environs of those cities. The tomb of the Said is the place of rendezvous, and instead of prayers, reciprocal declarations of love are not seldom made. In Bokhara, on the contrary, there is not a shadow of all this. Never have I seen there a man in the company of his wife. The husband slinks away from his other half, or third, or fourth, as the case may be; and it is a notorious fact, that when the wives of the Ameer pass by any place, all men are expected to beat a hasty retreat. Under such circumstances it is easy to see how society must constitute itself, and what shapes it must assume. Where the two sexes are so separated, it can never put on an appearance of gladness and geniality; all becomes compulsion and hypocrisy; every genuine sentiment is crushed by these unnatural laws which are imposed as God's ordinances, and as such expected to be observed with the strictest obedience.

To study that part of their lives which is before the public eye, we must first pay a visit to the tea-booths, which are the resorts of all classes. The Bokhariot, and the remark applies indeed universally to all Central Asiatics, can never pass by a second or third tea-booth without entering, unless his affairs are very urgent indeed. As I before mentioned, every man carries with him his little bag of tea: of this, on his entry, he gives a certain portion to the landlord, whose business is rather to deal in hot water than in tea.

During day-time, and particularly in public places, the only tea drunk is green tea, which is served without sugar, and with the accompaniment of a relish or two, consisting of little cakes made of flour and mutton suet; for the making of these Bokhara is famous. As any attempt to cool tea by blowing upon it, however urgent on account of its heat some such process may be, is regarded as highly indecorous—nay, as an unpardonable offence—the Central Asiatic is wont to make it revolve for this purpose in the cup itself until the temperature is tolerable. To pass for a man *comme il faut*, one must support the right elbow in the left hand, and gracefully give a circular movement to the cup; no drop must be spilt, for such an awkwardness would much damage a reputation for *savoir faire*. The Bokhariot can thus chatter away hours and hours, amidst his fellow tea-drinkers; for the meaningless conversations that are maintained weary him as little as the cup after cup of tea which he swallows. It is known to a second how much time is required for each kind of tea to draw. Every time the tea-pot is emptied, the tea-leaves that have been used are passed round: etiquette forbids any one to take more than he can hold between finger and thumb, for it is regarded by connoisseurs as the greatest dainty.

They seek to find amusements of a higher kind in excursions to the environs of the city. These are made sometimes to the tombs of the saints; sometimes to the convents of certain Ishans (sheiks), in the odour of sanctity; sometimes to the Tchiharbag Abdullah Khan, situate near the Dervaze Imam. The visit to a Khanka, that is to a dignitary of religion still instinct with life, is an act of more importance and involving greater outlay than the pilgrimage to a grave. The sainted men, whether departed or still living, have equally their fixed days for levées and receptions. In the former case the descendants of his Sanctity receive the tribute, in the latter a man has the good fortune to have his purse emptied by the holy hands themselves. On the occasion of these formal visits the Ishans are tuned to a higher pitch than ordinary, and as the holy eye distinguishes at once by the exterior of the visitor the amount of the offering that is to be received, so does that measure serve to fix with precision how long or how short the benediction is to be cut. Scenes of this kind, in which I performed my part as a spectator, or stood by, were always full of interest to me; and one, over which I have had many a hearty laugh, has made an indelible impression upon my mind. In the environs of Bokhara, I entered the residence of a sheikh to ask for his blessing and a little assistance in money. Upon the first point no difficulty was made, but the second seemed to stagger him. At this moment a Turkoman was announced as an applicant for a Fatiha. He was allowed to enter. His holiness made his hocus-pocus with the greatest devotion. The Turkoman sat there like an innocent lamb, and after being subjected to the influences of the sanctifying breath, energetically administered, he dived into his money-bag, from which he extracted some pieces of coin, and, without counting them, transferred them to the hand of him from whom he had received the benediction. I noticed that the latter rubbed the money betwixt his fingers, and was really astounded when he beckoned to me, and without once looking at the number of pieces, handed them over to me in the presence of the Turkoman. That was real liberality, the reader may say. I thought so myself until coming to the bazaar and seeking to make a purchase from a baker, one of the coins was rejected by him as false. I tendered the others, and they were all pronounced to be bad—valueless. The nomad, as crafty as he was superstitious, had paid for the spurious ware with spurious money, and as his holiness on his side had at once detected the cheat by the touch, he had no scruple in making it over to me.

On the occasion of their excursions to the environs of the city, persons of wealth are in the habit of taking with them their tea-things, and a servant to prepare tea. Those who are not so well off have recourse to establishments that are to be found at these places of resort. Visitors evince just as much desire to hide themselves, where possible, in the booths, as they do to avoid encamping close to the road. As it is the approved custom to invite every passer-by, be he of what rank he may, to take some refreshment of food or drink, each host entertains an apprehension, not unjustified by experience, lest those whom he accosts, not content with returning for answer the ordinary word expressive of gratitude—khosh (well)—may actually close at once with the invitation. Still, not to give it is everywhere regarded as a mean sin. Conditional acceptance only is usual in some places. These rules of hospitality so exaggerated, and at the same time so specious, operate oppressively and unpleasantly, both on him that takes and him that gives; and the confounded, I might almost say the aghast, air of the host who is taken at his word always produced upon me the drollest effect.

Tha spectacle which these private parties of pleasure generally afford is one of no great gladness, they rather seem to produce a deadly-lively effect. The significant joke, the peal of laughter, the loud cry are, it is true, none of them wanting on these occasions; but where the crown of society, woman, is absent, all is in vain, and never can life assume its real aspect of genuine enjoyment.

If I do not err, it is the Tchiharbag Abdullah Khan that still preserves most of the characters of a public place of entertainment. It is a spot well shaded by lofty trees; a canal flows through it, to whose banks the pupils of the numerous colleges and the young men belonging to the wealthier classes, resort generally on Friday afternoons. The inevitable tea-kettle is here again in requisition, and tea is the article for which the place is renowned; but not the only one, for the combats of rams are here celebrated also. The savageness with which these sturdy animals rush against each other when irritated, the fearful shock of their two heads, particularly when they struggle to push their antagonists back, present a spectacle very attractive to the inhabitant, not only of Bokhara, but of every part of Central Asia. What the bull-fight is in Spain, and horse-racing in England, these combats of rams are in Turkestan. The rams are trained to this sport, and it is really surprising how these brutes support with obstinacy often as many as one hundred charges. When they first make their appearance on the avenue, the bystanders begin to wager as to the number of shocks their chosen champion will support. Sometimes the weaker combatant beats a retreat; but very often the battle only ends with the entire discomfiture of one animal, consequent upon the cracking of his skull. It is a cruel spectacle; still the cruelty does not seem so great in the middle of Tartary as some of the sports in which so many civilised nations of the West still find amusement.

Let me now attempt to portray in the following slight sketch the external mode of living in Bokhara. In the morning—I mean by the term before sunrise, as by religious compulsion every man is an early riser—one encounters people, half-asleep, and half-awake, and half-dressed, hurrying one by one to the mosques:

any delay in arriving not only entails reproach, but is considered as meriting punishment. The stir made by these devotees in running through the streets rouses the houseless dogs from their lairs in the out-of-the-way corners or upon the heaps of dung. These famished, horrid-looking animals—yet contrasted with their Stambouli brethren, presenting a princely appearance—are crying proofs of the miserly nature of the Bokhariots. The poor creatures first struggle to rear their gaunt frames, mere skin and bone, from sleep; then they rub their rough, hairless carcases, against the mouldering walls, and this toilette at an end, they start upon their hunt for a *dejeûner à la fourchette*, for the most part made up of a few fleshless bones or carrion, but very often of kicks in the ribs administered by some compassionating and charitable inhabitant of Bokhara. At the same time as the dogs, awake the hardly-better lodged Parias of the Tartar capital—I mean the wretched men afflicted with incurable and contagious skin diseases, who sit at the corners of the streets *en famille*, and house in miserable tents. In Persia they are met with, remote from cities and villages, on the high roads; but here, owing to the absence of sanitary regulations, they are tolerated in the middle of the city. Their lot is far the most terrible to which any son of earth can have to submit, and unhappily they are long livers too. Whilst the mother is clothing her other accursed offspring with a scanty covering of rags, the father seats himself with the most disfigured one amongst them by the roadside, in order to solicit charity and alms from those who pass. Charity and alms to prolong such an existence!

After the sun has looked long enough upon this miserable spectacle, the city in all its parts begins slowly to assume animation. The people return in crowds from the mosques; they are encountered on their way by troops of asses laden with wood, corn, grass, large pails of milk, and dishes of cream, pressing from all the city gates, and forcing their way in varied confusion through the narrow and crooked streets. Screams of alarm from the drivers, the reciprocal cries issuing from those who buy and those who sell, mix with that mighty hee-haw of the asses for which Bokhara is renowned. To judge by the first impression, it might be supposed that the different drivers would be obliged to fish out their wood from milk, their grass from cream, charcoal from corn, silkworm-cocoons from skimmed milk. But no, nothing is spilt, nothing thrown down; the drivers are wont to flog each other through in right brotherly fashion, till in the end all arrives in safety at its destination.

At an hour after sunrise the Bokhariot is already seated with his cup of Schirtschaj (milk-tea): this beverage is composed of tea made from bricks of tea in the form of Kynaster, and abundantly flavoured with milk, cream, or mutton fat. This favourite drink of the Tartars, in which large quantities of bread are broken, would be more rightly described as a soup;

and although the treat was highly commended to me, I had great difficulty in getting accustomed to it.

After tea begins the day's work, and then one remarks particular activity in the streets. Porters loaded with great bales hurry to the bazaar. These goods belong to the retail dealers, who every evening pack up their shop and transport it to their own house. And then a long chain of two-humped camels that have no burdens are being led into the Karavanserai, destined to convey the produce of Central Asia in every direction. Here, again, stands a heavily-laden caravan from Russia, accompanied on its way by the prying eyes of the custom-house officials and their cohorts, for those long bales contain valuable productions of the industry of the unbelievers, and are destined accordingly to be doubly taxed. Merchants of all religions and from all nations run after the caravan; the newly-arrived wares find customers even before they are unpacked, and at such moments Afghans, Persians, Tadjiks, and Hindoos, seem to get more excited than is the case even with the heroes of the Exchange in Paris, Vienna, or Frankfort-on-the-Maine. The Kirghis camel-driver, fresh from the desert, is the quietest of all; he is lost in astonishment, and knows not whether most to admire the splendour of the mud huts, the colour of the dresses, or the crowds swaying to and fro. But the greatest source of amusement to me was to observe how the Bokhariot, in his quality of inhabitant of a metropolis,

jeers at these nomads; how he is constantly on the
alert to place the rudeness of the sons of the desert in
relief by contrasting it with his own refinement and
civilisation. Whilst the bazaar life, with all its alarm,
tumult, shrieks, cries, hammering, scolding, and knocking, is in full force, the youths greedy of knowledge
swarm about the numerous Medresse (colleges), there
to learn to extract from their useless studies lessons of a
more exalted kind of stupidity and a more grovelling
hypocrisy.

The greatest interest attaches to the primary school
posted in the very centre of the bazaar, and often in
the immediate neighbourhood of between ten and
fifteen coppersmiths' workshops. The sight of this
public school, in which a Mollah, surrounded by
several rows of children, gives his lessons in reading,
in spite of the noise, is really comical. That, in a
place where sturdy arms are brandishing hammers,
hardly a single word is audible, we may readily suppose. Teachers and pupils are as red in the face as
turkey-cocks from crying out, and yet nothing but the
wild movement of the jaw and the swelling of the
veins indicate that they are studying.*

In the afternoon (I speak here of summer-time, for
of the winters I have no personal experience), there is
more tranquillity both in bazaar and street. On the

---

* Schools thus placed in the middle of the bazaar are also met with in
Persia: these are the cheapest schools for children, still it is incredible that
the Orientals should suffer such a stupid practice to exist, and that they do
not remove these establishments for instruction to some less disturbed situation.

banks of the water reservoir and of the canals, the true believers are engaged in performing the holy ablutions. Whilst one man is washing his feet from their layer of sweat and dirt, his neighbour uses the same water for his face, and a third does not scruple to quench his thirst with it. Water that consists of more than one hundred and twenty pints is, according to the texts of Islam, blind; which means that filth and dirt lose themselves therein, and the orthodox have the privilege to enjoy every abomination as a thing pure in itself. After a service in the mosques, all becomes again animated; it is the second summons to work during the day, for a period by no means so long. The Mussulman population soon begin their evening holiday, whilst Jews and Hindoos still remain busy. The former, who are for the most part employed in the handicraft of silk dyers, move stealthily and timidly through the streets, their spirits broken by their long and heavy servitude; the latter run about like men possessed, and their bold bearing shows that their home is not far off, and the time not so remote when they also had a government of their own.

It is now within three hours of sunset. The élite of society betake themselves to the Khanka (convent), to enjoy a treat, semi-religious and semi-literary. It consists in the public reading of the Mesnevi, which is declaimed at that time of the day by an experienced reader in the vestibule of the Khanka. This masterpiece of Oriental poesy presents in its contemplations of terrestrial existence much elevation of thought. Versification, language, metaphors, are, in reality, full of charm and beauty; but the audience in Bokhara are incapable of understanding it, and their enthusiasm is all affectation. I often had seated at my side on these occasions a man who, in his excitement, would emit deep-drawn sighs, and even bellow like a bull. I was quite amazed; and when I afterwards made enquiry as to his character, I heard that he was one of the meanest of misers, the proprietor of many houses, yet ready to make obeisance for even the smallest copper coin. No one is at all inclined to adopt the sentiment he hears there as the rule of his life, and still it is regarded as becoming to be deeply impressed by the beauty of the expression. Every one knows that the sighs and exclamation of his neighbour proceed from no genuine emotion, and still all vie in these demonstrations of extraordinary feeling.

Even before the last beams of the setting sun have lost themselves in the wide waste of sand on the west, the Tartar capital begins to repose. As the coolness commences, the stifling clouds of dust subside. Where canals or water-reservoirs are near at hand, they are rendered available—the ground is watered and then swept. The men seat themselves in the shade to wait for the Ezan (evening prayer); that heard, an absolute stillness ensues, and soon all are seated before the colossal dish of pilau, and after they have well loaded their stomachs with this heavy and greasy meal, any desire they may have felt to leave the house is quite extinguished. Two hours after sunset all the thoroughfares are as silent as death. No echo is heard in the darkness of the night but the heavy tread of the night-watchman making his rounds. These men are charged to put in force the strictest police regulations against thieves and seekers of love adventures; they scruple not to arrest any man, however honourable his position, if his foot crosses his threshold after the beat of the tattoo has issued its order that all the world should sleep.

What in this mode of town life so pleases the Bokhariot—what makes him give so marked a preference to his own capital—is not difficult to divine. His mind has become familiarized with a simple mode of living, in which, as yet, little luxury is to be found, and which, in externals, admits not much perceptible distinction between ranks and conditions of men. A universal acquiescence in the same poverty, or to use a more appropriate expression, the absence of different degrees of visible property, makes Bokhara, in the eye of many Asiatics, a favourite residence. I once met a Persian in Teheran who had been a slave in Bokhara fifteen years. And there, in the middle of his fatherland, and surrounded by his relatives, he sighed and pined for the Tartar capital. At the outset he was delighted with the bazaars, filled with articles of European luxury; he contemplated them with childish delight; but later he saw how the wealthier alone made their purchases, and how all despised a man like him, clad in a cotton dress, the costume of the poor. No wonder his wish carried him again back to the spot where, at the time unconscious of his happiness, he was permitted to share great physical comfort, without a thorn in his eye or a pang in his heart.

CHAPTER XII.

BOKHARA, THE HEAD QUARTERS OF MOHAMMEDANISM.

"Bokhara, mirevi divanei
Laiki zen djiri zindankhanei."

Thou wilt to Bokhara? O fool for thy pains,
Thither thou goest, to be put into chains.

MESNEVI.

It has frequently been noticed by travellers in Central Asia, and we have likewise remarked upon it, that Bokhara considers itself the great pillar of Islamism, and the only pure fountain of the Mohammedan religion. Nor is it the Bokhariots alone who take this view, but all the rest of the Mohammedan world, in whatever region or country, unite in looking up to and extolling the Turkestan capital for possessing this exclusive privilege. The pilgrim from Central Asia, whether travelling in Asia Minor, Arabia, or Egypt, is received with marked veneration and respect, and is regarded as the very embodiment of every Islamitic virtue. The Western Mohammedan, especially the Osmanli, deeply wounded by the innovations our civilization has introduced into his native country, turns to his kinsman and co-religionist from the far East, and gazing at him with a look of extreme piety, finds comfort at the aspect of him, who in his eyes still represents the religion of the Prophet, pure and undefiled. Heaving a sigh, he exclaims: "Ha Bokharai Sherif!" (yes, the noble Bokhara), which utterance is meant to express his whole mind.

The difference that exists between Eastern and Western Mohammedanism in Asia is indeed a remarkable phenomenon, and deserves a closer examination. Upon my asking the Mollahs in Bokhara how it happened that they were better Mohammedans than the people in Mekka and Medina, where Mohammed had actually lived and taught, they answered: that "the torch, although sending its light into the far distance, is always dark at the foot,"—Mekka being meant by the foot of the torch, and Bokhara the far distance. In an allegorical sense this may be correct, but Europeans are not silenced by similes of that sort; and, since the fact deserves attention, we will endeavour to ascertain, first—the essential points of the difference in question; and, secondly—the causes for it. Upon examining in detail the various points of contrast between Eastern and Western Mohammedanism, the chief characteristic feature is, no doubt, the wild fanatic obstinacy with which the Mussulman, in the far East, clings to every single point of the Koran and the traditions, looking with terror and aversion, in the true spirit of the Oriental, upon any innovation; and, in a word, directing all his efforts to the preservation of his religion at that precise standard which marked its existence in the happy period (Vakti Seadet) of the Prophet and the first califs. This standard, however, is not sufficiently apparent, since Islamism, in those countries, has assumed a form such as a few eccentric interpreters among the Sunnites desire, but which, so far as our knowledge extends, *has never existed in reality*.

Fanaticism, the chief cause of hypocrisy and impiety, has disfigured every religion, so long as mankind, living in the infancy of civilization, has been unable to perceive the pure light of the true faith. All nations and all countries have given proof of its existence, but nowhere does it appear in such glaring colours, or wear such a disgusting aspect, as in the East. Here, religion, in order to improve the mind, deals chiefly with the body; here, in order to exercise moral influence, the devotee is occupied with physical trifling, and, neglecting the inner man, as may be supposed, every one strives for outward appearance and effect. In Bokhara the principle reigns paramount: "Man must make a figure,—no one cares for what he thinks." A man may be the greatest miscreant, the most reprobate of human creatures; but let him fulfil the outward duties of religion and he escapes all punishment in this as well as in the next world.

The very popular prayer of the thief Abdurrahman

(Duai-duzd Abdurrahman) illustrates most strikingly this opinion. It consists of about fifteen to twenty sentences, and its substance is as follows: "When the Prophet (the blessing of God be upon him!) lived in Medina, he went one afternoon upon the terrace of his house, in order to perform his devotions. He looked about with his blessed eyes and saw in his part of the town a funeral procession pass through the streets, followed only by a few persons, and the coffin surrounded by a marvellous brilliancy, not unlike a sea of rosy light. As soon as he had finished his prayer he hastened to the spot, joined the funeral procession, and saw, to his great amazement, that the shine did not leave the coffin, even when let down into the grave. The Prophet could not recover from his surprise; he went to the wife of the deceased, and asked what and who her husband had been. 'Alas!' she answered, with tears, 'God be merciful unto him, his death is a blessing to all, for throughout his life he was a highwayman and murderer; and the tears of widows and orphans he has caused to flow, are more than the water he has drunk. He lived only to cause unhappiness to others. I have often remonstrated with him, but in vain. He lived as a sinner, and as a sinner he died!' 'What!' exclaimed the Prophet, with ever-increasing astonishment, 'Did he possess no single good quality, has he never shown repentance?' 'Alas, no!' she sobbed out; 'the only thing he used to do every evening after his wicked daily work, was to read over these few lines (and she showed the prayer), and then fell asleep, and woke to sin anew on the morrow.' The Prophet looked at the prayer, and recognising at once its marvellous efficacy, he has left it behind to exercise the same virtue upon all orthodox Mussulmen." The moral drawn from this narrative needs no explanation; and it is easy to imagine how many Central Asiatics, furnished with such a recipe, *à la Tetzel*, will commit the most atrocious deeds, and retain withal the consciousness of being pious and religious men.

What strikes a European most of all, in seeing this principle of outward formulas reduced to practice, are the laws of cleanliness, which, in Central Asia, are observed with strict and scrupulous exactness, although, as is well known, the most disgusting filthiness is to be met with. By the Mohammedan law the body becomes unclean after each evacuation, and requires an ablution, according to circumstances, either a small (abdest) or a great one (gusl). The same has to be observed with respect to the clothes, which are subjected to a purification if touched by the smallest drop of water.* The cleaning of the body is strictly performed amongst all Mussulmen; nor, on the whole, is the law about the clothes lost sight of; but I have

---

* In the eyes of Eastern people, dogs and Europeans are classed together, as making water against the wall. Throughout the East people squat down during the action, for fear lest in a standing position a drop might touch and thus pollute their clothes.

never seen people in the West of Asia, as in Bokhara, repeat their prayers stark-naked, from a religious scruple, that their clothes might have been defiled without the eye having detected it. It is extremely ridiculous, that in any religion, as is the case in the Mohammedan, whole volumes should be written as to the manner in which its followers are to cleanse their body after each large or small evacuation. The law, for instance, commands the istindjah (removal), istinkah (ablution), and istibra (drying), *i.e.*, a small clod of earth is first used for the local cleansing, then water, at least twice, and finally a piece of linen, a yard in length, in order to destroy every possible trace. In Turkey, Arabia, and Persia, only one of these acts is performed,—the istinkah; but in Central Asia all three are considered necessary; and in order to prove the high standard of their piety, zealous Mohammedans carry three or four such clods of earth, cut with a knife that is used for no other purpose besides, in their turbans, to have a small store at hand. This commandment is often carried out quite publicly in the bazaars, from a desire to make parade of their conscientious piety. I shall never forget the revolting scene, when I saw one day a teacher give to his pupils, boys and girls, instructions in the handling of the clod of earth, linen and so forth, by way of experiment. It never occurs to any one that such a tenet is disgraceful, nor does any body perceive that these extremes of physical cleanliness lead directly to the extremes of moral impurity.

The extreme severity with which the law of the Harem is executed in Bokhara, is looked for in vain among the Western Mohammedans, or even among the fanatic sect of the Wahabites. This law, so contrary to nature, has necessarily been the cause of a certain vice equally contrary to nature, and which, although it exists among Turks, Arabs and Persians, is confined within a comparatively narrow limit, and condemned as a "despicable sin" by the interpreters of the Koran as well as by public opinion. In Central Asia, especially in Bokhara and Khokand, this atrocious crime is carried to a frightful extent, and the religious of these countries considering it a protection against any transgression of the law of the Harem, and declaring it to be *no* sin, marriages *à la Tiberius* have become quite popular; nay, fathers feel not the smallest compunction in surrendering their sons to a friend or acquaintance for a certain annual stipend. Our pen refuses to describe this disgusting vice in its full extent; but even the few hints we have thrown out are sufficient to show the abyss of crime to which an exaggerated religious fanaticism degrades mankind.

It is just the same with the prohibition of spirituous liquors. The Koran commands not only abstinence from wine, but from all intoxicating drinks, for this reason, that a state of intoxication would be attended by neglect of prayer, or of any other pious duty. The Western Mohammedans interpret this commandment as referring only to wine (sharab) in the strict sense of the word, and consider drinking arak (brandy) already a much less offence; many, indeed, are of opinion, that since it has not been expressly mentioned in the Koran, it would not be regarded as a sin to drink it with water. In Turkey and Persia brandy is as much in favour among the better educated classes, as wodki in Russia; but in Bokhara both brandy and wine are very rarely met with. Even those who do not confess the Mohammedan religion, such as Jews and Hindoos, cannot drink it except clandestinely, and the mere pronouncing the words sharab and arak, is a sin in the eyes of the orthodox. With facts like these one would expect the greatest sobriety among the people, but alas! how terrible is the substitute hypocrisy has invented!

The Central Asiatics make a distinction between fluid and solid spirits. The former are strictly forbidden, whilst the latter, by which all narcotics are understood, are looked upon as perfectly innocent. The famous opium-eaters of Constantinople, who, at the present day almost extinct, were seen daily, at the beginning of the century, in the notorious square of Direkalti, and admired by all passers-by — the various hashish-eaters in Egypt—the lovers of the comparatively harmless teryak in Persia,—all these are as nothing in comparison with the bengis* of Central Asia.

* Beng is the name of the poison which is produced from the canabis indica.

In the first-named countries opium has a rival in "pater bacchus," and holds, therefore, a divided empire; but in Turkestan, where the "jolly god" is a stranger, it reigns paramount, and its destroying power is fearful. The number of beng-eaters is greatest in Bokhara and Khokand, and it is no exaggeration to say that three-fourths of the learned and official world, or, in other words, the whole intelligent class, are victims to this vice. The Government looks on with perfect indifference, while hundreds, nay, thousands, commit suicide. It never occurs to any one that a prohibition should be made on this subject, but if a man were convicted of having tasted a drop of wine, he would be beheaded without any further ado.

These errors, together with many others of the same kind, must no doubt be ascribed to an eccentric scrupulousness in observing the existing laws. Strange as they are, they appear less surprising when compared with those views and opinions which arose in Eastern Mohammedanism in consequence of a different interpretation of those traditional dogmas, which are not only rejected as erroneous, but flatly condemned by the learned Mohammedans of the West. Among these we are struck first of all with the religious orders or pious fraternities, which are spread in an extraordinary manner over Central Asia, and are subject to such strict regulations, and conducted with a fervour which contrasts singularly with the character of Eastern nations, especially the Central Asiatics. In the Western Islamitic countries we meet with the various orders of the Oveisi, Kadrie, Djelali, Mevlevi, Rufai, Bektashi, &c., which, at all times treated with civility by the Ulemas, were never able to attract within their magic circle more than a few individuals of a heated imagination; whereas, on the contrary, the Nakishbendi, Makhdumaazami, in Bokhara and Khokand, embody large masses of the population, who are appointed, guided, and governed by the officers of the order, representing the temporary supreme chief. Every community, however small in numbers, comprises one or more Ishans (priests of the order) beside the lawful Mollah, Reis, &c.; and I have often felt astonished at witnessing the blind obedience and respect paid to the members of the order as compared with the former. It need scarcely be added, that these influential Ishans stand frequently in the way of the Government, but it has never ventured to offer them any check or resistance, regarding, as they do, religious orders as inseparable from Islam. Mohammed expressly stated, "*La Ruhbanitum fil Islam*"— " no monks in Islam." Nevertheless the Khan, his ministers, even many Ulemas, in spite of the latter, regarding the Ishan as powerful rivals, and hating them accordingly, are in the habit of adopting the outward attributes of one or the other order, out of deference to public opinion.

The judicial procedure of Eastern Mohammedans is

equally remarkable. They entirely reject the Urf, *i.e.*, the decision of the judge, based upon his own judgment and convictions, in cases where the Sheriat (the laws of the Koran) is insufficient; as also the Kanun, *i.e.*, laws framed by later legislators. The latter they regard as heretical innovations, and they take the Sheriat, or the code of laws emanating from the Koran, as their sole and infallible guide. That the laws Mohammed framed twelve hundred years ago for the social wants of the simple Arabs, should not suit every clime and epoch, can be no matter of surprise. In Turkey and Persia the necessity for reform has long been felt. The Governments of these countries have tried in all cases to supply the deficiencies of their primitive codes by supplemental additions, however much the opinions of the Ulemas resisted such a step, naturally foreseeing from it, as they did, the downfall of their power. In Turkestan, not only the Mollahs, but the Government, and everybody in fact, is highly indignant at the very idea of a supplement. In their eyes the Koran is "as fine as a hair, as sharp as a sword, and satisfies all possible wants of life;" whoever thought differently would be treated as a wicked man and an infidel. People eat, drink and dress, in strict conformity with the precepts of the Koran; it is the standing rule, by which all taxes and toll-moneys are levied, the standard, by which all wars are conducted, and the guide for directing their relations with foreign powers! Upon the same principle, any innovation in domestic life is strictly forbidden as *sin*. England, Russia, and other modern states, of whom the Koran makes no mention, cannot be recognised by the Tartar rulers *de facto*; on the contrary, they consider it their duty to oppose them as intruders by the law of the Djihad (the religious combat), a policy which will, of course, as already sufficiently shown, lead them to entire destruction.

With regard to the Shiitish Persians, the Eastern Mohammedans stand in a very different relation to them from their Western brethren. This religious schism, as is well known, has often been the cause of long and bloody wars,—under the pretext of a temporary quarrel. Ever since the first dissensions took place between the dynasties Akkoyunlu and Karakayunlu, Turks and Arabs have frequently been opposed to the Persians in destructive and calamitous wars: deep hatred and bitter resentment separated the two sects, and the former succeeded in ejecting their Shiitish enemies from the bond of Islamism. The Persian is looked upon as an heretical Mussulman, but always as a Mussulman; he is admitted to the holy cities and all places of pilgrimage, the orthodox Sunnite does not object to pray with him in the same mosque, and in modern times the hatred between the Osmanli and Persian has already so far diminished that the latter is permitted by law to intermarry with the former.

In Central Asia there exists no trace of anything of

the kind. Here the Persians are hated and persecuted as fiercely as on their first appearance among the Shiitish sect. In the year 945 of the Hidjra, they were declared outlaws and infidels by the fetwah of a certain Mollah, Shemseddin Mohammed, a native of Samarkand, and living in Herat at the time of the Sultan Husein Baikera. This fetwah has done much injury to the poor inhabitants of Iran, for, although the marauding Turkomans would have taken them prisoners without any form of law, they would not have been sold in the market-place of fanatical Bokhara, had not the brand of the Kafir qualified them for it, only such men being saleable. Whatever cruelties were practised on them, were all committed under the pretext of punishing an unbeliever, and though Eastern Mohammedans try to vindicate the Mollahs of Turkestan, by pointing out that the Persians recognize one and the same Koran, and one and the same prophet, yet they declare the fetwah to be just and proper, and protest against all assertions to the contrary, of the West-Mohammedan learned men, as ignorance and error.

There are essential distinctions also in the ritual of the Eastern and Western Mohammedans. I doubt very much whether, even at Bagdad and Damascus, during the most brilliant period of Islamism, officers (Reis) were daily traversing the streets, stopping everybody in the midst of their daily occupations in order to hear them the prayer Farz-i-Ayin, and punishing the ignorant on the spot. This is actually being done in Bokhara at the present day. In the various ceremonies of circumcision, marriage, and burial, the Central Asiatics have several customs of their own, entirely heterogeneous to Western Islam; their daily prayers, which have to be repeated five times, consist here of more Rikats (genuflexions) than in other countries; and it is curious, at the Ezan (call to prayer), the Turkestans most carefully avoid all tune or melody, and recite it in a sort of howl. The manner in which the Ezan is cried in the West, is here declared sinful, and the beautiful, melancholy notes, which, in the silent hour of a moonlit-evening, are heard from the slender minarets on the Bosphorus, fascinating every hearer, would be listened to by the Bockhariot with feelings only of detestation.

In addition to the above let us bear in mind the many mosques, medressas, all filled to overflowing with worshippers, the Karikhanc, *i.e.* houses, where blind men recite the Koran the whole day long, the numerous Khanka, where fanatics roar out their Zikr day and night, and with which institutions every city is crowded; then let us picture to ourselves the various gestures, the severely earnest looks and the whole appearance of the Mollahs, Ishane, Dervishes, Kalenters, and ascetics, one of wild fanaticism, and it might perhaps be possible to form an idea of Bokhara, of this pillar of Islam, these headquarters of an overstrained religious zeal, and where the religion of the

Arab Prophet has degenerated into a form, such as the founder no doubt never wished his work should assume. From here it has spread with the same tendencies over Affghanistan to India, Kashmir, and the Chinese Tartary, and northwards as far as Kazan. In all these places the spirit of Bokhara has taken firm root, for Bokhara is their teacher, and neither Constantinople nor Mekka, but Bokhara is looked up to as their sole guide. It is here that our civilization will encounter more serious obstacles than in Western Asia, and Russia most likely has already made this experience with respect to the Nogai Tartars. It would be a matter of regret, if the English Government should not as yet have felt this to be the truth with her 40 millions of Mohammedan subjects in India. The consequences would be sure and inevitable.

So much at present for the difference between Eastern and Western Mohammedanism, and without much research we shall find the principal causes to be as follows:

Firstly, Asia, the chief seat and fountain-head of religious fanaticism, is found, the more we advance eastward, the more true to its ancient type. As in general the inhabitants of India, Thibet, and China are more eccentric, more religiously fanatical, or, in other words, more Asiatic, than the followers of Islam, in the same measure the Eastern Mohammedans are more zealous than their Western co-religionists.

Secondly, the same eccentric fanaticism, which the

Central Asiatics displayed when professing the doctrines of Zoroaster, has been the cause why their conversion to Islam cost the Arabs so much time and trouble. It took more than 200 years, before the religion of Mohammed had completely supplanted the old faith. No sooner had the conquerors left a town than the newly-converted inhabitants returned to their old faith, and the town had to be re-conquered and re-converted. But when the iron perseverance of the Arabs had at last succeeded in making them Mohammedans, they attached themselves to the new religion with the same fervour they had manifested in the old. As early as the beginning of the rule of the Samanides, we find in Transoxania men of high reputation, throughout Islam, for their learning and their exemplary piety. Belkh had already then acquired the name of Kubbetül Islam, the dome of Islam. The city and neighbourhood of Bokhara were crowded with the tombs of saints and learned men, and we can easily understand how it happened that these Turkestani cities had in piety and learning become successful rivals of Bagdad, the then centre of the Mohammedan world, where devotional zeal was eclipsed by the splendour of worldly grandeur.

After the extinction of the dynasty of the Samanides, but especially during the Mongol conquests, no doubt all religious life suffered a temporary check, but the edifice has never been shaken to its foundations as in Bagdad, where Helagu, in destroying the phantom caliphate of Motasimbillah, broke the chief strength of Islam and scattered it to the winds. In Transoxania, on the other hand, its energies were being silently strengthened and matured. Timur aimed at making his native home the chief seat of Mohammedan learning, and his work was continued, though in a different spirit, by the rulers of the Sheibani dynasty. It can therefore excite no wonder that Bokhara has been able to preserve to the present day, that precise standard of religious asceticism which characterized Islam in the middle ages.

Thirdly, the great body of the Sunnites has been separated by the schism of Persia practically, if not morally, into two distinct parts, and the separation is certain to continue. The pilgrimages to the holy cities of Arabia have by no means compensated for the undoubtedly greater intercourse, which, in the times of the caliphat, could be carried on without fear of disturbance from the Eastern to the Western frontier of Islam. Sectarian animosity has been purposely kept alive, and has rendered Persia a dangerous country to any Sunnitish traveller. Whilst great political changes, as well as constant intercourse with Christian Europe, combined to bring the Western Sunnites under the influence of foreign social relations, the Eastern Sunnites, left entirely to themselves, had no opportunity offered them of introducing either changes or reforms. They looked with quite as much abhorrence as the Chinese and 'Hindoos upon heretical

Persia, the only country which afforded them the means of communication with the West.

The observation which I have offered, that the influences of European Christianity have divided western from eastern Islam in many cardinal aspects of faith, may lead many of our readers to hope, that the ever-increasing communication and interchange of ideas will gradually effect a total transformation in Asia, or, as many sanguine travellers of modern times believe, that Asia will be Europeanised.

The question is naturally one of interest to every one who wishes (and who does not wish it) for an improvement of the social relations in Asia, and far too important for a mere passing examination. Nevertheless, in order to obviate certain misinterpretations or false constructions, we must remark, that the above observation is not to be regarded as offering an infallible test of Western Mohammedan advancement. We have to be careful, not to mistake for precious metal the tinsel of European civilisation and modes of thought, with which Young Turkey and Persia endeavour to garnish their innate barbarism. I must confess the result of European influence in these countries is hitherto alas! very small and ineffectual. The inexperienced eye of a tourist is deceived by their having partly adopted our dress and furniture, but all else is now just as it was in olden times, and will probably continue so for a very long time to come.

It is taken for granted that our relations, as Europeans with Asia, are those, as it were, between a son and his mother, the latter possessing a certain amount of superstition, with which she finds it difficult to part. From Asia we received our descent, mentally and materially, as well as our education, but nobody would reproach us with ingratitude or want of respect, if we reject the views and opinions of "our aged parent," and for her own benefit occasionally press upon her our ideas instead. I use purposely the expression "press upon," for whatever has been adopted of European civilisation in Asia up to the present day, has not been the result, either of conviction or a liking for our social relations, but simply that of fear. A forced love never lasts, and were we to base our speculations as to the future of the whole of Asia upon the changes hitherto effected in Western Asia, they would inevitably prove fallacious.

CHAPTER XIII.

THE SLAVE TRADE AND SLAVE LIFE IN CENTRAL ASIA.

THE last cannon-shot fired by the victorious champions of the Union against their seceding brethren, although it has not entirely put an end to the slave trade in the Western hemisphere, has nevertheless dealt it a very severe blow. The flag of Great Britain in the waters of Eastern Africa and the recent conquest of the whole Caucasus by the Russians have, to a great extent, crippled the same abominable traffic among the Mohammedans of Western Asia. The indolent, enervated Orientals may still regard with bitter resentment and rancour the efforts of Europe in the cause of humanity; but the sale and purchase of human beings is everywhere practised with a certain reserve arising from a sense of shame, or, to speak more correctly, of fear of European eyes. This trade is now to be found unfettered and unembarrassed only in Central Asia. Here, in the ancient seat of Asiatic barbarism and ferocity, thousands every year fall victims to this inhuman trade. These victims are not negroes, occupying the lowest place in the human race, but belong to a nation celebrated now, as of old, for its culture and civilisation. These not only exchange freedom for slavery, but at the same time the comforts of comparative civilisation for the miseries of semi-savage life, and are torn from their smiling homes to pine away in the desert. The lot of such captives is even harder than that of the negro. Inasmuch as to this day Europeans have had very little information with respect to the miserable state of things which prevails in the distant regions of Central Asia, it may not be out of place if I here recount my own experiences of them somewhat in detail.

What the Portuguese slave traders and the Arabian ivory merchants are in Central Africa, that are the Turkomans in the north-eastern and north-western portions of Iran, indeed we may say in all Persia. Wherever nomad tribes live in the immediate neighbourhood of a civilised country, there will robbery and slavery unavoidably exist to a greater or less extent. The poverty-stricken children of the desert are endowed by nature with an insatiable lust for adventure, and frames capable of supporting the most terrible privations and fatigues. What the scanty soil of their native wilderness denies them, they seek in the lands of their more favoured neighbours. The intercourse between them, however, is seldom of a friendly character. As the plundered and hardly used agriculturist cannot, and dare not, pursue the well-mounted nomad across the pathless deserts of sand, the latter, protected by the nature of the country, can carry on his career of plunder and rapine without fear of chastisement. In former times the cities on the borders of the Great Sahara and of the Arabian desert were in the same plight. Even at the present day the caravans in the latter country are exposed to the greatest dangers. But Persia has to suffer from these evils to a still greater extent, as the deserts which form her northern boundary are the most extensive and the most savage in the world, while their inhabitants are the most cruel and least civilised of nomads.

The wars of hoary antiquity between the Iranians and Turanians, sung by the master singer of the Shah Nameh, "the Book of the Kings," seem to have had their origin in acts of violence perpetrated by the latter. It is true that the combatants of that period are represented in the poem as belonging to one and the same race, but we find that at the period of the expedition of Alexander the people of northern Iran called on the great Macedonian to afford them protection against their northern neighbours, whom they described as terrible beings of inhuman aspect—probably they were of the true Mongolian type, which differs widely from that of the Iranians. Alexander built a great wall from the Caspian Sea to the Kurdistan mountains. This immense work, however, did not come up to the expectations of its founder. Like the Great Wall of China, built for a similar purpose,

it could not permanently keep out the barbarians.
Their impetuous fury burst through such feeble obstacles, and nothing could check their devastating incursions except the energetic rule of some exceptionally vigorous sovereign, who instead of protecting his subjects by a stone wall, did so with a well-disciplined army. This is the case at the present day. The Turkomans and Œzbegs direct their forays according to the peaceful or disturbed state of the adjacent provinces, or the energy or indolence of their respective governors. During the disorders which attended the establishment of the Kadjarish dynasty, individual bands of Yomut Turkomans pushed their predatory incursions as far as the neighbourhood of Ispahan, although the greater number of them were serving under the banner of Aga Mohammed Khan. At the same period the Tekkes pressed forward on the north-east as far as Seistan. At the present day it is the two provinces of Khorassan and Mazenderan which suffer most. The Turkomans first of all inquire into the character and administration of a newly appointed governor, and if they find in him signs of cowardice or neglect of duty (which is often the case), they make repeated incursions with terrible speed on the defenceless province committed to his care. On the other hand, they hardly dare to show themselves in those places where a vigorous and active officer is at the head of affairs. At the time of my journey through Khorassan the roads were so safe that tra-

vellers could go alone through districts which were formerly so fraught with danger, that the largest and best appointed caravans could pass there only when accompanied by a body of troops and a battery of cannon. At that time the governor, Sultan Murad Mirza, kept the nomads in check. Every movement of theirs was reported to him by his spies, and, as soon as they showed themselves, they were attacked in their own haunts, and received severe punishment. In Astrabad, on the contrary, where a fool was entrusted with the administration, the neighbourhood was so unsafe that the Yomuts carried off Persians captive from the very gates of the town.

There are several tribes of Turkomans both on the edge and in the interior of the desert, who consider the robbery of human beings so indispensable a means of livelihood as to deem their existence in the steppes impossible, if they were to be deprived of this productive source of wealth. As other nations talk about "the prospects of a good harvest," so they talk about "the prospects of open roads to Iran." The time which elsewhere is employed in ploughing, irrigating, and sowing the fields, is spent by them in training their horses, burnishing their arms, and in mock combats. Custom has raised their detestable occupation to the rank of a recognised trade. It is looked upon as a Djihad, or religious war, against the Shiite schismatics, who are declared to be no better than infidels. As the heroes set out on their adventure they are publicly dismissed with the blessings of the ministers of their religion; and in case of any one of them paying with his life for his enormities (which very seldom occurs), he is at home declared to be a martyr, a mound of earth adorned with flags is heaped over his remains, which are seldom left in the hands of the enemies, and the devout make pilgrimages to the holy place, where they implore with tears of contrition the intercession of the canonised robber.

The terrible extent to which the most exposed provinces suffer from these excursions is explained by the courage and resolution of the Turkomans. No war, no devastation caused by the elements, can be compared to the misery which their depredations occasion. Not only is all trade and commerce on the highways crippled, but even the husbandman must provide himself with a tower in which he can take refuge, when suddenly attacked by them during his labours in the fields. The smallest village is surrounded by a wall. Even these measures do not suffice, for the robbers often come in large bands and lay siege to such fortified places, and not seldom carry the whole population, men, women, and children, into captivity with all their moveable property. I have seen in Eastern Khorassan villages whose inhabitants, although in the immediate vicinity of large forests, pass the winter without fires, because none dare venture out to cut wood beyond the walls. Others suffer hunger, as their water-mills are outside the village. Travelling is, of course, regarded as a most desperate venture, which no one undertakes save in cases of the most urgent necessity, or under the protection of an armed force.

The readers of my book on Central Asia will have already formed some idea how far this fear of captivity among the Turkomans is well-founded. The lot of the negro, confined in the close hold of a ship during his passage from Africa to America, is sufficiently hard, yet it is not less hard to be bound behind the saddle of a nomad with the feet tied under the belly of the horse, to be insufficiently supplied with food and water, and to be thus transported for days across the weary desert, far from one's dear country and the bosom of one's family. These privations of savage life in the tent of the rude nomad and under an inclement sky are the harder for the Persian to bear, as at home he is accustomed to cooked food and the comforts of civilised life. In addition to these sufferings he is loaded with heavy chains, which are not removed by night or by day. He is continually the object of the revilings, curses, and blows of his tyrannical master. Indeed the first stage of his slavery is the most grievous.

At the present day the occupation of stealing men is followed by the Œzbegs and Turkomans alone. Of the first race the inhabitants of Khiva are to be especially noticed, but they only follow it when in the course of their hostilities with the Turkomans they are driven towards the frontiers of Iran. The Bokhariots have not approached those frontiers since the commencement of this century, and the inhabitants of Khokand may be said to have never come in contact with them. Of the Turkomans, the Tekkes and the Yomuts are most addicted to this traffic; the first seeking their victims in Khorassan, Herat, and Seistan, and even along the western frontier of Afghanistan; the latter along the southern shores of the Caspian Sea. After these the Salors and the Sariks are to be mentioned, who, broken in power and diminished in numbers, seldom, but then with so much the greater fury, make their incursions. The Alielis and Karas can only now and then get hold of a caravan of Hindus, Tadjiks, or even Afghans, and these only on the road to Bokhara. The Tchaudors, who dwell between the lower part of the course of the Oxus and the Caspian Sea, since the Russians are no more marketable, nor indeed easy to catch, have scarcely any field left them for exercising their man-stealing propensities.

The majority of the slaves in Central Asia are Shiite Persians, more especially from the provinces mentioned above, though many from the remaining provinces are also captured, either in war or during their pilgrimage to Meshed. Besides them there are Sunnite Persians from Khaf and Herat; the last are generally caught while cultivating their fields, or while gathering the pistachio nuts. Djemshidis and

Hezares, who fall victims to their mutual feuds, are less often to be met with, and still smaller is the number of Afghans and Hindus. Nay, Osmanlis and Arabs, in spite of the high esteem in which they are held, are sold as slaves, but, as far as I know, there are not more than four or six of them. Jews alone, who have the reputation of being sorcerers, are regarded with too much horror by the inhabitants of Turkestan to be a marketable commodity.

It is difficult to estimate the number thus carried year by year into captivity, because, as I have explained above, it varies according to the state of things in Persia. Nor is it easier to estimate the number of those at present living in slavery in Turkestan. Not all persons who fall into the hands of the Turkomans are sent to the Khanats for sale. Taking into consideration the distribution of property in Iran, we may reckon that about one-third of those captured in Mazenderan and along the shores of the Caspian are ransomed. This is a clear gain to the nomad robber, as he, in the first place, saves the expense of keeping his merchandise for a long time on hand; in the second place, he is not exposed to the risk of the market, for should his captive prove physically deficient in some important respect, he will not be able to sell him at all. Still, however, the proportion of those who are thus ransomed is not everywhere the same. The greater part of those who fall into the hands of the robbers are poor men, who are most exposed to this danger during their work out in the fields. These, of course, can rarely be ransomed. But if, in the case of those who are captured in Mazenderan, we may estimate those who are ransomed at a third, we cannot assume the same of those who are seized in the much poorer provinces of Khorassan and Seistan. I have heard, out of the mouth of a slave dealer who had grown grey in his trade, that from these districts scarcely a tenth part are ransomed, the remaining nine-tenths being forwarded for sale in the markets of the Khanats. The Turkoman never retains a slave for his own use, except (1) when his captive is old or crippled, and yet not so much so but that he works enough to earn his meagre sustenance; if he cannot, he is at once mercilessly cut down; (2) infants who are brought up as Turkomans to become the wildest of robbers; (3) when Cupid makes some pretty brunette of an Iranian so dear to him that he cannot make up his mind to part with her. This last case, however, happens but seldom, as the Turkomans are notoriously the greatest misers in the world. As, besides, they are wanting in that feeling of delicacy for which the Circassian Huri-dealers are so renowned, the harems of Khiva and Bokhara receive many flowers which have lost their freshness in Turkoman hands. The only Persians who are to be found among the inhabitants of the steppes are such as in their own country would not be much better off, or else escaped criminals who have to continue their former courses of misdoing, of murder and robbery, in conjunction with the nomads.

It is the ordinary practice of the men-stealers to keep their booty by them not longer than two or three days. They are by that time transferred to the slave broker, who by way of advance has already furnished the robbers with money or provisions. These conscienceless usurers derive the largest profit from the abominable traffic, for the robbers are for the most part dissolute characters, who, contrary to the usual practice of the nomads, gamble away, or squander in vicious enjoyments, their money as soon as they get it. Slave brokers are of two kinds. (1) Turkomans, who carry on the commerce which exists between the inhabitants of the steppes and the Khanats. They wait until they have got together thirty, forty, or fifty slaves, and then travel in a caravan to Khiva or Bokhara. In the meantime their human merchandise are let out for hire as day labourers, in order to lighten the expense of their maintenance. (2) Sunnite inhabitants of the Persian frontier. These men play a very curious and ambiguous *rôle*, and are the most detestable of all engaged in the whole business. On the one side they serve the Persians as go-betweens, employed to find out such persons as are kept in slavery in the steppes or in the Khanats; on the other they are the most useful spies of the nomads, whom they furnish with the best intelligence about a village or a caravan. Many, especially such as live on the eastern frontier of Persia, have buildings for the reception of slaves in Herat, Maymene, and Bokhara, and just as once in the year they lead to the market a string of miserable slaves of both sexes, so on their return they bring back with them a number of captives redeemed through their mediation. From the family of one of these unfortunate creatures, they take regularly three times the ordinary amount of the ransom, and talk largely about the difficulty of finding him, and of persuading his captor to accept of the money, while all along they know the very place where he is, and have probably already spoken about the price. It is amusing to observe how these scamps change their sentiments, their religion, and political opinions, according to circumstances. On their way to Bokhara, while playing the part of slave holders, they act the zealous Bokhariot, abuse the heretical Shiites, and exult in the just measure dealt out to the Persian slaves. On their return to Iran, when playing the part of slave ransomers, they are loud in their abuse of the brutality and cruelty of the Bokhariots, shed bitter tears over the misfortunes of the poor Persians, and are, in one word, the softest-hearted creatures in the world.

In the caravan in which I myself travelled from Bokhara to Herat, there were two such slave brokers, who came from Khaf and Kain. Both of them bore the title of Khodja, or descendant of the prophet, of which they were not a little proud. The tenderness and care with which they treated the liberated slaves in their charge was almost unexampled. Yet these very men, as the leader of the caravan assured me, had only a few months before led a train of miserable captives into slavery. In the Khanats of Khiva and Bokhara the slave dealers, called there Dogmafurush, form a regularly organised guild. It is remarkable that as regards their nationality they are for the most part Sarts, Tadjiks, and emancipated Persians, and not so often Œzbegs or of any other tribe belonging to the Turko-Tartaric race. The sale takes place either in the dealers' magazines, or in some market-place outside the town, to which place the goods are removed some days previous. The most important depôts are to be found in the Khanat of Khiva, first of all at the capital, then in Hezaresp, in Gazavat, in Görlen, and in Kohne. Besides these, every place of any pretensions has a retail dealer, who is in connection with the large wholesale dealers, or sells goods on commission. In Bokhara is to be mentioned first of all Karakul, and next the capital; besides these, Karshi and Tchihardjuy. It is to be observed that, eastward from Samarcand, this abominable traffic declines more and more, so that in the Khanat of Khokand there are no large slave dealers, and the majority of the slaves to be found there are bought in the territory of Bokhara. In the steppes lying to the north of the Khanats, thanks to the spread of Russian sway, slaves are only found as articles of luxury in the houses of the rich begs.

The price of slaves in the markets of Central Asia,

like that of every commodity, varies according to the quantity at any one time on sale, which in time of peace is less, in time of war greater. The difference of price in male slaves of the same age depends for the most part on their physical condition and their nationality. The Turks of northern Persia are most preferred; first, because they sooner learn to make themselves understood in the Turkish dialects of Central Asia, which are akin to their own; secondly, because they have robuster frames and are more accustomed to hard work than the other inhabitants of Iran. The Afghans fetch the lowest price, not only because they have the greatest dislike to hard work, but also on account of their vindictive and revengeful character, which in the case of a brutal master may lead to unpleasant consequences. As for the female slaves, they do not by any means enjoy the position which is occupied by the daughters of Circassia and Georgia in the harems of Turkey and Persia. On the contrary, their position is rather to be compared with that of the negresses in those countries. It is very easy to explain why. In the first place, the daughters of Turkestan correspond better to the ideas of beauty entertained by Œzbegs and Tadjiks than the Iranian women, who with their olive complexions and large noses, would never bear off the apple of Paris from the fair, full-cheeked Œzbeg women. In the second place, in consequence of their poverty the inhabitants of Central Asia do not indulge in polygamy to such an extent as the Mohammedans of the West. Besides this, the Œzbeg has generally too much aristocratic pride to share his bed and board with a slave, whom he has bought for money. In Bokhara it is true that we find instances to the contrary, but that is only among the high functionaries of state, and even they only take such women as have been brought as children into the country. In the middle classes such *mésalliances* are very rare phenomena. Besides, marriage is much easier here than in other Mohammedan countries. Hence female slaves are kept only as articles of luxury in the harems of the great, or as domestic servants.

As regards male slaves the case is quite different. This yearly contingent of human arms has become for centuries necessary to the support of the Œzbegs, who have a horror of steady agricultural labour. Indeed without their slaves they could hardly obtain from the ground enough to support life. The truth of this assertion is shown by the fact, that the price of cereals in the Central Asiatic markets is determined not simply by the rise and fall of the waters of the Oxus, but also by the greater or smaller number of slaves sold during the year. The use to which slaves are applied is principally agriculture, and in the next place care of cattle; and the larger the estate of an Œzbeg landlord, the larger the number of slaves which he requires. In a land like Turkestan, where the military element preponderates, and every free man, either from instinct or from political necessity, lays hold of the sword rather than the plough-tail, it is necessary that the arms, thus subtracted from profitable labour and employed in murder and devastation, should be replaced by others accustomed to labour. That this is so, is best shown by the fact, that in those districts in which the population are most addicted to war and robbery, there the number of slaves is greatest. In this respect Khiva stands first of the three Khanats, Bokhara second, and Khokand third. In Khiva the greater part of the population is Œzbeg, and, as they are surrounded on all sides by nomad tribes, they are continually engaged in war, and anarchy prevails among them more often than in the two other Khanats. In Bokhara, where the population is strongly mixed with peaceable Tadjiks, things have been rendered more stable by an older established and better organised government. In Khokand, which also contains many Tadjiks, wars are infrequent, owing to the notorious cowardice of its inhabitants, and when they do occur they are by no means so destructive in their character.

A small proportion of the slaves are employed as private servants by the government officials (Sipahi) as also by the sovereigns themselves. For such purposes, however, only such are used as were brought in their earliest youth to Central Asia. These receive a thoroughly Œzbeg education, and beyond the opprobrious title of *kul* (slave), bear few traces of the servile condition. Like the Circassian slaves in Turkey, they often attain the highest posts in the administration, as their innate Iranian quick-sightedness enables them to supplant their Œzbeg competitors. Thus, many who have now under their rule whole provinces, were brought into the Khanat as slaves. In Bokhara, where the Œzbeg aristocratic is of little moment by the side of the predominant Persian element, the sovereigns often take slaves for their lawful wives. Such was the mother of the present Emir, such is one of his wives, both of them of Iranian origin.

In the purchase of a male slave the first point looked to is a strong and robust physical frame, but his value is increased if it be found out later that he has a good character. The seller must engage himself to take him back during the first three days in case any hidden physical defect be found out; for, although the buyer at the time of sale examines him carefully all over like a beast of burden, makes him show the strength of his arms, chest, back, and voice, he is still obliged to be on his guard against the tricks of the broker. For instance, it is very difficult to ascertain the age of such a Persian slave. As is the custom in Iran, the Turkomans also dye the beards of their captives if they have any grey hairs. It is thus possible to make a mistake of twenty, nay, even of thirty years, and it sometimes happens that a slave who, when bought, had a fresh, youthful appearance, and a coal black beard, a few days afterwards turns out to be a grey-haired old man. It is easier to practice such tricks, as the slave, subdued by fear and harsh treatment, does not dare to make the least objection to any assertion of his Turkoman master. This is especially the case with slaves who belong to the Sunnite sect. As they profess the religion of the Central Asiatic, they are not allowed to be made slaves of by the commandments of their religion; but in consequence of the threats of the dealer they deny their own faith. The Central Asiatic, when he sees an Afghan or a Herati for sale, knows that he has been compelled to renounce his faith, yet with disgraceful hypocrisy considers it no sin to buy him and keep him as a slave. I have myself seen in Khiva and Bokhara, even in houses of Mollahs of great renown for learning and piety, Sunnite slaves, and when I called them to account for conduct so inconsistent with their profession, they answered, " At the time I bought him he was a Shüte; that he is now a Sunnite is to be attributed to the influence of the sacred soil of Turkestan." Thus is religion employed to cheat religion.

If we now pass on from the details of the slave trade to consider the condition of the slave, we shall find that the hardest time for him to bear is when he is first captured and trained by the Turkoman or the broker; when the Iranian, justly proud of his superior civilisation, is treated like one of the lower animals by the coarse and brutal Turanian, whose very name is in Iran held in derision. The Persian is from his childhood accustomed to the most refined politeness, and to a flowery, elegant conversation; and must of course suffer mentally a great deal when first introduced to the savage manners and habits of Turkestan. His physical sufferings are by no means so great. The majority of them, destined for agricultural labour, generally gain the confidence and affection of their master by their good behavior. If a slave has during a year not incurred punishment, he is soon looked upon as a member of the new family. Indeed, many receive, after a certain time, either monthly wages, or else a share of the produce of the land or cattle committed to their care. As the Iranian is in general more active and frugal than his Turanian neighbour, the slaves in Turkestan, in a remarkably short time, get together a little capital. This is employed by most of them in ransoming themselves from slavery, which they have the right to do after seven years' service. This term is occasionally shortened as a reward for peculiar diligence, or from great good nature on the part of the master; and the slave is surprized by an azad (letter of freedom), in the same way that we make a present to a faithful servant. Such a document is confirmed by the kadi and the temporal magistrate, and he who is in possession of it becomes at once master of his own actions. The act of emancipation is everywhere accompanied by certain solemnities. Sheep are slaughtered, guests invited; the freedman embraces one after the other the male members of his master's family; and after he has taken his place upon the same piece of felt carpet as his master, his freedom is proclaimed. Among the Kirghiz it is the custom for the master on such occasions to fasten a white bone to the girdle of the freedman, which denotes that the latter is raised from the ranks of the "black-boned" (subject people) to that of the " white-boned " (nobility).

So much for good-tempered and obedient slaves. Where the contrary qualities show themselves, Œzbeg barbarity and cruelty make themselves felt in all their force. It is enough to make one's hair stand on end to read the list of punishments used to compel a refractory slave to obedience. The master has legal right of life and death over his slave. It very seldom happens, however, that he actually kills him, as he thereby loses the whole of his purchase money; but the miseries which he inflicts on him are worse than death itself. Many are kept for years together on mere bread and water in the midst of the lonely deserts; others, a few days before their seven years have expired, are sold again—not, however, in the Khanats, where, their character being already known, they would be unsaleable. In such cases of imposition the victim is generally a Kirghiz, unversed in the tricks of the slave trade. Thus the Persian passes from the city into the northern desert, whence, even if emancipated, he seldom, if ever, returns home.

It is certainly striking that, out of the large number of slaves of Persian origin who are continually brought into Central Asia, only half of those who obtain their freedom go back to their native country. Such as do return are induced to do so either by the necessity of setting their family affairs in order, or by extraordinary home-sickness. He who has lived eighteen years in Turkestan will seldom change it for Iran. The slaves, as observed before, are for the most part originally poor; and when they have secured in Turkestan a certain means of gaining their livelihood, or have got together some property, they in few cases think of returning to their native land, where, on account of general habits of industry and activity, existence is much harder to support; where the necessaries of life are more expensive, and the luxury and splendour of the wealthy excite many ungratified desires in the breasts of the poor, which are not aroused in the midst of the barbarous simplicity of the Khanats. Still, it is to be observed that the emancipated slave can never get rid of the disgrace implied in the word *kul* (slave), however great may be the wealth he may have accumulated, or however high the post to which he may be promoted. Although he may be living in the utmost splendour and magnificence, the kul can never hope to obtain the hand of a free Œzbeg, the poorest of whom would reject his proposals with scorn. I know an instance in which an Œzbeg refused his daughter to a freedman, although the latter's suit was backed by the command of the khan; he preferred rather to encounter the anger of his sovereign than to call one who had once been a slave his son-in-law. Even the khanezads* (children of slaves), who are not allowed to be sold, are treated in the same manner, and can only marry the daughters of other emancipated slaves, or sarts. Only in the fourth generation is the disgrace attached to the word *kul* somewhat softened down, but by no means quite obliterated. In a country like Central Asia, in which courage is looked upon as the highest virtue, the slave is regarded as the *ne plus ultra*—a man who, for want of a contempt of death, allows himself to be put in chains; and it is this vice which is so difficult to be forgiven. This way of looking at the subject is further strengthened by the boundless feeling of aristocracy which distinguishes the Tartars, whether settled or nomad, in which not even the wildest Tories or the proudest marquis of the Faubourg St. Germain can surpass them—a feeling which is entertained not only against the foreign Iranian, but even the native Tadjiks, the eldest inhabitants of the land.

It will be understood that it is only the moral stigma of slavery which the freedman has to suffer from. In his civil rights he is as well protected as any one else. Thus, as the Oriental is even more a creature of habit than we are, I found it very easy to understand how the Persian soon finds himself completely at home in Turkestan, which country he once so despised and

---
* The sale of a khanezad is regarded as a disgraceful action, and one who commits such an act is branded as a thief and a robber.

dreaded, and dwells contentedly in a foreign land, only occasionally solacing himself with a visit to his relations or to the shrine of some Shiite saint in Iran.

Unfortunately, it is the material comfort and prosperity of the slave which the Central Asiatic, like other Mohammedans, alleges in his defence, when we express our abhorrence of the disgraceful traffic in human beings. As in Turkestan, so in Turkey we may often hear this argument:—" The sons and daughters of the wild Circassians were in their native land poor people, who in their free mountains could hardly get bread enough to eat; here with us they become rich government officials, pashas, nay, even princesses, whose powerful influence affects the policy of government." They further point out how kindly the slaves are treated in the houses of persons of distinction, where they are put on the same footing as the members of the family. But they forget that these cases are exceptional, and that such good fortune depends for the most part on the personal beauty of the favoured few. What becomes of the greater number, whose charms are not such as to gain the favour of their master? What shall we say of this majority, exposed as they are to the oppression and cruelty of a tyrannical master, and constantly employed in the hardest labour?

Such things are of course not taken into account, any more than the original cruelty of the slave merchant, who tears his victims from their homes and their friends. On the banks of the Bosphorus, as on those of the Oxus, few persons care to picture to their minds the horrors of that first moment of separation. How many orphans, how many widows, how many aged and helpless parents, are left behind to wring their hands in sorrow for their bread-winner, who is carried into captivity! It is impossible to count them, it is impossible to describe the miserable condition of so many villages and districts which are exposed to the terrible scourge of the slave trade. The traveller in those regions stumbles at every step over the most melancholy traces of the devastation which it causes. However certain he may feel of the splendid destiny which awaits this or that individual captive, he must still exclaim: "This is the most execrable occupation that has ever defiled the hands of man, and its suppression is the first and holiest duty which our western civilisation has to perform for the cause of humanity!"

The suppression of the slave trade in Central Asia is, moreover, much easier than many might at first sight suppose. The root of the evil is to be sought, not so much in the Turkomans as in the inhabitants of the cities. All nomad tribes were and are ready for such a trade, if they only find settled tribes who will buy their captives of them. The Bedouins of the Arabian desert could never addict themselves much to the traffic, inasmuch as the markets of the surrounding cities were closed by the religion of Islam against the sale of their booty. In the same way the Turkomans would soon abandon the practice, if the sale of Persians, Afghans, &c., in the Khanats were declared illegal. The Djemshidis, the Firuzkuhis, and Hezares, afford the strongest proof of this. As the transport of their captives to Bokhara is rendered unsafe by the intermediate Turkoman tribes, while at the same time their sale is forbidden in the Afghan town of Herat, they have either to suppress their slave-trading propensities altogether, or come to a compromise with the Turkomans, much to the advantage of the latter.

Sultan Murad Mirza, an enlightened prince, and the governor of Khorassan, once expressed to me his surprise that England, which spends so many thousands in checking the slave trade in African waters, can look on unconcernedly while the same trade in the middle of Asia lays waste such a country, whose ancient civilisation was of profit to Europe itself. In like manner I, too, cannot conceal my astonishment at the apathy which Europe, and especially that State whose flag is in the East ever the harbinger of the dawn of a newer, a happier era, has displayed on this question. Sentimental newspaper writers, in their political rhapsodies, may yet for a long time take under their protection the feelings of independence of many a savage Asiatic tribe, to whom freedom means nothing more than anarchy, plunder, and murder. But the dreams of Rousseau have had their day, and we can with the fullest confidence say, that whenever Europe shows herself in the East, whether in the peaceful garb of the missionary, or in the terrible panoply of her warlike power, she brings only blessings in her train, and scatters the seeds of a new order of things. The more light is poured from the West upon the East, the sooner will the evil customs of the old world be eradicated, and our brother men be made happier.

CHAPTER XIV.

PRODUCTIVE POWER OF THE THREE OASIS COUNTRIES OF TURKESTAN.

In arguing about the Russian conquest of Central Asia, we are wont to say that the Court of St. Petersburg, in those far-reaching schemes which she pursues towards the Hindu-Khush with so much toil, at so heavy a cost, seeks some richer recompense than is to be found on the shores of the Yaxartes and the Oxus. Well; it is true that Russia's policy does not confine itself to the possession of the plains of Bokhara, Khokand, and Khiva. But in the meantime let us not undervalue the immediate gain of these conquests. It is right that we should learn the comparative worth of the three Khanats, the nature and extent of their produce, both as it is, and as with proper management it might become.

The very name of "oasis countries" contributes towards creating an impression, that the inhabited part of Turkestan must be unimportant as regards productive power; add to this the poverty and the extremely primitive and simple mode of life of its inhabitants, and it is not surprising that the great distance and the consequent want of knowledge should have begotten and spread erroneous notions. The natives themselves, as well as oriental travellers and geographers, such as Idrisi, Ibni Haukal, Ebulfeda, and the learned Prince Baber, fall into the opposite extreme, by representing Turkestan as the richest country on the face of the globe, India alone excepted. This opinion prevailed in former times,* not only throughout Western Asia, but even very lately I have met with it in several localities, and never felt more astonished than when I heard the egotistic Persian eloquently praising the wealth of Turkestan, a country he looks upon with deadly hatred and aversion. As for ourselves, we will try to form as far as possible an impartial estimate, although we must maintain at the outset, that Turkestan by far surpasses the known parts of European and Asiatic Turkey, Afghanistan and Persia, both in the wealth and variety of its productions; nay, that it might be difficult to find in Europe, flourishing as it is, and rich in every blessing, a territory that would rival the oasis countries of Turkestan.

The great variety of productions is to be ascribed essentially to the climate of the countries bordering the Oxus and Yaxartes. It is neither harsh, nor could it exactly be termed mild. On the average it cor-

* The plain of Sogdiana or the Zerefsha—valley between Bokhara and Samarkand—is spoken of as an earthly paradise, and Hafiz calls the towns of Bokhara and Samarkand the greatest treasure, and yet surpassed by his beloved.

responds to the climate of Central Europe, though it must be remarked, that the winter is far more severe on the shores of the Sea of Aral and in the mountainous parts of Khokand, and the summer, on the contrary, much warmer in those districts that lie to the south, and often almost tropical in the immediate neighbourhood of the great sandy deserts. The Oxus is frozen over every winter, from Kerki and Tchardshuy to its mouth; in Kungrad, Khodja Ili, and on the right bank, where the Karakalpaks dwell, the winter is generally very severe; the snow lies often for weeks on the ground, and tempestuous north winds (Ayamudjiz) are not unfrequent. Under such conditions there can be no question of a mild climate, and yet in Khiva I have found the heat unbearable as early as the beginning of June, while in August, near Kerki and Belkh, it was more sultry and oppressive, even in the shade, than is the case in really tropical countries. This great variation in the climate produces corresponding local differences in the vegetation of even a small extent of country. Thus, for instance, the cotton of Yengi Üergendj is far better than that in the more northern districts, and the silk of Hezaresp is considered throughout the Khanat of Khiva to be of first-rate quality. Görlen produces the finest rice, and the finest fruit is found in the environs of Khiva, which lies farther south. In Bokhara and in Khokand we see the same effects produced by the climate, and hence the reason why each of the three Khanats contains, on a comparatively small area, such various and manifold productions, as are usually met with only in larger countries, which lie between several zones.*

The extraordinary productiveness of the soil is to be ascribed partly to the "blessed" rivers, so-called by the natives, which intersect the oasis-countries, and partly to the quality of the soil. Of these rivers the Oxus is the most important. From its fertilizing influence upon the land it may be compared to the Nile; although, when used as drinking-water, the latter still surpasses it in its pleasantness to the taste. Next comes the Zerefshan, whose name, "Scatterer of Gold," sufficiently indicates the blessing it scatters over its shores. Nor are the smaller rivers, such as the Shehr Sebz and the tributaries of the Yaxartes, of less importance. When we finally add, that the irrigation of the fields is carried on with as much care, and much more ease, than in other parts of Western Asia, we shall cease to marvel any longer at the rich resources of the soil, however grand and important they may still appear.

I have already noticed in my "Travels in Central Asia" that the irrigation is carried on—firstly, by natural canals, called *arna*, which are formed by the

---

* The difference in the harvest time in Turkestan best illustrates the above remark. In Belkh, for instance, and in the neighbourhood of Andkhuj, the harvest is at the beginning of June; in Hezaresp, Khiva, and Karaköl, towards the end of June; in the oasis-countries, in July; in Kungrat, and in the north of Khokand, not before the beginning of August.

irregular course of the Oxus; secondly, by *yaps*, *i.e.*, smaller artificial canals, by which every village and colony is surrounded and intersected. In all places of any importance there is a high official, called Mirab (prince or warden of the water), who inspects the various aqueducts, and orders them every spring to be freed from the accumulated sand. During the winter the sluice-gates of all the principal "arnas" are closed as a protection against the inundations which naturally follow the breaking up of the ice. The cleaning of the canals takes place at the beginning of April, and the great object in view is to make them constantly deeper and narrower. The sand that is taken out is heaped up on both sides of the bank, which have thus for miles the appearance of intrenchments, and with their cooling shade protect the precious water from the burning rays of the summer's sun. To the general purposes of communication, however, these intrenched ditches are very prejudicial, although of real advantage to agriculture. Hence, the more expensive kahriz—subterranean canals—in Persia, are far more advantageous, and, moreover, preserve the water purer and cooler. The yaps and arnas in Central Asia form great obstacles to the traveller. Bridges are either very bad or altogether wanting. Let the reader imagine the trouble and the dreadful loss of time incurred, when a caravan with its heavily-laden camels has to cross from ten to fifteen of such embanked canals in one day's march. How prejudicial it is to the rivers to have so much water drawn off, we see clearly in the Oxus. Formerly it flowed, no doubt, into the Caspian Sea, now its embouchure is in the Sea of Aral,* and this great change in its watercourse must be ascribed, if not wholly, yet in a great degree, to the evil of the many small canals.

It is difficult to decide which of the three Khanats is the most fertile, especially now, when since the death of the much-lamented Conolly, nobody is able to furnish a succinct account of the nature and resources of the soil. To judge from all I have seen in my journey to Samarkand, and learned from my fellow-travellers, of Khokand, the native home of most of them, I should feel inclined to give the preference to the Khanat of Khiva in point of vegetation. The two other Khanats have more land under cultivation, but Khiva surpasses them by far in the quantity and quality of its productions, with the exception, perhaps, of fruit, which Bokhara furnishes in greater variety, and of finer flavour. Bokhara also deserves the prize with respect to all mineral productions; but the breeding of the finest cattle and horses is the exclusive property of the nomads.

The land is measured by *tanab* (cord,—a tanab is

---

* Burnes (Travels in Bokhara, ch. ii. p. 188) doubts altogether whether the Oxus had formerly a different watercourse, and, amongst other reasons, supports his view by the opinion of the natives. No one will feel surprised that I heard them assert the very contrary. Among the Turkomans there exist numerous contradictory legends in connection with the former watercourse of the Oxus.

equal to sixty square yards), and in Khiva and Khokand consists of (1) *Mülk*, freehold property, which is subject to the payment of taxes; (2) *Khanlik*, arrear estates, *i.e.*, such land which the Government has either reclaimed and brought under cultivation, or which has devolved upon it by confiscation and conquest. Of this land a third of the net income is claimed by the State. (3) *Yarimdji*,* all land that belongs to the medresse (schools), mosques, or any religious institutions, and which is liable to a fourth of the net income. The Khanlik estates in each district are under the control of a certain number of officials, called *Müshüriib*, who at the same time collect the taxes. Church property, on the contrary, is under the management of the mutevalis, as in other Islamitic countries.

The quality of the land in general may be judged best by my stating, that the richest soil under cultivation produces one hundred batman (one batman is equal to twenty-four pounds) on a tanab, and that of least productive quality never less than sixty batman. And taking into consideration that the cultivation of the ground here, as everywhere in Asia, is done in the most negligent manner, and is in the highest degree primitive, a competent judge can easily form an idea of the great fertility of the soil.

It is impossible for me to say how many square miles of cultivated land, or of land capable of cultivation,

---

* These were formerly let on the system of half-profit, as indicated by the name.

the three Khanats possess. The frequent wars and unsettled times sufficiently explain the numerous ruins of former flourishing colonies. Of the Khanat of Khiva thus much at all events may be assumed, that the area of territories laid waste and turned into deserts is larger than the land at present under cultivation. With the exception of a few single productions, with which the three Khanats carry on an export trade among each other, and with Russia, only so much of the rest is grown as is required for home consumption. There is no doubt that not only might the quality of all present productions be essentially improved, but also considerably multiplied.

A short survey of the productions of the three Khanats will help to explain and confirm in detail all I have hitherto stated.

1. THE VEGETABLE KINGDOM.

Wheat and barley are the most important among the cereals grown in the oasis countries of Turkestan. There are four kinds of wheat:—

1. *Bukhara budayi* (Bokhara wheat) is considered the finest; it has a long, thin, and reddish grain, with a greenish top. Of this sort the delicious bread is baked, in the preparation of which the town of Bokhara excels, and which is famed far and wide under the name of *shirmaye* (milk-marrow).

2. *Tokmak bash* (cuneiform top) has a round, thick

grain; it is very substantial, and most like our wheat. The best quality is found in Khiva.

3. *Kara süllü* (black-haired) has a thin and dark-brown grain; it is chiefly used as food for horses, not being of a particularly good quality.

4. Yazlik (summer-fruit) takes a very short time to grow; it is exceedingly light, and, when used, is mixed with other kinds of wheat.

Barley is not so good in Central Asia as in Persia or Turkey. There is, besides the usual sort, an inferior one, called *karakalpak* in Khiva, which is here used, as everywhere in the East, as food for horses. The average prices of all cereals are exceedingly low, as compared with the countries of Western Asia. The price of a Khiva batman of the best wheat varies from two to three tenge (one tenge, seventy-five cent.), whilst barley costs often less than one tenge, and seldom more.

Rice is grown in enormous quantities, but it is far inferior to the Herat or the excellent Shiraz rice, called tchampa and amberbuy (amber perfume) in quality. It is more like the Egyptian, called in Turkey dimyati (damietter), but would no doubt surpass the latter, if cultivated with more care and attention.

Djügeri (holcus sorghum) is grown and consumed in far larger quantities in the three Khanats than anywhere else in Asia. It is eaten in a milky state, but when dry it is used as fodder, principally for young colts, being less heating, and also more nourishing, than barley, from the quantity of saccharine matter it contains. Bread is made of it, either alone or mixed with wheat.

Mekke djügeri (Turkish wheat) never grows higher than a small span's length. Two kinds of it are found, one with a yellowish, the other with a red, small grain. It is never dried, and always either eaten in its milky state or used as fodder.

Tari (groats) is an important article of consumption in Central Asia, and is therefore much grown. There are several sorts.

Besides the well-known kinds of pulse, such as peas (burtshak), beans (lubie), lentils (jasmuk), &c., there are several others which we do not know; as for instance, the *konak*, which has smaller but thicker seeds, and a lower shrub than our lentil; *mash*, rather larger than millet, of a brownish colour, and several others, which are of no interest to the general reader.

Of oil-plants, I must mention first of all the *kündshi* sesame, which thrives very well, and provides the Khanats amply with oil for cooking and burning. Then there is the *zigir*, a plant similar to millet, which bears on one stalk several fruits, which are like apples, and the yellow seeds in which are not bigger than poppy-seeds. This oil is fit in food, especially in pastry. Then the *djigit*, the seeds of the cotton-capsule, the oil of which, however, is not fit for food. *Kender* (hemp), of which an inferior sort of linen is made, and which also furnishes the very popular narcotic, called beng. Lastly, indau, a small shrub, from the greenish seeds of which a bitter oil, and of a disagreeable smell, is made, which is used as a medicine for animals, and especially for camels.

Among the plants, which produce dye-drugs, the following are most esteemed:—*ruyan* or *boyak*, an excellent species of madder, which thrives in all three Khanats, and is exported in considerable quantities to Russia. In the year 1835 this article was very little in request, and in the year 1860 as many as 24,523 Russian pud (883,000 English pounds) were imported.* *Isbarak* or *barak*, whose small yellow flowers, when dried and powdered, give a fine yellow colour. *Görtchük*, a plant resembling clover, with small red flowers; the leaves, when boiled, give a fine black colour. *Buzgundjh*, a plant with a fruit similar to gall-nuts, only grows in southern Maymene, and in the Badkhiz mountains, north of Herat, and is said to produce the finest red colour; it fetches a high price in the place itself.

Although not belonging to the same class of plants, I must mention here the *terendjebin*, a resinous and very sweet substance, which grows on a thorn, called khari shutur (camel's thorn). The *terendjebin* shows itself suddenly and quite unexpectedly towards the end of the summer during the night, and has to be collected at once in the early morning, before it grows hot. It resembles a gum, is of a greyish white colour, exceedingly sweet, and can be eaten in its raw state; in Central Asia it is made into shire (syrup), but in

* Mitchell. "The Russians in Central Asia," p. 462.

Persia it is used in the sugar-manufactures of Meshed and Yezd.

As regards fruit, we find in the Khanats almost every species (with the exception of fruits of the South) in great quantity, and of excellent quality. A very considerable export trade is carried on in it to Russia, and even to "rich" India. The Central Asiatic is not a little proud of his superiority in this respect, in Asia the glory and value of a country being determined by the quality of its water, air, and fruit. Each of the three Khanats has in the latter its spécialité; Khiva is distinguished for its melons and apples, Bokhara for its grapes and peaches. It may be that some parts of Persia and Turkey surpass Bokhara; but for melons, Khiva is unrivalled, not only in Asia, but I feel inclined to say, throughout the world. No European can form an idea of the sweet taste and aromatic flavour of this delicious fruit. It melts in the mouth, and, eaten with bread, is the most wholesome and refreshing food that nature affords.

The celebrated Nasrabadi melon alone, near Ispahan, reminds one, though very feebly, of this fruit of Central Asia, unique in its kind. There is a great variety of species. The principal summer melons are the following:—1. *Zamtche*, which ripens earliest; it is round, of a yellowish colour, and has a thin skin. 2. *Görbek*, of a greenish colour, and with a white meat. 3. *Babasheikhi* is small, round, and with a white meat. 4. *Köktche.* 5. Shirin *Petchek*, especially mellow and sweet, of a small round shape. 6. *Shekerpare.* 7. *Khitayi.* 8. *Koknabat.* 9. *Aknabat.* 10. *Begzade.** The winter melons are not ripe until the beginning of October, but they keep the whole winter, and are most palatable in February. There are the following kinds:—1. *Karagulebi.* 2. *Kizilgulabi.* 3. *Beshek.* 4. *Payandeki.* 5. *Saksaul Kavunu.* These are mostly exported to Russia.

The Oxus chiefly contributes to render the melons of Central Asia so incomparably excellent, since the finest quality thrives only on its banks. The melons of Bokhara are very indifferent, and in quality even inferior to those of Khokand.

Khanikoff mentions in his interesting work† ten different kinds of grapes he found in Bokhara. In Khiva I met with the following:—1. *Huseini*, with oblong seeds and a thin skin, very sweet, and keeps throughout the winter. 2. *Meske*, with large round seeds. 3. *Sultani.* 4. *Khalide* are ripe first of any. 5. *Shiborgani.* 6. *Taifi.* 7. *Khirmani.* 8. *Sayeke.* All these different sorts of grapes grow on the level ground, and are either made into shire (syrup) or dried for eating; wine being made only by the Jews in Bokhara, and in a very small quantity.

There are four sorts of apples grown, and that of

* I observe with pleasure, that of the seeds, which I brought with me from Central Asia, several kinds have succeeded in Hungary. These will undoubtedly be the best melons we have in Europe.

† "Bokhara, its Emir and its People."

Hezaresp may boldly challenge the productions of our European horticulture.

The mulberry, too, is larger, more varied, and sweeter than ours, and to this superiority we must, perhaps, ascribe the fact, that the silk of Central Asia is better than the Italian and French, and that a certain disease among silk-worms, common with us for many years, is there quite unknown.

The rearing of silk-worms came originally from Chinese Tartary, especially from Khoten, where, as M. Reinaud* correctly remarks, it was introduced in the first century of our era from the interior of China. Silk stuffs of native manufacture were known in Bokhara in pre-Islamitic times, according to the testimony of a certain Manuscript,† which treats of the ancient history of Bokhara. It is no exaggeration to assert that the cultivation, spinning, and dyeing of silk, is a still more primitive process in the three Khanats than in China itself, where industrial progress, no doubt, effected many changes, whilst here everything has remained as it was years ago. The Khanat Bokhara supplies most of the raw silk; it is produced in the capital, in Samarkand, and among the Lebab-Turkomans. Much also comes from the Khanat of Khokand, in the neighbourhood of Mergolan and Namengan. Khiva contributes but little, and this little is inferior

---

* " Relations Politiques et Commerciales de l'Empire Romain avec l'Asie Orientale," p. 197.

† Tarichi Narschachi.

in quality to the productions of the other Khanats, though, as competent judges have assured me, it is far superior to the silk of Gilan and Mazendran, in Persia. The manipulation, however, is very imperfectly performed. I was struck with the manner of winding off the cocoons, which were placed in a cauldron of boiling water and stirred with a broom, until a certain number of threads unwind themselves, which are then wound round the broom. The dyeing is almost exclusively in the hands of the Jews, the weaving is done by the Tadjik and Mervi, who, in accordance with the taste and fashion of the country, prepare only stuffs of glaring colours.

In former times, especially during the Arabian occupation, the silk stuffs of Central Asia were celebrated throughout the East; but when the cleverest of the artisans were transferred by the conquerors to Damascus and Bagdad, the old art gradually disappeared, and is now gone for ever, in spite of the efforts of Timur to transplant it back from Transoxania. How great is the quantity of silk produced here, is shown by the circumstance, that the greater part of the cotton stuffs, called *aladja*, that are generally worn, are strongly intermixed with silk; that not only the rich, but every man of middle rank, possesses one or more garments, several table-cloths and pocket-handkerchiefs made of silk; and that a considerable export trade in silk is carried on, not only with Persia, India, and Afghanistan, but to a large extent with Russia.

The cotton in Central Asia promises to become an important article for the future. It is cultivated in large quantities in the three Khanats, furnishing the material for the upper and under garments of every body, high and low, for their bed-clothes, and cloths of every kind. The cotton in Turkestan is better than the Indian, Persian, and Egyptian, and is said to equal the far-famed American cotton. At present, however, Russia alone consumes this article in her manufactures at Moskau, Wladimir, Tverskoy, &c., and in quantities which increase annually in a surprising degree. The manufacturers complain greatly of the clumsy management of the planters, especially of the insufficient cleansing of the cotton from the seeds, as well as of the dishonesty of the traders, who wet the bales, or fill them with stones, to make them heavier. Nevertheless, the cotton, which is imported from Khiva and Bokhara by Orenburg, is almost indispensable to Russian industry.

In Central Asia the cultivation of cotton is comparatively easy and convenient, the cotton fields requiring no irrigation, and the rain being considered, if anything, prejudicial even in the spring. A hard, stony ground, called *Soga*, is always chosen, and is ploughed once; on the whole, the cultivation of cotton is the least troublesome of all field occupations. According to the statistical dates of the Orenburg custom-house the greatest quantity of cotton is produced in the Khanat of Bokhara; this statement, however, rests upon an error, since the caravans of Khiva, when crossing the Jaxartes, frequently join the Bokhariots, or they give themselves out for Bokhariots; these latter standing on a much better footing with the Russians, whilst the people of Khiva are in very ill favour with them. I know from my own experience, and have convinced myself by frequent inquiries, that not only is the cultivation of cotton far more flourishing in Khiva, but its quality is far superior to that in the two sister Khanats. The pod, here called gavadje, is smaller than that of Bokhara; but the cotton is much finer and whiter even than the guzei sefid, that is, the first quality of Bokhariot cotton industry. The Central Asiatics themselves give the preference to the Khiva production, a fact which tends to confirm our opinion. In dyeing and weaving Bokhara stands pre-eminent, but the stuffs from Khiva are better paid in her capital than her own manufactures. They are exported to Afghanistan, India, and Northern Persia, and are a highly-prized article even among the nomads.

There is no doubt that the cotton of the oasis countries will one day considerably increase in value. Several circumstances of paramount and urgent necessity must combine to further this object. Above all things, it is requisite that important improvements should be introduced in the mode of cultivation; our European machines should come in aid of the cleansing and packing, and the roads should be rendered, as far as possible, secure. By these means the cotton would not only be improved in quality, but, without any great additional expense, the quantity might be considerably multiplied. It is very probable that Central Asia may one day, although not in the immediate future, be to Russia what New Carolina is to the manufacturing towns of England at the present day.

The immense increase in the exportation of cotton from Central Asia is shown very clearly in the Blue Books of 1862 and 1865, in the list which Mr. Saville Lumley, former secretary to the English embassy at St. Petersburg, has contributed. According to this official statement the Khanats exported to the value of—

	BOKHARA. Roubles.	KHIVA. Roubles.	KHOKAND. Roubles.
1840—1850	2,065,697	470,781	16,851
1853	280,514	133,799	The dates are wanting.
1854	509,600	248,347	
1855	513,023	185,683	
1856	501,225	36,050	
1857	578,483	66,776	
1858	634,643	59,729	
1859	495,065	2,274	
1860	721,899	22,429	4,907
Total...	4,234,412	755,087	4,907

From this list we see, that the exports of 1840—

1850 did increase more than double during the next ten years, and under favourable political circumstances would, no doubt, continue to increase.

We must add the remark, that although Bokhara shows in this list throughout the largest figures, it does not by any means follow that they are the result of its own exclusive production. Much Khiva cotton has been included, as well as the cotton which the Urgends traders carry to Orenburg on the Bokhara road. The Orenburg custom-house furnishes the list, and all the cotton is entered under the head of Bokhara. In like manner much Khokand cotton is mixed up with it. The Khokand traders give themselves out for Bokhariots on the frontier, on account of the frequent hostilities between their tribe and the Russians.

2. The Animal Kingdom.

We must mention first of all the domestic animals, and among these the genus, sheep. Two species are usually distinguished: 1, the *Kazak koy* (the Kirghis sheep); and, 2, the *Œzbeg koy* (the Œzbeg sheep). The Kirghis sheep is preferred to the latter, for its wool as well as its meat. Throughout Central Asia we meet with the fat-tailed sheep. Of these it is said, that their masters are obliged to fasten either cylinders or wheels under their broad, thick tails, which they drag after them on the ground, in order to render walking easier to them, or rather to enable them to walk at all—a story which is by no means exaggerated, however incredible it may appear. The so-called Bakkan koy, the fatted sheep, give often from two to three batman of pure fat. The meat I found, in point of taste and flavour, superior to any in all those parts of Asia I am acquainted with. The highly celebrated Kivirdjik and Karaman sheep in Turkey cannot be compared to them; and even the south Persian sheep, of which the Persians are exceedingly proud, are inferior to them.

The wool is not of the same excellence, and is used less for clothing (probably for want of knowledge in the preparation of it) than for carpets, travelling-bags, horse-cloths, and similar other coarse stuffs; it is little seen in the export trade. Black, curly lamb-skins, on the other hand, form an important article of trade. Its chief source is Bokhara, especially Karaköl; from here it is exported all over Asia, and even to Europe, where it is known under the name of Astrachan. The skin is drawn off the young lamb two or three days after its birth, and then softened in barley meal and salt. It is said, that washing it in the water of the Zerefshan gives it the beautiful lustre; and in the month of July thousands of them may be seen spread out for drying along its banks, between Bokhara and Behaeddin. The skins are everywhere admired, but mostly in request in Persia, where they are made into the fashionable hats of the country. If we take into account, that a külah (a hat, for which three or four skins are used) costs there as much as from ten to fifteen ducats, we may feel assured that our Astrachan of a considerably lower price is no Bokhara production. With the nomads of Central Asia the breeding of sheep is a chief means of maintenance, and we can easily form an idea of the innumerable flocks of sheep which graze and rove upon the steppes. The Kirghis send great quantities of sheep to the Khanats and to Russia, where the importation is constantly on the increase. In the year 1835 about 850,000, and in the year 1860 already 3,644,000 roubles' worth of sheep were imported.* In addition to this enormous quantity of sheep, raw sheepskins to the value of 75,000, and wool to the value of 86,000 silver roubles, passed the Russian frontier at Orenburg in the same year.

The *goat* is, after the sheep, one of the most important of domestic animals. Goats' flesh is not so palatable as that of sheep, but it is here better than anywhere else in Asia. The wool of the goat, according to Burnes, is far inferior to that of the Cashmir goat, but tolerably good; and waterproof stuffs are made of it.

Horses, of excellent breed, are found among the Turkomans, who export the finest to Afghanistan, India and Persia. The Turkoman horse, especially the Akhal and Yomut race,† is very little inferior to the Arab horse in point of swiftness and endurance, as well as in beauty of form. The Œzbeg horse, or the

* Compare " The Russians in Central Asia," p. 462.
† Compare " Travels in Central Asia," p. 420.

species met with in Bokhara, Khiva, and Maymene, possesses more strength than swiftness.

The *camels* of Central Asia, among which the breed of Bokhara and the two-humped Kirghis are considered the best of their kind, are surpassed in point of strength and swiftness only by the Arab, and especially by the Hedshaz camel. The story that the camels can preserve water pure and cool in their second stomach, and that travellers, when suffering from thirst, drink it in their utmost need, is perfectly unknown here; and on questioning the nomads on the subject, they only laughed and seemed highly amused. These animals are famous in Central Asia for their rare contentedness, satisfied as they are with the very worst water, and most miserable food, consisting of thistles and briars, and in spite of which they hold on for days, loaded with the heaviest burdens. They are at the same time entirely free from the spite and viciousness of the Arabian camel. They are exported to Russia and Afghanistan; less to Russia. Their hair is cut twice a year, and is used in the manufacture of ropes and coarse stuffs. Cattle on the whole are not very numerous, and in rather a poor condition. The finest cattle are said to exist in Khokand, and among the Karakalpaks on the Oxus, whose exclusive occupation is to rear them. Beef is, in Central Asia, still more tough and unpalatable than in Persia or Turkey, and the consumption of it is therefore limited to the poorest class of the people. Butter and cheese are made of cow's milk, but in comparatively small quantities. *Mules* are not found in Central Asia, from a religious superstition against disgracing the horse, the noble animal, "par excellence;" but all the greater care is bestowed upon the breeding of the ass, which undoubtedly is here the finest and most excellent of all I have seen in Asia. The ass is, in Bokhara, not only of a vigorous frame and high stature, but of surprising nimbleness, and in long caravan marches can be relied upon as much as the horse. The fowls are of the long-legged Chinese breed. Geese are smaller than those in Europe; and there are several species of ducks. Besides these, there are swans, partridges, guinea-fowls and pheasants, of which the finest sort is found in Khokand.

3. Mineral Kingdom.

My readers will not feel suprised that we should have but a scanty knowledge of the mineral riches in the three Khanats. Lehmann, and other Russian travellers, who, furnished with sufficient geological knowledge, might have made closer investigations, were thwarted in their efforts at every step by the jealousy of the Tartar officials. I incline, however, to the opinion of Burnes, that Central Asia possesses either no precious metals or extremely few, and that the gold dust in the Zerefshan is not the property of the country, but washed down by the small rivers that rise in the Hindukhush. According to a statement of the Central

Asiatics, the mountainous country round Samarkand and in Bedakhshan, the Oveis-Karayne mountains on the left bank of the Oxus (in the Khanat of Khiva), and the Great Balkan in the desert near the Caspian Sea, are rich in metallic wealth. That gold mines really do exist near the upper Oxus, is proved by a certain considerable quantity of gold annually obtained from it, although the gold-washing is carried on in the most primitive and negligent manner.

The gold-washing, or more correctly the gold-fishing, is done with camels' tails, of which several are hung up side by side between two poles. People beat them about in the water for some time, or they dip them into the river, and then hang them up. Those places are always chosen where the water is troubled, and the work is generally performed in June and July, the months in the year most fit for the purpose. I doubt whether any gold-dust is exported; it is not probable, since the smaller ornaments are made of native metal, as the Persian goldsmith in Bokhara informed me. Silver is found in Khiva in the above-mentioned mountains, and a considerable quantity of this valuable metal was really gained during the reign of Allahkuli-Khan, when the miners were worked for three years under the management of a native of India, who had been educated for this department. It is said that after the death of this prince he either fled or was murdered. Since that time the mines have been much neglected. I also heard some vague reports of the existence of silver mines near Shehri Sebz.

Of precious stones, we must mention first of all the rubies of Bedakhshan, which were formerly of high repute in Asia, under the name of Laali Bedakhshan; at the present day not many of them are found. Cornelian exists in large quantities in the mountain-rivers of Bedakhshan. It is very cheap, and is exported to Arabia, Persia, and Turkey. Lapis lazuli, which is used in dyeing, is of small value in Central Asia, and is exported to Russia and Persia. The turquoise of Bedakhshan and Khokand is far inferior in colour to that of Nishapur in Persia, and is purchased by none but the nomads and Nogay silversmiths; it is of a green instead of a blue colour, and liked far less than the latter.*

This sketch of the productions of the oasis countries in Central Asia will have convinced my readers, and especially those who are acquainted with Asiatic countries and their conditions, that Turkestan cannot be numbered among the sterile countries. Called by the natives "a jewel set in sand," from its own peculiar value and the barrenness around it, Central Asia will certainly play an important part one day among the countries of the far East, and occupy a prominent position, as soon as the beneficent beams of our European civilisation shall have dried up the stagnant pool of its miserable social relations, and as

* Compare Ritter, "Erdkunke," viii., 326.

soon as the grand results we have gained for industry and agriculture shall there likewise have received their acknowledgment. It is robbery, murder, and war, but not the barrenness of nature, which convert the shores of the Oxus and Jaxartes into a desert. In Bokhara, but especially in Khiva, agriculture is almost exclusively in the hands of slaves, of which there are in the latter Khanat more than 80,000. Their rude manners have placed the sword in the hands of the inhabitants,—the plough is considered degrading, and is entirely given over to slaves. When will these Khanats learn to see that a great part of their misfortunes, and the unsettled state of their political and social relations, originate in the perversity of their nature and conduct?

A government which endeavours to smooth existing relations deserves our full acknowledgment and cordial wishes for success, although it is premature to anticipate a complete change. Nor must we grudge it the natural wealth of the country. Setting aside the moral influence of such a Government, and its possible future political schemes, the material gain is, on the whole, not large; nay, I maintain, that it is small, when compared to the trouble and expense the occupation and administration of such a province require —a province, the communication with which must always be attended with endless hardships and difficulties.

CHAPTER XV.

ON THE ANCIENT HISTORY OF BOKHARA.

WHAT I have to impart in this chapter on the ancient history of Bokhara is taken out of a Persian MS., brought by the late Sir Alexander Burnes from Bokhara, which bears the name of "Tarikhi Narshakhi," the history of Narshakhi. The author, Mehemmed ben Djafer el Narshakhi, wrote this highly interesting work in Bokhara, in the year of the Hegirah, 332, under the government of Emir Hamid the Samanide, in Arabic. Later, in the year 522, it was translated into Persian, and augmented by quotations from a not less interesting work, Khazain ul Ulum, "The Treasures of Wisdom," which Ebul Hassan wrote at Nishapur. In consideration of its historical value it is well worth the trouble (in a quite literal translation) to give the whole. The distinguished orientalist, Monsieur de Khanikoff, has already done this, and it will very probably be put before the scientific world. We have here only selected that which is suitable to the outline of our sketches, and for this reason given an extract in a free translation, since this is less fatiguing to the majority of readers, and more acceptable.

BOKHARA, *i.e*, ITS ENVIRONS.

On the site of modern Bokhara there must have been in ancient days a morass, which arose from the yearly flooding of the river that comes from Samarkand. In summer, from the melting of the snow in the existing mountains in the neighbourhood, this was much augmented. This morass was dried up at a later period, and the fertile soil soon attracted settlers from all sides. From these colonists a prince was chosen, by name Aberzi, for their ruler. Bokhara itself existed not then. There were simply numerous villages, of which Beykem or Beykend (the village of the ruler) was the largest. Tyranny soon dispersed this little colony. A part of it drew back to northern Turkestan, founded the town Djemuket,* and soon enjoyed a flourishing condition. Later they returned to the assistance of their brethren whom they had left behind. Then Prince Shir Kishver, " Lion of the Land," conquered the bad Aberzi, put him in a sack full of thorns, and turned him round and round until he died. Bokhara gradually flourished again. Shir Kishver ruled for twenty years, and contributed much to the success of the colony, and his followers pursued the same path, and the whole neighbourhood was soon peopled and covered with villages. In what epoch the chronology of this place falls, is hard to con-

* This is very probably the modern Chemket, in the new Russian province of Turkestan.

jecture. It were a vain effort to attempt to penetrate the table of the oldest history of Bokhara. We prefer rather to give the interesting data of the MSS. on that neighbourhood, and to begin with Bokhara, which from ancient days was an important spot.

Bokhara, the Capital.

What the source of our information relates with regard to the religious importance of this spot, what pre-eminence its inhabitants had, what distinction awaits them at the day of resurrection, &c., will not much interest our readers. Siaush is stated to have been the founder of the fortress, where he was slain in a public square, before the Gate Guriun, by his own father-in-law. This place was constantly held in honour by the fire-worshippers, and every one took care to offer a cock there on Noruz (New Year's Day) before the set of sun. This commemorative festival was celebrated everywhere. Troubadours have long sung of it in their lays, though the story relates to facts that happened three thousand years ago. Other people affirm that Efrasiab was the founder. It may suffice to know that the fortress long remained desolate and uninhabited until Benden, or Bendun, the husband of Queen Khatun, rebuilt it, together with a castle over the gate, on which he caused his own name to be engraved in iron. In the year 600 Heg. this gate, together with the iron slab, was still conspicuous; later all fell in ruins, and every attempt to rebuild it was fruitless. After the opinion of the wise men of the day it was at length rebuilt in the form of the Pleiades, on seven pillars, and from that time all kings who inhabited it were victorious, and, what is still more wonderful, none of them died, as long as they continued to occupy it. This castle had two gates—the Eastern or Gurian Gate, the Western or Rigistan Gate—which were connected by a road, and the castle contained the dwellings of the chief officers, as well as the prison and treasury and divan. After these events there was a time of desolation, and it was again rebuilt by Arslan Khan, and enjoyed its former greatness, 534 Heg. When Kharezm Shah took Bokhara he permitted governors appointed from Sandjar to direct matters, and to destroy the citadel. Then, in 536 Heg., it was again restored. Similar events it experienced many times, till at last the Moguls, under Djengis Khan, reduced to ruins Bokhara and the fortress.

Of the palaces of Bokhara, the Seraï at the Rigistan must be mentioned in the first place, in which square the lords of this land, both in the pre-Islamite times and also later, were in the habit of living. In regard to circumference, that which Emir Said, the Samanide, caused to be built is the largest, and probably most splendid palace, where all the high counsellors, with the governors, are found in one and the same building.

After this, we must name Seray Molian, or that palace which was built on the canal of the same name.

This is described as an exceedingly charming dwelling-place, which was surrounded by the most luxurious gardens, the most beautiful meadows and flower-beds, brooks and fountains. The whole tract of country, from the gate of the Rigistan to Deshtek (little field) was quite full of beautifully-painted, sumptuous houses, with lovely lakes, and shadowy trees which allowed no sun to penetrate; and the gardens exuberant in fruits, as almonds, nuts, cherries, &c.*

The palace of Shemsabad is also worthy of notice, which the king, Shems-ed-din, caused to be built near the gate Ibrahim, and which is remarkable for its zoological garden, named Kuruk. This was a place of four miles in circumference, surrounded with high walls, where many dove-cotes, as well as wild animals, such as apes, gazelles, foxes, wolves, boars(!), in half-tamed condition, are found. After the death of Shems-ed-din, his brother, Khidr Khan, mounted the throne; then his son, Ahmed Khan, who continually increased the beauty of the palace; but when the latter was conquered and conducted to Samarkand by Melek Shah, it was abandoned, and fell into ruins. Besides these there were many country houses in the neighbourhood, nearer to the town, which belonged to the Keshkushans. By this name a certain people were indicated who came out of the west to Bokhara, but were not Arabs, and possessed a singularly good

* Almonds and cherries are, now-a-days, not to be met with as a product of Bokhara.

reputation. When Kuteibe, after the conquest of Bokhara, required the half of the houses for the Arabs, the Keshkushans formed the largest portion of those who gave up their houses and settled out of the town. Of these country houses only two or three remained to later periods, which bore the name of Köshki Mogan (Kiosks of the fire-worshipping priests). There were many temples in Bokhara known as those of the fire-worshippers, and the Mogan were accustomed to maintain them with great care. The first town wall which extended round Bokhara was built by the command of the governor, Ebul Abbas, in 215 Heg., in consequence of the inhabitants having complained that they had suffered so much from the inroads of the Turks. In the year 235 Heg., it was repaired and fortified, but later entirely ruined when the Mongol hordes laid waste the city and environs of Bokhara. Besides the above, mosques and other buildings are mentioned. We wish to spare our readers these details. The past prosperity of Bokhara is sufficiently shown, when we appeal to twelve canals or larger conduits which intersect the vicinity in all directions. The fruitful and bounteous nature of the soil has, in the East, become proverbial, and the great sums which have been levied on the town and environs prove it. After the fourth, *i.e.*, the final conquest of Bokhara by Kuteibe, the Khalif in Bagdad received 200,000, and the governor of Khorassan 10,000, dirrhems. In the time of the Samanides Bokhara paid, in Kerminch alone, more than a million dirrhems tribute, which is considered an immense sum according to the tariff of that period. In pre-Islamite times there was in Bokhara only barter. The first governor who struck silver money was Kanankhor. The coin had on one side his portrait, and was of pure silver: this lasted up to the time of Abubekir. The old coinage became lessened, and was replaced by the inferior mint at Kharezm. In the time of Harun al Raschid, Athref, the governor, struck a new mint of six different kinds of metal, which were named atrifi or azrifi. (I think that the word, common in Persia, eshrefi—ducats, is not from the Arabic, but derived from azrifi.)

In industrial arts also, Bokhara has exceeded the other nations of once famous Asia. The dress stuffs which were fabricated on the bank of the Zerefshan were sought for in Arabia, Persia, Egypt, Turkey, India itself. These were merely of three colours, white, red and green; but its silken stuffs were strong and heavy, and were worn for a long time as the favourite royal and princely robes in many lands. Next to these were the large carpets and curtains, which were woven in Bokhara. The former of these were so expensive that the town of Bokhara could pay, with one single carpet, the tribute to Bagdad. In the later devastations of Bokhara the clever artizans were scattered, and with them their art fell to the ground.

THE ENVIRONS OF BOKHARA.

Besides the chief city and its wonders, there are many places of the environs described in the manuscript before me. Some of these exist even now; others have passed nameless.

Kermineh. In this many other towns are comprised, and this region has produced many poets and poetesses. It is distant from Bokhara fourteen farsangs only, and was named Dihi Khurdek (little town).

Nur is a larger place, where there are many mosques and caravanserais, and it is the spot most frequented by pilgrims of the whole neighbourhood. In Bokhara much is thought of this, for a journey thither is esteemed as half a pilgrimage to Mecca.

Tavais (as the Arabians name it, for the proper name was Kud), a considerable spot, which was celebrated for its markets. They lasted commonly ten days, and were frequented yearly by more than ten thousand persons, who came from Ferghana (Khokand) and from all quarters. This circumstance made the inhabitants wealthy, and they were famous for their riches. Tavais lies on the high road to Samarkand, and is seven farsangs from Bokhara.

Ishkuhket, a large and rich town, carries on an extensive commerce in preparing kirbas (a kind of linen); has many mosques, caravanserais, and is considered one of the loveliest towns of Bokhara.

Zendiné produces the best kirbas in Bokhara, which

it exports to Arabia, Fars, Kirman, and other distant lands, and which is used everywhere by princes and great people for clothing. It is in high estimation, and is purchased at the same price as the heaviest stuffs.

Revane is a fortified spot, and was formerly the residence of the kings, and it is said that it was built by Shapur. It is on the Turkestan boundary, has a weekly market, at which much silken stuff is sold.

Efshana is a well fortified spot, has a mosque built by Kuteibe, and a weekly market.

Berkend, a large old village, which the Emir Ismael, the Samanide, bought, and divided the revenue between Dervishes and Seids.

Rametin is older than Bokhara, and was earlier inhabited by princes. It is said to have been built by Efrasiab, who fortified it also at a later period, when he was attacked by Kaykhosrev, who sought vengeance on him for the death of his father, Siaush, and son-in-law. In this place were the most celebrated temples of the fire-worshippers in all Transamana. Efrasiab was, after two years, seized and killed by Kaykhosrev, and his grave is found at the entry of that fire-temple, which stands on that high hill which is now visible close to the mountains of Khodscha Imam. These events are reported to have taken place three hundred years ago.

Yerakh'sha is one of the Bokhara towns, and is celebrated for its castle, which was built by Prince

Gedek, one thousand years since, and then lay long years in ruin. Later, Prince Hebek restored a portion, and Benyat, the son of Tugshade, is said to have died there. In the time of Islam, Emir Ismael, the Samanide, wished to make a mosque of it, and offered the inhabitants 20,000 dirrhem as a re-imbursement for the restoration, but they declined his offer. In the time of Emir Hayder, the Samanide, there were yet some wooden remains, which that person brought to Bokhara, and used for the building of his castle. Yerakh'sha has yearly fifteen markets, of which the last, which is held at the end of the year lasts twenty days, and also is called the Noruz market (New Year's Day market), which since that time (what time?) has become a Bokhara custom. Five days after the Noruz market comes the Noruz Mogan (New Year's Day of the priests of the fire-worshippers).

Beykend was considered a city, and its inhabitants are highly indignant if any one call it a village. Were a Beykender in Bagdad questioned as to his home, he would say Bokhara. It was once a considerable spot, had many beautiful buildings and mosques, and in the year 240 Heg. had yet many rabats (stone houses in the form of a caraverserai). The number of these exceeded a thousand, all inhabited by people who, in summer, dwelt at their own country seats, but in winter spent the fruits of their industry in the town, and thus were very gay. The Beykenders were also great merchants, who carried on a trade to China and the Sea. The fortifications of this town are older than Bokhara, and it gave Kuteibe much trouble to take it. In earlier times each prince had here his castle. Between Beykend and Farab is a tract of twelve farsangs, which goes through a sandy desert. Arslan Khan had raised here a magnificent building, and with much cost brought the Canal Djaramgam into this vicinity. In the neighbourhood of Beykend there are many beds of reeds and large lakes, which they call Barkent ferrakh or *Karakol*. According to a credible statement these are about twenty farsangs in extent, and abound in water-fowl and fish, beyond any other portion of Khorassan. Here the Canal Djaramgam had not sufficient water, so Arslan Khan wished to bring from these lakes a stream to Beykend, which place lies on a slight elevation. They began to dig, but they struck on an excessively hard rock, which rendered useless all their hammering and hewing. Loads of fat and vinegar were employed for the softening of the stone, but in vain, and the work was abandoned.

Farab has a large mosque, of which the walls and cupola are built of tiles, without a particle of wood visible. It had its own princes, who governed from Bokhara in a settled order, and, to a certain degree, independently.

Queen Khatun and the Four First Arabian Field Marshals.*

In the time of the Arabian occupation, or more properly speaking, in that time when the first outposts of the Arabian adventurer pressed to the distant East, there was in Bokhara a woman on the throne, who, during the minority of her son Tugshade, held for fifteen years the reins of government with both might and rectitude. Of this woman, who is considered to be the Nushirvan (emblem of justice) of Central Asia, it is reported that she went daily from her castle on the Rigistan† on horseback, and, surrounded by all classes, busied herself with state affairs. Towards the end of year 53 Heg., the Arabians, under the leading of Abdullah-ben-Ziad, crossed the Oxus, and took the once celebrated Peykend, through which victory they came into possession of much treasure, and about 4,000 prisoners.

In the year 54, Heg., they attacked Bokhara with a strong army and battering engines, and Khatun was cowed before the threatening peril. One messenger was sent by her to the Arabian field-marshal with presents, and instructions to obtain at least an armistice for fourteen days; another was sent to the northeast to a Turkish race, for quick aid. The stratagem was

* Khatun means in Turkish, *woman*, of which word we wish to avail ourselves instead of a name, as this is the practice in the MS. before us.

† *Rigistan* means in old Persian, an open space, which is strewn with sand (rig) and kept vacant.

successful. The Arabs, anticipating nothing, granted the armistice. Meanwhile the Turks approached, and Khatun felt herself strong enough to attack the besiegers and put them to flight. The defeat itself was not denied by the Arabian historians: they only add, that the Mussulman army took a rich booty in gold, silver, clothing stuffs, and weapons, in which were the golden and jewelled boots of the queen, Khatun, the worth of which was estimated at 200,000 drachmas. Abdullah-ben-Ziad felled all the trees in the vicinity, and destroyed all the towns. Khatun felt anxious for the fate of her land, and concluded peace with the Arabians, which she bought, they say, for one million drachmas. In the year 56, Heg., Said ben Osman was named governor of Khorassan. He crossed the Oxus and fell on Bokhara. Khatun wished to buy a peace for a similar sum to that which she gave Abdullah ben Ziad. Despite of this offer, Said, who stood with 120,000 men in Kesch (Shehr Sebz) and Nakhsheb (Karschi), refused compliance, gave battle, and after he had beaten the army of Khatun, made peace. The queen was obliged to submit, and entered the army of the Arab as a vassal.* The submissive State gave eighty hostages, and Said ben Osman went to Samarkand, which he also took, and thence, laden with rich treasures, returned back to Medina. The report goes,

* Report says, that Said ben Osman and Khatun, who was a celebrated beauty, loved each other; and even in later years the popular ballads were extant which sung of this adventure.

that the hostages which Khatun gave to the Arabian field-marshal were officers who doubted the legitimacy of Tugshade, and plotted together against the queen. According to agreement, they wanted merely to accompany the Arab army as long as they remained in Bokhara, but Said wished to have them with him as trophies of his victory when he entered Medina. This moved the deceived Bokharians; and when they saw their ruin unavoidable, they wished, at least, to die avenging themselves. They slew Said, and then severally destroyed each other. In his turn, Muslim ben Ziad was named ruler of Khorassan. He hastened quickly to his post, drew together a considerable army, and fell on Bokhara, again become faithless. Khatun quickly perceived that she, alone, was no match for him, and sought everywhere help. She gave her hand to Terkhan, Prince of Samarkand, to purchase protection for her country; also the mighty Turkish prince, Bendun, was called in to aid. When all the assistance had been promised, Khatun hastened to conclude a truce: the Arabs consented; when Bendun appeared with 120,000 men, and induced the reluctant queen to violate the truce. The Arabian field-marshal was extremely incensed, and sent one of his officers, by name Mehleb, to Khatun, to remind her of her blameable neglect of duty. Mehleb took from each company a man with him, quitted secretly the camp by night, with the intention to surprise, on some point, the enemy's army. He was already arrived on the banks of the river (Zerefshan), when some Arabs, thinking that the question was a matter of booty, joined him. Their united force was not more than 900 men. The enemy's cavalry discovered this, and at the first onset cut down 400 of them. The rest fled quickly back, but were followed, and towards daylight reached near to Khoten. The Turks opened a bloody battle; Mehleb was surrounded on all sides, and announced, by a powerful shout, his position to the nearest Arabian camp. The signal was heard; Muslim knew the voice of Mehleb, heeded it but little, and only Abdullah, who blamed the indifference of the commander-in-chief, mounted his horse in order to assist his brother, who was hard pressed. This approach gave courage to Mehleb and his followers. The battle was renewed; Bendun fell, and the Turks were put to flight with great loss. An immense booty fell into the hands of the conquerors; and it is said that each horseman received about 1,000 dirrhems. After this incident Khatun made peace, and did homage to the Arabs. She also appeared in the camp, and did homage again. She requested to see Abdullah, whose heroic deeds had astonished the whole army. Muslim called him. He wore a blue tunic with red girdle, and favourably impressed the Queen by his noble appearance, and she made him great presents. The fourth Arabian field-marshal was Kuteibe ben Muslim. He went to Khorassan, under the Kaliphate of Hudjadj, conquered on his way the provinces of Tocharistan, and crossed the Oxus, in 88 Heg. Peykend was apprised of his approach, a strong walled fortress, the taking of which cost him a hard struggle. The Arabs were forced to besiege it fifty days, and suffered considerably. Since force could produce no effect, he was obliged to employ stratagem, and caused it to be undermined, and the fortress was thus surprised. He pardoned the inhabitants, made peace with them, and leaving Varka ben Nasr-ullah as governor, went to Bokhara. Intelligence soon reached him that the Peykendis had killed the governor, whom he had left behind, and who, as it proved, had provoked the revolt by his cruel deeds. Kuteibe hastened back, plundered the city, destroyed it, killed all the men able to bear arms. The rich and mighty Peykend, which maintained an extensive commerce in teas from China and other goods, was utterly destroyed. Some portions were restored later, but its prosperity was gone for ever. They relate that the Arabs, among abundant treasures, found a silver idol, which, with the robes, was worth 150 miskal. Among things most worthy of remark, were two pearls, as large as a pigeon's egg. These, according to the report of the Peykendis, were brought into the temple by a bird. Kuteibe sent such things to the Khalif Hudjadj as a present, who, in a letter of thanks, expressed both his admiration for the objects, and the high spirit of the sender. From hence he went to Vardun, (now Vardanzi) which he spoiled, with all the other villages belonging to it.

These successful advances of the Arabian army terrified the small princes of that neighbourhood, and they united, and attacked, with joint forces, the invaders. As the Arab historian affirms, Kuteibe was greatly distressed. He was also destitute of arms;" and they say that a lance was bought for 5 dirrhems, a helmet for 50, the cuirass for 900. Happily, the ruler of Samarkand, by cunning and deceit, had withdrawn from the alliance to go over to the Arabs; and the Turkish leader having obtained information that fresh auxiliary troops had arrived in Kesh and Nakhsheb, retreated to Vardun; and Kuteibe remained undisturbed in the possession of the conquered province in Transoxiana.

Tugshade and Mokanna, the Veiled Prophet of Khorassan.

Tugshade, who, after the death of his mother, was chosen King of Bokhara, had to thank Kuteibe, alone, for his throne, since he supported him against his powerful neighbour, the Governor of Vardun, who invaded Bokhara repeatedly, but was always driven back by Kuteibe. This feeling of gratitude may have been the principal cause that Tugshade went over to Islam, and distinguished himself by his remarkable ardour in favour of the new opinions. He reigned thirty-two years, not so much as an independent prince, but as the vassal of Kuteibe, who found in him a mighty aid in propagating by force the doctrine of Mohammed, which the inhabitants of Bokhara were much disposed to reject. As the Arabian adventurers made conversion to Islam the chief condition in submitting, the Bokhariots, at each capture of their capital, acknowledged, in appearances, Islam, but after the departure of their conquerors returned to their beloved national religion, the Parsi. Kuteibe wished to check this. He ordered, therefore, that the half of the houses of the whole town should be given up to the Arabs. The proselytes were placed, by these means, in the immediate neighbourhood of men who continually watched them, and urged them to the new doctrine. In the year 94 Heg., he permitted a large Mosque to be built, in which all were to assemble for prayer on Fridays, and in which the Koran should be read, in an emphatic manner, in the Persian language. This mosque existed even in the time of our author's writing, who besides adds that upon the doors figures of animals were cut, (which, as is known in every place of Islam, to say nothing of a mosque, is treated as a gross offence): the reason of this, they say, was, that these animals were taken from an earlier temple of the Fire-Worshippers, and retained afterwards.

Tugshade reigned thirty-two years. After his death, Kuteibe, his son, (whom he so named, from attachment to the Arabian field-marshal), took the throne. At the commencement of his reign he affected the Musulman, but, as it was soon apparent that he was secretly attached to the old religion, he was executed by order of Ebn Muslim, the ruler of Khorassan, and in his stead, Benyat, also a son of Tugshade, was named Lord of Bokhara. Under both these latter reigns, it happened that the Sefiddjamegan (the white-clothed), as the followers of Mokanna, the Veiled Prophet of Khorassan, have been called, raised, with the new doctrine, the standard of rebellion against the Arabian conquerors. In like manner with Kuteibe, the son of Tugshade, did the other son, Benyat, go over to the rebels, and was put to death by order of the Khalif, 166 Heg. The family of Tugshade held the throne of Bokhara till 301 Heg., when Ibn Ishak, the son of Ibrahim, the son of Khalid, the son of Benyat, ceded his rights to Emir Ismael, the Samanide.

As to the history of Mokanna and the Sefiddjamegan, this movement might have had, certainly, dangerous consequences for Islam in Central Asia, if the authorities in Bokhara, and particularly the Khalif Mehdi, had not used all proper precaution. Mokanna, (as is related in the MS. lying before me), the veiled prophet of Khorassan, whose real name was Hashim bin Hekim, was born in the village of Geze, near Merw, and early occupied himself with many kinds of knowledge, but especially with enchantments and secret arts.

He was named Mokanna, or the Veiled Prophet, on this account, because he covered his head constantly with a veil, for he was deformed in features, one-eyed, and, moreover, bald. He had, no doubt, under Ibn Muslim a high military rank, as he there once came out in his character of prophet; he was seized, sent to Bagdad, and there put in prison. He escaped thence and came back to Merw, and when he showed himself among his people, for the first time, he demanded, " Know ye who I am?" They said unto him, that he was Hashim bin Hekim. He replied, " You are in error. I am your God, and I am the God of all people. I call myself what I will. I was earlier in the world in the form of Adam, Ibrahim, Moses, Jesus, Mohammed, Ibn Muslim, and now in the form in which you see me." " How is it, then," they asked of him, " that these make themselves known as prophets, but you wish to be God?" " They were too sensual, but I am through and through spiritual, and have constantly possessed power to appear in any form." He lived, then, in Merw, but his agents moved about everywhere in order to gain followers, and his letters of mission began thus:—

"In the name of the Merciful and Gracious God, I, Hashim, son of Hekim, Lord of all lords. Praised be the One God, He who was before in Adam, Noah, Ibrahim, Moses, Christ, Mohammed, Ibn Muslim; He who was manifested before all these, namely, I Mokanna, lord of might, brightness, truth,—rally round me and learn, for mine is the lordship of the earth, mine the glory and power. Besides me there is no god; he who is with me goes to Paradise; he who flies from me goes to hell."

Among his adherents an Arab, named Abdullah, principally distinguished himself, and, in the vicinity of Kesh, misled very many. At a later period the greater part of the villages around Samarkand and Bokhara went over to him. The professors of the new sect became from day to day stronger, and with their numbers increased also both uproar and riot, and the alarm and cries of the Musulmans. When the governor of Khorassan was informed of this issue he wished to seize Mokanna; who then kept himself concealed a long time, and though all the passes of the Oxus were guarded, he succeeded in escaping over to the Transoxanian side, and effected a retreat into a strong fortress on the mountain of Sam, near the town of Kesh (the modern Shehr Sebz). The Khalif Mehdi also was struck with terror at the intelligence. He sent first troops, and then arms in person to Nishapur, for it had become a question whether the partisans of Mokanna would not obtain the upper hand, and Islam sink to the ground. At that time in the new sect robbery and murder having been permitted, immense hordes out of Turkestan joined the revolters, the Musulmans were hard pressed on all sides, their villages plundered, their women and children carried away to prison. In the year 159 Heg. the commandant of Bokhara went against them with a considerable force, and the contest between the partisans of Mokanna and the Mohamedans lasted in that country many years. The Veiled Prophet moved not from his fortified position, his spiritual influence was sufficient to stimulate his followers.

The Arabian garrison of Bokhara, with the few which remained true to Islam, soon felt itself too weak against the number and fanaticism of their far superior enemy. Aid was sent from Bagdad under the command of Djebrailo bin Yahya; and the well fortified place, Narshakh, which was a residence of the Sefiddjamegan, was first attacked. After a close and vain siege the walls could only so far be damaged as to allow a ditch that was fifty yards long to be filled with wood and naphtha: this they fired, and the cross beams of the wall became consumed, and the whole mass without support fell. With sword in hand the Mohamedans rushed into the fortress, many were massacred, many yielded under the condition of retreating with their arms. The fortress was evacuated, yet when the Sefiddjamegan heard that their commanders were put to death in a traitorous fashion, they themselves took up arms in the enemy's camp. A fresh contest arose, in which the Arabs conquered, and the supporters of Mokanna were partly destroyed, partly put to flight. After Narshakh, Samarkand had to be forced, the inhabitants of which, in great part, were known to belong to the new sect. The sieges and battles of these places lasted more than two years (because a great number of the Turks had joined the Samarkanders without any result being obtained).

Mokanna, the mysterious prophet, kept himself during this period always in his fortress, attended by one hundred of the loveliest women of Transoxiana. The interior of the castle was kept only for these with himself and one male page; besides these was no earthly eye permitted to penetrate into his sanctuary. They say that 50,000 of his followers lay at the gate of the fortress, and earnestly implored him to show but once his god-like splendour. He refused, sent his page with the message:—" Say to my servants that Musa (Moses) also wished to see my godhead, but the beams of my splendour he could not support. My glance kills instantly the earth-born." The enthusiastic adherents assured him that they would gladly offer their lives as a sacrifice if this high enjoyment was allowed to them. When he could not furthermore deny them, Mokanna consented to their entreaty, and appointed them to come at a certain time before the gate of the fortress, where he promised to show himself. On the evening of the appointed day he ordered that his women should be placed in a line, with looking-glasses in their hands, as the beams of the setting sun were reflected in the looking-glasses, and when everything was illuminated by that reflection, he ordered them to open the doors. The splendour blinded the eyes of his devoted adherents, who fell prostrate, and called out,—",God ! enough for us of thy glory, for if we see it more all will be destroyed!" They lay long in the dust supplicating him, until at length he sent his page with the message:—"God is pleased with you, and he has given you for your use the good of all the world."

Fourteen years long Mokanna is reported to have lived in this fortress consuming his time with women in drinking and carousing. The Arab field marshall, Said Hersi, had at last, after a hard siege, driven him into straits. The outer part was taken, and there was only the inaccessible citadel on a higher eminence. With the extinction of his ascendant star Mokanna was abandoned by his followers, and when he saw the inevitable ruin nigh he decided, in order not to fall into the hands of his enemies, rather to destroy himself with his women and treasures. He gave to the women at a last carouse a strong dose of poison in wine, and challenged them to empty a goblet with him. All drank but one, who poured the wine into her bosom, and as an eye-witness, told later the whole catastrophe. According to her, Mokanna, after all the women had fallen dead, cut off the head of his faithful page, and, quite naked, burnt himself, with his treasures, in a furnace, which had been heated for three days. He announced before that he wished to go to heaven to call the angels to his help. "I have long watched the furnace," said the fortunate woman who escaped, "but he never came back in that fashion." After the death of Mokanna there were many curious sects and creeds, but they concealed themselves from the ever increasing power of Islam. Under the Samanides the doctrine of Mohammed spread more and more, and Transoxanian countries became soon famous for their religious zeal.

CHAPTER XVI.

ETHNOGRAPHICAL SKETCH OF THE TURANIAN AND IRANIAN RACES OF CENTRAL ASIA.

THE TURKS OF EASTERN ASIA.—PHYSIOGNOMY AND CUSTOMS.

I THINK that there are few points upon the whole terrestrial globe, which are of greater importance for our historical researches than the oases of Central Asia. These in the primitive times were inexhaustible floodgates for those warlike hordes, who often inundated and conquered the most beautiful spots of Asia, streaming towards the west in wild torrents, and even occasioning alarm among Europeans. No people can be so interesting for us upon the subject of Ethnography as the Turko-Tartars, who, under such various names and forms, have appeared on the scene of the events of the world, and have had such powerful influence over our own circumstances. Is it not surprising that of all nations we are the least acquainted with these? Huns, Avars, Utigurs, Kutrigurs, Khazars, and so many others, float before our sight only in the mist of fable. The clash of arms which sounded through them from the Yaxartes to the heart of Gaul and Rome has long since ceased. In vain should we inquire even into their origin, did we not find in the scanty dates of the Western chronicles of that period some points of reliance. These dates show us that between the Tartar tribes of that age and the present inhabitants of Central Asia there did exist an analogy of an unmistakeable character. We detect this in descriptions of them—in the accounts of their manner of living—all evincing much resemblance to the customs and physical condition of the present inhabitants of Turkestan. A similar life to what Priscus describes in the Court of the King of the Huns is met with to-day in the tent of a nomadic chief. Attila is more original than Djingis or Taimur, but as historical personages they resemble each other. Energy and good fortune could now almost produce upon the borders of the Oxus and Yaxartes one of those heroes, whose soldiers, like an avalanche, carrying everything before them, would increase to hundreds of thousands, and would appear as a new example of God's scourge, if the powerful barriers of our civilisation, which has a great influence in the East, did not stop the way. The people of Central Asia, particularly the nomadic tribes, are, in the internal relations of their existence, the same as they were two thousand years ago. In these physiognomical signs we find already changes from a mixture of Iranian and Semitic blood (chiefly after the Arabian occupation). The features of the Mongolian-Kalmuck type here and there approach the Caucasian race. The Tartar in Central Asia is no longer what we see him represented by the Greek-Gothic writers, for even in the times of Djingis he was no longer the same. It is, therefore, of great interest to mark how this change in physiognomical type continually decreases from the east to the west—how this Deturkism, if I may so express myself, is perceptible among the various races of Central Asia, and in what degree their various gradations through social circumstances came, more or less, in contact with foreign elements. This will especially be seen by a cursory view of the Turkish nations of Central Asia from Inner China to the Caspian Sea; but those Turks who stretch hence up to the Adriatic, or to the banks of the Danube, are West Turks, and cannot be included in the unity of race so much by physiognomical type as by analogy of speech, characters, and customs.

With the former, whose masses have retained compactly together the unity of the race, in spite of all those ways in which the Central Asiatics differ remarkably from one another—in spite of our ethnographical names,—the distinction shows itself clearly in their features and common physical type. Whatever views we may entertain of the origin of the Turks, so much is certain, that they are closely related to the Mongols; the relation being much closer than those which subsist between the Indians and Persians in Iran.

Much, very much indeed, is to be done before we have investigated the mutual relations of the whole Turko-Tartaric race, which stretches from the Hindu Kush to the Polar Sea, from the interior of China to the shores of the Danube. Our present sketch is only a weak attempt at a small portion—general views upon all that personal experience has presented to our observation; and it may here and there exhibit somewhat of novelty. Through the extent known to us from East to West, we divide the Turks into the following classes:—

1. Buruts, black or pure Kirghese.
2. Kirghis, properly Kazaks.
3. Karakalpaks.
4. Turkomans.
5. Œzbegs.

BURUTS.

These are pure, or black (Kirghis), and dwell on the eastern boundary of Turkestan, namely, the valleys of the Thian-shan chain of mountains, and inhabit several points on the shores of the Issik Köl, close upon the frontier towns of Khokand. As I am told (I have only seen a few of them), they are thick-set, but of powerful stature, strong-boned, but remarkably agile, to which last quality their warlike renown is attributed. By their physiognomy alone are they to be distinguished from the Mongolians and Kalmucks: the face is less flat, their cheeks less fleshy, their foreheads somewhat higher, their eyes are less almond-shaped than those of the latter. With regard to their colour, they can be little distinguished from the neighbouring nomadic races; red or fair hair and white complexion (by which type our European scholars would claim relationship for this race with the Finlanders and other north Altaic races) are rarely found; at least, my Khokand friends assured me that among hundreds there were scarcely one or two.* In all likelihood the Kiptchaks, of whom I have made mention in my travelling journal at page 382, are no other than a division of the Buruts, who are settled down in and around Khokand, and have caught, both from Islam and from their social relationship with Turkestan, far more than the rest of the Buruts, who, through their contact with Kalmucks and Mongolians, now and then profess themselves more or less Islam. Their language also contains many more Mongolian words than the dialect of the Kiptchaks. From this most original Turkish people we pass over to the second gradation, which is—

* Klaproth, and Abel Remusat, in his "Researches on the Tartar Languages," counts this stock with the Hindu-Gothic race, which assertion is now considered by every one an error. Castren may, without doubt, be right, if he in his investigations in south Siberia finds relationship in a light-coloured Turkish stock; but these are not Buruts. I believe that even the learned Mr. Schott is deceived, when, following Chinese sources, he favours this opinion, in his treatise, "Upon the Pure Kirghese." Berlin: 1863. It appears that the Buruts are confounded with the Uisuns, who dwell further north, are light-coloured, and probably are the remnant of a Finnish stock. See "The Russians in Central Asia," by Mitchell, p. 64.

THE KIRGHIS.

Among the Kirghis or Kasak (as he calls himself), the character of the Mongol Kalmuck type is no longer to be met with in such a striking manner as among the Buruts, although he is hardly to be distinguished from the latter in language and manner of life. In colour, he nearly resembles the rest of the inhabitants of the deserts of Central Asia. The women and youths, in general, have a white and almost European complexion; still this becomes soon altered, through the manner of living in the open air, in heat and cold. The Kirghis are of thick-set and powerful frames, with large bones; they have mostly short necks,—a real type of the Turanian, opposed to the long-necked Iranian; not very large heads, of which the crown is round, more pointed than flat. They have eyes less almond-shaped, but awry and sparkling, prominent cheek-bones, pug noses, a broad flat forehead, and a larger chin than the Buruts. Their beards have little hair on the chin, only on both ends of the upper lip; and it is remarkable, that they lament this deficiency, and by no means find such delight in this physiognomical characteristic as in the projecting cheek-bones, small eyes, &c., which are esteemed by them as beauties.*

* That many nomads censured this deficiency in projecting cheek-bones in myself, as a disfigurement, I have already mentioned. This need not astonish us; and it appears to me truly remarkable, that Dr. Livingstone, in his book, "The Zambesi and its Inhabitants," can assert that he has seen African women, from the Makololo race, who, standing before the mirror, strove to lessen the broad mouth, which is common among them, with the intention to make themselves more beautiful.

Since, as we have said, the type of the primitive race is no longer so striking among them and universal as among the Buruts and Kalmucks, so also we find their ideal of perfect beauty derived only from their neighbours, with whom they gladly intermix; and Lewschine* has rightly stated a fact, when he mentions the preference they allow the Kalmuck women before their own. That from their great extension through the northern desert lands of Central Asia, perceptible shades may be met with in the external traits is scarcely to be doubted;† but one easily comprehends that our classification into great, little, and middle hordes, is unknown to them; for, from the mutual tie of the manner of living, customs and dispositions, they remain always the same, in spite of the many subdivisions into branches, families and lines, which they, like the Turkomans, gladly consider as decided separations. Whether on the shores of the Emba or of the Sea of Aral, as well as in the environs of the Balkhash and Alatau, there is little difference to be found in the dialects spoken by them. Many tales and songs, many national dishes, and national games, are, throughout the year, to be met with in like manner; and although they may occur but seldom, still, love of travelling and warlike disturbances have often brought together the most distant races.

* " Description of Kirghese Kazaks," by Alexis de Lewschine. Paris: 1840; page 317.
† *See* the former work, page 300, chapter II.

In their dress, the Kirghis are to be distinguished from the rest of the nomadic tribes and settlers: in Central Asia, mostly by their head-gear. The men wear, in summer, a felt hat (*kalpak*); in winter, a cap (*tumak*), with fur covered with cloth, the back-flaps of which protect the neck and ears. Besides these, they have still a little fur cap (*koreysh*), which, however, is employed more for in-door use. The women wear a *sheokele*, which is distinguished from the Turkoman head-dress in that it is more conical, and allows the veil to fall not before, but down the back to the loins. The hair, also, is dressed in a different fashion. The young Turkoman women plait the hair in two plaits; the Kirghis with eight thin ones, four on either side. They cover their heads with a *letshek*, in cloth, which covers head and neck. In negligé attire, the girls twist red handkerchiefs round their heads, but the women white or dark-coloured ones. The upper garments have the same tasteless form, with many folds, as everywhere in Central Asia, only more of the bright and glittering colours are liked; and in the north of Khokand it is the custom for the young Kirghis to prepare for themselves a garment from the raw hide of the fox-coloured horse, besides which they let the horse's tail hang down from the neck as an ornament. In their coverings for their feet, the only distinction is, that the western have adopted the Russian form of boot; the eastern, on the contrary, the Chinese; namely, with pointed, curved toes, and slender, high heels.

The religion is almost universally the Mohammedan; still, in a very lax condition, which is the case with nearly all the nomadic tribes in connexion with Islam.* Before and long after the Arabian occupation of Central Asia, the Kirghis professed Shamanism, and it is not to be wondered at, considering the little influence which the teachers of Mohammed could maintain there, that much of the early faith remains there now, and out of a whole tribe, which consists of many hundred tents, there are often only one or two persons among the chiefs who can read the Koran a little.

The greater part of them are the bad students out of the schools of the three Khanats, who for pay go into the army in the deserts. The true proselyte zeal has long become extinct, and the able seek employment in the town.† To keep a Mollah or an Akhond is besides more fashionable, for it points out the affluent condition of a party. To the nomadic tribes their material condition is of more consequence; they look upon religion as a secondary object. They call themselves Mohammedans, but prayers, fasts, and other religious acts are little observed by them, and it

* The Islam of faith was established, according to Fischer ("History of Siberia," pages 86, &c., and elsewhere) towards the middle of the sixteenth century, by one Kutshum. This date is admitted by those in the north, as well as by the dwellers in South Siberia, still in Turkestan that conversion is reported to have taken place much earlier.

† Lewschine says the same in his above-named work upon the Kirghis, page 353.

will in consequence not appear at all remarkable that
superstition, that reminiscence of the infancy of all
people, still plays here an important part. Chiro-
mancy, astrology, casting out devils, breathing on the
sick, and other humbugs we will not mention, since
we find them in the educated Islamite countries, as
Persia, Turkey, and even in enlightened Europe. Of
the superstitions of the Kirghis those only are most
interesting for us which relate especially to the earlier
faiths of these nomadic tribes, and furnish us thereby
with some ideas as to their earlier social relations.
That sacrifices were offered, the still existing oracle
upon the shoulder-blades and entrails proves. The
first, called Keöze süyeghi, consists in placing on the
fire, clean and pure, the shoulder-blade of a sheep just
slaughtered, keeping it in the flames until it is quite
reduced to powder. It is then carefully laid down,
and the experienced person, who is generally a grey-
beard, a Bakhshi, or a Quack (Kam) studies the cre-
vices of the burnt leg with the greatest seriousness
and a countenance full of importance.* When the
cracks run parallel with the broad end of the leg it
signifies good fortune, but if in the opposite direction
a misfortune. The latter, naturally, is seldom detailed.
Still this is no wonder, for when the civilized Greeks
were cheated at Delphi and Dodona, why should not

* Dr. A. Bastian has found the oracle of the shoulder bone even among the
Buruts who profess Shamanism, and it is considered by the Kirghis as a
remnant of the same religion. See Ausland, No. 23, 1869.

this happen among the Kirghis deserts. To prophesy from the position and twisting of the entrails is a rare knowledge, in which the Kalmucks pretend to be particularly distinguished. It is remarkable that this oracle is only consulted when they are curious to know the sex of a child that is to be born. Fire also must probably have been held in high honour, because it was not allowed to spit on it. Ceremonies and dances are held around it, a custom which exists in a wonderful manner in so many parts of Asia, Africa, and Europe, and is still carried on in this district as well as in Khiva and Khokand. To blow out a light is considered very ill bred by the Kirghis in the whole of Central Asia; and finally from the colour of burning oil, fat, &c., many prognostics are divined. The superstition of the women is enormous, and really deserves the trouble of a particular study. A girl, when only in her fourth year, is possessed with it as completely as an elderly nomadic matron who has passed her whole life in the lonely desert which de-developed all her intellectual faculties in that direction. Each individual part of the tent, each utensil, has some superstition in connexion with it, which is strictly observed in pitching a tent, in milking, cooking, spinning, and weaving, far more than the laws of Islam, which are never particularly taken to heart. But the favourite divination of these soothsayers is from fresh-spun thread. Four stones are laid down, two white and two black; in the midst is a thread, *strong twisted*, and the other end suddenly set free. If the thread in its fall sink down to the black stones, it signifies misfortune; to the white, the contrary. From the hand of the twister no action is descried, for the oracle must be infallible. This is called Tyik Yip, and is to be found everywhere in Central Asia.

Of food which is peculiar to the Kirghis we will name Sürü, which consists of smoke-dried flesh (horse or sheep's flesh) cut into small pieces, roasted in fat. The preference for this arises from its keeping for weeks carried about without spoiling. Ködje, ordinary wheat, is cooked in water and eaten in sour milk.

As national games of the Kirghis, we may mention tadjak-kisimo (stocks). It consists in leaping over a rope held high. The winner is applauded, the clumsy, on the contrary, are pressed between two chairs, and exposed to the jeers of the company. Further, "eshek yagiri" (wounded asses' back), in which in running they must leap over three or four squatting playfellows.

3. KARAKALPAKS.

These form the third division in the race, and are essentially different from the Kirghis in physiognomical expression, although allied in language and customs. The Karakalpaks are distinguished by a tall, vigorous growth and a more powerful frame than all the tribes of Central Asia. They have a large head with flat full face, large eyes, flat nose, slightly projecting cheek-bones, a coarse and slightly pointed chin, remarkably long arms and broad hands. Taken as a whole, their coarse features are in good harmony with their not less clumsy forms, and the nickname of the neighbouring people

Karakalpak.
Yüze yalpak.
Üzi yalpak.

Karakalpak, (has a flat face, and is himself totally flat). This sobriquet has not been uttered without reason. The complexion approaches that of the Œzbegs, particularly that of the women, who long retain their white complexion, and with their large eyes, full face, and black hair, do not make an unpleasant impression. In Central Asia they are highly renowned for their beauty. The men have pretty thick, but never long beards. The Karakalpaks, who are sometimes falsely ranked with the Kirghis, are at present only to be met with in the Khanat of Khiva, to which they moved at the beginning of this century. A man of this tribe relates to me that they lived earlier on the banks of the Yaxartes, and certainly near its mouth, whilst another portion abides in the neighbourhood of the Kalmucks, probably in the government of the Semipalatinsk.

The first part of this report does not seem to me to be a mere invention, for Lewschine (in the above-cited work, p. 114), reports, speaking of the ruins of Djem-kend, that even in the last century Karakalpaks had lived there. According to all probability they have separated for a long time from the Kirghis, to whom they approach nearest, and now they form, with respect to their physiognomy, the transit point from the latter to the Œzbegs. In their dress they draw nearer to the Œzbegs than the Kirghis. The men wear large *telpek* (fur caps) which fit low in the neck and cover ears and brow; the women have a cape like a cloak round the throat, and are delighted with red and green boots. The tent of the Karakalpaks is much larger, and of stronger construction than that of the rest of the nomadic tribes, and is guarded by a species of large dog, only to be met with among this tribe. In their dwellings in general they are distinct from the other nomadic tribes in dirt and uncleanliness; they evince also in their food and clothing a carelessness, which makes them abundantly ridiculed and disliked by their neighbours. To their national dishes belongs the *torama*, which consists of finely chopped meat, and is cooked with a large quantity of onions (which vegetable is much liked there) and mixed meal. *Kazan djappay*, meal baked in a pan in fat, which is considered a dainty. Lastly, *baursak*, a meal which consists of a four-cornered piece of pasty filled with meat.

A favourite game is *kumalak*, resembling the game in Europe. It is played with dried excrements of sheep. Many of them devote themselves to games of chance.

4. THE TURKOMANS.

These, which I designate as the fourth gradation of the Mongolian Turkish race in their westerly extension, possess many of the peculiarities of the Kirghis as well as of the Karakalpaks. The pure Turkoman type, which is to be found among the Tekke and Tchaudor, living in the heart of the desert, is denoted by a middling stature, proportionately small head, oblong skull (which is ascribed to the circumstance, that they are not placed at an early period in a cradle, but in a swing, made of a linen cloth), cheek-bones not high, somewhat snub noses, longish chin, feet bent inwardly, probably the consequence of their continual riding on horseback, and particularly by the bright, sparkling, fiery eyes, which are remarkable in all sons of the desert, but especially in the Turkomans. As regards colour, the blond prevails, and there are even whole tribes, as, for example, the Kelte race among the Görgen Yomuts, which are generally half blond. On the borders of the desert, but particularly at the Persian frontiers we find this principal trait already quite altered by the frequent and considerable intermixture with the Iranian race, in which one sees many men with thick black beards, and often without the least trace of the Mongolian Turkish race. Indeed, the Göklens are those who, with the exception of the formation of the eyes, most resemble the majority of the Persians.

Slave-dealing, which from immemorial times has been practised in the northern provinces of Persia, has there, where the intermediate trade with Persian slaves takes place, left many traces behind. Still, only upon the borders, for those living in the interior of the desert and occupying themselves more with the peaceable occupation of keeping cattle than with alamans (foray) have, on the average, preserved the marks of the pure Turkoman type. As the nomads are generally more agile and quick than the settled tribes, which is naturally to be attributed to the endless wanderings of their adventurous existence; so the Turkomans are to be distinguished in this peculiarity from all the dwellers in tents in Central Asia. And their slender frames, hardened by a very poor food, can outdo even the Arab in privations and endurance. Taken as a whole, the Turkomans cultivate (spite of the type of a family unity) a strange mixture of customs and habits, which are found either here and there among the neighbouring nomads and Œzbegs, or only among themselves. While their language approaches to the Azerbaïdjan dialect, their customs have the pure Turko-Tartarian stamp; and in their social relations, as well as in their warlike existence and their abundant religious usages, they have more in common with the Kiptchaks than with the Kirghis, Karakalpaks, and Œzbegs, with whom they have lived in close connexion for so many centuries. That they separated themselves early, very early, from the greater part of the Turko-Tartarian nations, admits of no question. There is no doubt, according to their own assertions, that they moved first from the east to the north-west, namely, towards the southern frontier of the former main horde, and thence towards the south. This assertion is very probable, and as alleged proofs of it, we may cite the small number who have remained behind on the road as remnants, and are still now to be found. As such, are cited the Turkomans to the north of Kermineh and Samarkand, who, in the midst of kindred elements have remained true to their nationality. Their emigration from Mangishlak, unquestionably the oldest abode of the Turkomans, is indicated by the Central Asiatics themselves in the following chronological order. As the oldest in their present native country, we name the Salor and Sariks; after them come the Yomuts, who, before the period of the Sefevides, stretched from the north towards the south along the shores of the Caspian. It is said that the Tekke, at the time of Taimur, were transplanted to Akhal in small numbers, in order to paralyse the great strength of the Salor. The Ersaris, towards the end of the last century, from Mangishlak have settled upon the shores of the Oxus; whilst, finally, the Tchaudors, of the more recent period of Mohammed Emin Khan (Khiva), from the shores of the Aral and Caspian Seas, are shifted to the opposite bank of the Oxus, although many of that tribe are to be found in the old places. As the Turkoman's chief employment aims at pillage, it is natural to expect that many of their customs should harmonize with this. Their attire, although in its origin of the Khiva fashion, is made shorter and closer, that they may be able more easily to take hard exercise: the heavy fur cap is replaced by a smaller one. Their drawers, which supply the place of trousers, are very wide, and remind one of the national 'garb of the Hungarian peasants. The curls of hair which hang down behind the ears far over the shoulders of the young, are peculiar to this tribe. These are allowed to grow by the young; during the first year of married life, they are worn concealed in the cap, and only after its lapse cut off. This ornament gives to the young cavalier a stately appearance whilst riding, and he is not a little proud of it. The dress of the women, also, has some peculiarities, to which belong the upper garment, hanging down, long-armed, like the Hungarian jacket; the head-gear, and the masses of silver ornaments,—as bracelets, necklaces, amulets, etuis, &c. It is not unusual to meet among the women perfect beauties, not inferior to the Georgians in growth and regularity of features. Though the young girls in all nomadic tribes are tolerably practised riders, the young Turkoman women stand pre-eminent in this art. With regard to their religious zeal for Islam, their proneness to superstition is the same as that of the Kirghis; and as the readers of my "Travels" are more acquainted with them, we will pass from them to the Œzbegs.

ŒZBEGS.

These may be considered the established and civilized inhabitants of Central Asia, and they have retained only feeble traces of the Mongolian-Turkish race, owing to considerable intermixture with the ancient Persian elements, and also the great number of slaves, who are brought there out of the present Iran. In their broad faces, sound of voice, the sharp angle which the temples form, and especially the eyes, we recall their Tartar origin. The Œzbegs were always pointed out by the Tadjiks by the nickname of Yogunkelle (thick skull), and really this part of their body is thicker and coarser than that of the rest of their Turanian fellow races. Besides the diversity that reigns among them in the three Khanats and in Chinese Tartary, you may further observe that the dwellers in villages generally possess more signs of the national type than townsmen. For instance: Œzbegs of Khiva are to be recognised by the broad, full face, low, flat forehead, large mouth; the Œzbegs of Bokhara, by the somewhat more arched foreheads, more oval faces, and long, pointed, oblong chin, and the great majority by black hair and eyes. Also in colour there are some shades of resemblance. In the neighbourhood of Kashgar and Aksu yellowish-brown to blackish tint prevails; in Khokand, brown; in Khiva, white is the reigning colour. Indeed, the Œzbegs are bastards of the Turanian race, in the same manner as the Tadjik and

Sarts (the aborigines of the ancient Transoxiana, Sogdia, and Fergana*). Of the origin, immigration, and settlement of the Œzbegs, we have but little information, and that highly confused. Whilst some maintain that the name of Œzbeg was the name of one of their most renowned princes, who, in the time of Djingis, ruled over the whole desert; others discover, in the etymology of the word Œzbeg (independent prince, independent head), the signification of that actual independence for which the tribe was distinguished, as it disengaged itself from any ruler, and attempted, on its own account, its march of conquest toward the west. The name becomes prominent with the family of Sheibani, viz., with Ebul Kheir Khan, as founder, in the foreground; for, although Taimur may belong to the same tribe, still the Turkish state is more prominent than the Œzbeg.

If I am not deceived, it appears to me, at least, that the Œzbegs of to-day form a tribe, which, as a colony, highly inconsiderable in numbers, only increased after it had received into its bosom contingents of the various nomadic tribes passing from the north to the south. This assertion is, perhaps, bold, still the following circumstances render it not impossible.

1st. The already indicated diversity which shows itself between the Œzbegs of Turkestan from Komul

* "Gibbon;" edited by Dr. W. Smith. London, 1862, page 296. Here it is justly remarked, "The Œzbegs are the most altered from their primitive manners. 1st.,—by the profession of the Mohammedan religion; and, 2nd.,—by the possession of the cities and harvests of Great Bucharia.

to the Sea of Aral, whereby the degree of resemblance which exists between the latter and those nomadic tribes living in the vicinity is not to be mistaken, who, induced by certain circumstances, in which riches and religion play an important part, settled in towns, and are amalgamated with Œzbegs.

2nd. Many names of branches and families of the Œzbegs are common amongst the rest of the tribes of Central Asia. Thus, for example, we find the tribes Kungrat, Kiptchak, Naiman, Taz, Kandjigale, Kanli, Djelair, by which the thirty-two chief divisions of the Œzbegs are named, figuring also among the Kirghis. The Turkomans and Karakalpaks can produce some, which, from the great importance the nomadic tribes attach to family names, certainly would not be the case if earlier mutual relations had not existed. We know little of their origin, little in regard to the time of their settlement. The opinion of Persian historians, that the Œzbeg power rose upon the ruins of the Taimur dynasty is, indeed, correct, but forms no guide to the Œzbegs themselves. The name only is apparent; but who can tell us to which tribe that Turkish population professed to belong, which at a period long anterior to Taimur, and before Djingis, in the time of the Kharezmian princes, Sahi Charezmian, and even further back in the thirteenth century, were established in the three Khanats? In Khiva I often heard of the brilliant period of ancient Ürgendj, namely, before the inroad of the Mongolians, described as

Œzbeg. Was this merely national vanity, or had the Turks at that time at Khiva really called themselves Œzbegs? Turks were already settled during the Arabian occupation, as may be seen in the ancient history of Bokhara, although not directly in the centre, certainly in the neighbourhood of the old Persian towns, in the time of the Samanides; and it would be highly interesting to know to which type they really belonged. In the customs of the Œzbegs, also, much foreign admixture has been introduced chiefly through Islam, and the restless manner of existence pursued by them; but not nearly so much as with the Western Turks, who through the foreign elements that they receive are already quite denationalized. The Œzbegs are pious —one might say zealous—Musulmans. Nowhere in Islam, Kashmir excepted, does the tendency to asceticism flourish more than here: a third of the inhabitants of a town are Ishan, Khalfa, Sofi, or aspirants to those holy titles, and nevertheless the doctrine of Mohammed has little limited their customs in regard to all this. In Khiva, and in some parts of Chinese Tartary, they have remained truest to nomadic customs. They build houses, which are used as stables and granaries; but for dwelling-places, they prefer always the raised tent in the court-yard;—building durable dwellings is scoffed at by the pure Œzbeg, and ridiculed as even now usual only with the Sart (Persian aborigines). A general habit is marked out in the proverb: "Sart baïsa tam salar—as soon as the Sart becomes rich, he builds a house," in contradistinction to the Œzbeg, who procures rather a horse or arms. Also in food and clothing but few refinements have crept in, the chief towns excepted. Whilst in the towns the Harem life is in full force, one finds in the country all Œzbeg women unveiled, for, to the great anger of the Mollah, they resist that restriction, to which their nature is averse. Ceremonies at burials, weddings, births, contain much of what is not only foreign to Islam, but even criminal. This false step is a striking contrast with the otherwise enthusiastic feelings of Central Asiatics. Not less does the rigid adherence to a warlike existence, in which the Œzbegs are distinguished from the rest of the established nations of Central and Western Asia, deserve our attention. Agriculture and durable dwellings render people more peaceable; but this is not the case with the Œzbegs, because they excel so many nomadic tribes in bravery.

CHARACTER.

However great the extent over which the diverse branches of Turkish tribes may be found, however variously the influence of strange elements may have acted upon their social relations, still the features of a common type of character cannot be denied;—a picture in which more traces of analogy are to be found than in the physiognomy and other physical signs respectively. The Turk is everywhere heavy and lethargic in his mental and corporeal emotions, therefore firm and stedfast in his resolves; not, perhaps, from any principle of life philosophy, but from apathy, and sincere aversion to everything which would alter his adopted position. This lends him an earnest and solemn aspect, which is so often extolled by European travellers. As upon the shores of the Bosphorus the Osmanli, in his *keïf*, can gaze for hours on the clear sky, while he only makes as much movement as will blow the blue wreaths of smoke from his pipe towards the yet bluer firmament; so the Œzbeg or the Kirghis can sit for hours, motionless, in the narrow tent, or in the immeasurably wide desert; for, while the former turns his gaze upon the colours of the felt coverlet or carpet, already seen thousands of times,—the latter looks on the waving, curling quicksands, which are to amuse him. As those who go about briskly and nimbly, or even gesticulate, are only compassionated by the Osmanlis as living proofs of partial insanity and misfortune; so each quick movement of the feet and hands is considered by the Œzbegs as highly unseemly. Indeed, when I called out to one of my Tartar fellow-travellers to save himself from some falling bales of goods by a side-spring, he exclaimed, indignantly: "Am I, then, a woman, that I should disgrace myself by springing and dancing!" With this profound seriousness and marble-cold expression of countenance, we find everywhere among the Turks a great inclination to pomp and magnificence; but this does not degenerate into frivolity or fanfaronades, as is the case with the Persians. In Constantinople one often hears the proverb: "Intellect is peculiar to Europe, riches to India, and splendour to the Ottoman." The solemn processions (alay) of the sultan and of the great nobles are alike celebrated in the East and the West, and the imposing exterior which is exhibited on such occasions is nowhere to be found so faithfully reflected as among their fellow tribes in Central Asia. An Œzbeg or Turkoman, when upon his horse, or seated in his tent at the head of his family, has the same proud bearing, the same self-consciousness of greatness and power. He is quite convinced that he is born to rule, and the foreign nations which surround him to obey,—just in the same way as the Osmanli thinks with regard to Bulgarians, Armenians, Kurds, and Arabians. His love for independence is boundless, and is also the chief cause why he cannot long remain under the chieftain whom he loves in many respects; and he would rather command ten or twelve miserable highwaymen or adventurers than stand at the head of a well-equipped, elegant troop, who might, in common with himself, own a greater master. Coinciding with these traits of character, is also the predilection of the Turks for repose and inactivity; for, although diligence and activity, according to our European notions, are not to be met with anywhere in Asia, still, work is not so much abhorred, either by the Iranian or Semitic nations, as by the Turks, who consider hunting and war alone worthy of man. Upon them husbandry is only forcibly imposed, and is considered ignominious. A wondrous prosperity has never befallen Turkey. The peasant was always idle and careless; the number of craftsmen limited. Officials had only wealth when the Janitchars came back from their pillaging excursions, laden with treasures.

In Central Asia, agriculture is exclusively in the hands of the Persian slaves; commerce and business with the Tadjiks, Hindoos, and Jews; for even the Œzbegs, settled there for centuries, meditate robbery and war, and if they can procure no foreign enemy they attack each other mutually in bloody brother strife.

As concerns intellectual capacity, I have found that the Turk is everywhere far inferior to other Asiatic nations, namely, the Iranian and Semitic; and that, through narrowness of mind, he loses those prerogatives which his superiority in other respects would acquire for him. This weakness is denoted by the word Türklük (Turkdom), of which Kabalik (coarseness), and Yogunluk (thickness), are synonyms. By Türklük, one understands also rudeness and roughness in manners; and if here and there this defect is palliated by the appellation, Sadelik (simplicity), still, for the most part, they are subjoined to the Turkish name as insulting epithets. As the Osmanli is over-reached by the Armenian, Greek, and Arab; so is the Œzbeg baffled by the subtle and yielding Tadjik, and the no less crafty and avaricious Hindoo. Whether this is to be ascribed to a national defect or to an extreme nonchalance, it were hard to determine; still, it is highly remarkable that the Turk in the far east, as well as in the immediate vicinity of the civilised western country, shuns meditation, and that nowhere are his attempts at wit particularly brilliant. This disadvantage is partially the reason that among the Turks more honesty, frankness and confidence, is to be met with than among the remaining nations of Asia.

Türklük, by which strangers understand the above-named fault, is often used by the Turks themselves as a mark of plainness, simplicity, and uprightness. The lights and shades of Türklük have been at all times observable and discoursed on, whenever parallels are drawn between the character of the Turks and of other nations, especially the Persians. People praise the acuteness, the refined manners of the latter; but still, he who wants to find a faithful servant, an attached soldier, or an upright man, will always give the preference to the Turks. Therefore, we find in earliest times that foreign princes liked to use Turkish troops; they call them into their country, and invest their officers with the highest dignities; and as bravery, perseverance, and love of governing, is more innate in them than in any other Asiatic people, it is very easy to explain how they rise from simple mercenaries to governors; and how they subjugated Iranian and Semitic peoples, from their home up to the Adriatic, many of whom are still ruled by them. In my opinion, it is not only superiority of physical powers which has sustained the Turkish dynasties upon foreign thrones, and still does so: this is also greatly ascribable to their superiority of character. They are unpolished, and by nature wild, uncultivated, but seldom cruel out of malice. They enrich themselves at the cost of their subjects, but again divide generously the collected treasures. They are severe towards their subordinates, but seldom forget the duties that they have to fulfil towards the latter, as patriarchal heads. In a word, in all deeds and works of the Turks a sort of kindness is perceptible, which is, perhaps, more to be ascribed to indolence and laisser-aller, than to a fixed purpose to do good; but still it works as a virtue, whatever may be its origin.

Finally will we mention hospitality, in which the Turks are better versed than the Iranian and Semitic nations, and certainly for very simple causes. As acknowledged, hospitality is observed in proportion to the degree in which a nation advances from a nomadic condition to a settled manner of living, and as Asia is generally far more prominent in this virtue than Europe, so are the Turks, the majority of whom are incarnate nomads, to be distinguished from the rest of Asiatics, who, long settled there, rejoice in an older civilisation. This must be considered a mere sketch of the common character of the Turks. Concerning the gradation of different races, we find the Buruts wilder, more savage than the remaining nomadic fellow races.* They are more superstitious, but also less malicious than, for example, the Kirghis and Turkomans, because, without having wholly deserted Shamanism, they know but little of Islam; and it is well known that the weaker a nomadic people's ideas of that religion are, the fewer are its vices, and the more tractable are they with strangers. The Kirghis, on the contrary, are in the chief features of character less warlike, although they can easily make up their minds to undertake a baranta (pillaging expedition). They form the greater part of Turkish nomads, are for the most part devoted to a wandering life; and whilst the Turkomans are in many places to be met with in a half settled state, for example, along the left shore of the Oxus, from Belkh as far as Tchardjuy, and in Khiva, one can only find very few examples among the Kirghis. They are easier to subjugate than other nomads, because they, as already stated, are more peaceable and less brave, still their colonization appears almost verging upon impossibility; at least it will require a gigantic task of Russia, if such be her design. The Karakalpaks, through their remarkable simplicity, are often considered foolish and dull. They represent the idiot among Central Asiatic nations, and many droll anecdotes are composed at their cost. In bravery they are even inferior to the Kirghis; they

* Radloff also confirms the same in his Report upon the Acad. Imp. of Sciences of St. Petersb. See the bulletin of the society named, vol. vi., p. 418.

have seldom appeared as conquerors, and are seldom employed by others even as mercenaries. As they occupy themselves chiefly in breeding cattle, and like best to sojourn in woody regions, they are called by the Œzbegs, ayik (bear). Still, activity, benevolence and faithfulness, are everywhere adjudged to them. The Turkomans are notorious among all the races of Central Asia as the most restless adventurers, and rightly; for not only there, but throughout the whole globe, hardly can a second nation be found of such a rapacious nature, of such restless spirit and untameable licentiousness as these children of the desert. To rob, to plunder, to make slaves, is in the eye of the Turkoman an honourable business, by which he has lived for centuries. He considers those who think otherwise as stupid or mad, and yields in such a manner to this passion that he often commences plundering his own tribe, indeed, often his own family, in case he is baulked in foreign forays. As a very weak apology, it may be argued that they inhabit the wildest and most savage countries, where even keeping of cattle gives only a scanty revenue: still the fruits of their detestable trade hardly ever alleviate their pressing poverty, for they are just as dirty niggards, as avaricious, and starve often in the possession of riches as much as the poorest being. The Œzbegs play the fashionable among their fellow-races in Turkestan. They are not a little proud of the education which, through Islamitish civilisation, they obtained, and, starting from this point of superiority, wish to govern their nomadic brethren. Highly praiseworthy with them is their tenacious adherence to so many good points of their national character; which, in other places, is too easily transformed and disgraced by Islam. With the Œzbeg, there is, in spite of the hypocrisy and pretended holiness, which endeavour to spread themselves by Mohamedanism, still always very much honesty, uprightness, and Turkish open-heartedness, in which qualities they are considerably to be distinguished from the reprobate and vicious Tadjiks, and are truly worthy to govern the latter. The Œzbeg is, as far as personal knowledge has shown to me, the only Turk, from China to the Danube, who represents all the best side of the national character of the Turks.

CHAPTER XVII.

IRANIANS.

The Turanian people, but especially the already mentioned Turko-Tartaric tribes, have made themselves renowned in antiquity by their warlike disposition, and the wild untractable rudeness of their habits; but the Iranians, in strong contrast with these, have always been known for the delicacy of their habits and a brilliant state of civilisation. The former have ever appeared among their neighbours as spoilers, destroyers, and plunderers; the latter, on the contrary, as civilisers, propagators of the arts, and milder social relations.

For it is not only the whole Mohamedan region which embraced Persian civilisation, but even we Europeans have borrowed much from these wonderful people, which, partly through the channel of the ancient Greek and Byzantine culture, partly by a later contact of the Western with the Eastern countries, as, for example, in the Crusades, has naturally always reached us second hand. Iràn from time immemorial was the seat of civilisation, and in the entire record of the civilisation of mankind we could in vain seek for a nation which, notwithstanding grand political revolutions, notwithstanding the copious foreign influx of the ancient spirit of its civilisation, could preserve so long and faithfully the character of its national existence as the Persian. There is a great difference between the doctrine of Zoroaster and that of the Arabian Prophet, and yet in the modern Persian almost all the features of the former character may be discovered, which the Greek historians trace out in the ancient Persian. In a hasty superficial glance this will not strike the eye so easily, for, according to outward appearance, it would be most difficult, amidst the agglomeration of tribes in the Persia of to-day, to find out the genuine Iranian. Yet a deeper insight would soon convince us of the truth of what has been said, and we should see that the Iranian has not only borrowed nothing in his customs and manner of thinking from the Semitic and Turanian elements, which for more than a thousand years have endangered his nationality, but has rather exerted over the latter a powerful influence. The cradle of the Iranian nation, as asserted by a modern ethnographer, namely, the learned Russian traveller, M. de Khanikoff, in his Memoirs, "Sur l'Ethnographie de la Perse," is the Eastern portion of modern Persia, and especially Southern Sigistan or Sistan, and Khorassan, which stretches out to the north-east. It is not only ethnography, but also history, which accords with this assertion. As Sigistan, the native place of Rustem, and other celebrated Iranian heroes of the classical age, is used as the scene of action by the narrators of fiction at this day, whenever they wish to describe something highly potent and ancient, so the old *Belkh* in Khorassan is declared to be the original source of religion and polite education, and Merv is pointed out as the spot where Adam received from the angel the first lesson in agriculture. In a word, whatever refers to the early ages is to be met with in the East, but never in the West.

The Iranian race, on its dispersion, as has been already remarked in a foregoing paragraph, took a direction from East to West; the Turanian scattered from South to North, and in two directions, one towards the North-East the other towards the North-West. The emigration occurred in those very ancient ages, of which we can have hardly the faintest conception; yet even here there are features of a common type which guide us like glittering stars through a night of uncertainty, and though the Iranian race has suffered much in modern times from the Turko-Tartar tribes, so superior to themselves in number, one can nevertheless detect in the groups lying scattered around, the separate rings of the former chain; precisely also as one recognises in the Western remnants, though in continual contact with Turanian and Semitic elements, the avowed Mede, so in the Eastern remnants one may recognise the primitive genuine Iranian.

This preceding opinion formed from personal conviction, and every one who carefully observes the Persian of modern Iran and Central Asia must perceive the same, receives a further confirmation in the learned investigations of our arrow-headed writings;* and it is

* Ritter, *West Asia*. Vol. ii. p. 86.

chiefly the Iranian catalogue of people in the arrow-headed writings at Persepolis which enumerates all the nations of Iran, starting from the centre of the empire, Persepolis, and continuing in a west and eastern direction. Of course nothing positive will be perceived in these with reference to higher or lower antiquity concerning the physiognomical distinctions of one or another branch of the families, but that a substantial difference existed already in the early ages is hardly to be doubted. " The Semitic influences in the West," says Fr. Spiegel, " began very early during the existence of the Assyrian and Babylonian kingdom, and lasted through the whole Achœmenian period. After the overthrow of the Achœmenian kingdom occurred the amalgamation with Greeks as well as Semitics, and so forth."* As is rightly observed, for in the Southern provinces of Farsistan, Laristan, and Luristan, where the contact of the Iranian and Semitic elements from the earliest ages has remained undisturbed, we find in the person of the modern Persian the same physical characteristics that were described to us in these people by Herodotus, and later Greek authors. The spare form, which is more natural to the Western than to the Eastern, strongly reminds one of the principal feature of the Arabian, who is represented by Unsemitic tribes as *nahif*, haggard, and thin, whilst the Turk is *kesif*, blunt, and stout, the genuine Persian *zarif*, noble, and elegant.

* " The Ethnographical Position of the Iranian tribes." *Ausland*, 1866, No. 36, p. 853.

The Semitic elements have commenced in south and east Persia, from Benderbushir until near to Kirmansah, and have especially left behind with the inhabitants of the towns perceptible traces, which strike the eye all the more when we compare the physiognomy and stature of a Sigistanian with those of an Isfahanian. This is best perceptible in the Ghebrs (fire worshippers), who sojourn among the West Iranians, and are very different from them. As one misses among them the predominating numbers of thin, slender forms, so also one seldom meets with the narrow chin or the thin, small nose. The Ghebr, in company with the Khafi, will certainly strike us less than in the midst of a group of Isfahanians; and since the Ghebrs, who are only sparingly scattered in the west of Persia, are to be considered as the remnants of the primitive Iranian people, having remained most pure from the mixture of foreign elements, one can assert with certainty that the distinction of physiognomy between East and West Iranian must always have existed. The Greek historians of the Alexandrian campaign, who came in contact with the Eastern as well as the Western nations of the then great Iranian kingdom, have disregarded in their descriptions the ethnographical side of the question, which is of the highest importance in our studies. In the same way we gather but little information from the sculptures which descend from the Sassanides. The figures on the bas reliefs of Nakshi Rustem, Nakshi Redgeb, and, near at hand, of Kazerun, may furnish faithful representations of the former

Persian, but of the nationality of the same there is no accurate account; and however wide the opinion may extend with regard to stature and features, these appear rather to belong to the West Iranian than to the East Iranian, for the striking resemblance to the modern inhabitants of West Iran must be apparent to the eye of every one. Recent European travellers only cause us to observe the existing difference.

So we find that Gareia Silva Figeroa,* who in 1627 visited Persia on a diplomatic mission, already calls our attention to the difference between the East and West Iranian, though without entering into any details of the physical characteristics. Chardin, who travelled through this country in 1664-1677, is more explicit, for he says that the Ghebrs, in whom he perceives the remnant of the ancient Persian, are of a disagreeable exterior, clumsy figure, coarse skin, and dark complexion, and form a strong contrast to the present inhabitants of West Iran, who have a mixture of the Chirkassian and Georgian blood in their veins. This opinion is also positively expressed by Peter Angelus (Labrosse), a contemporary of the former, in his "Gazophylacium linguæ Persarum," published in 1684, under the article, "Georgians."†

Since, therefore, no doubt can remain about the distinction between the East and West Iranians, we will bring the divergence to a common point of view, and

* Khanikoff's "Memoire sur l'Ethnographie de la Perse." Paris, 1866, page 45.
† Above cited work, page 47.

TURANIAN AND IRANIAN RACES. 319

then represent the separate branches or members of the two powerful races in such a way as we observed the same on our journeys, not leaving unnoticed the observations of our predecessors with reference to this subject.

	a. WEST IRANIAN.	*b.* EAST IRANIAN.
FIGURE.	In *surpassing numbers, though not slim, yet of a haggard and thin form;* of a light, supple movement, and graceful demeanour; but very rarely very thin or very fat, or strikingly tall or very short.	Of a somewhat thick-set figure; bones of a powerful and large construction, but also clumsy in movement, although far less awkward than the Turanians.
HEAD.	Oval, narrow, and middling high forehead, flattened at the temples; *oblong* skull and narrow chin.	Much less oval than *a*, almost to be called round; a wider forehead, also larger jaw bones, and more *fleshy* cheeks; the chin, however, oblong, and less pointed than the Turanians.
EYES.	Large, black, with long upper lid, and arched eyebrows.	Black, oblong cut, close and thick eyebrows.
NOSE.	Long, thin, often arched.	Less long, sometimes thick at the *root,* but never so stumpy and wide as the Turanians.
MOUTH.	Moderate-sized; perceptibly thin compressed lips.	Often wide and thick lips.
HAIR.	Black, of a thick and powerful growth; particularly long, thin, beard.	Black, of thick growth; beard thicker, but less long than the West Iranian.

In consequence of this diversity of the physical externals, there is also a distinction not to be mistaken in the moral *properties* of these two races. The East Iranian, although far superior to the Turks in vigour of mind and body, is far inferior to the Persian of modern Iran; and it appears as if the stamp of the mental superiority of the latter was imprinted in the symmetrical formation of their limbs and elegance of their features.

East Iranians.

We can form the following subdivisions or branches according to the geographical position of their northeasterly extension? 1. Sigistani or Khafi. 2. Tchihar Aymak. 3. Tadjik and Sart; each of which counts many subdivisions or degrees. As in our progress towards the West we lose, in the Turanian race, the Mongolian character in physiognomy more and more, and find in the single branches a continually increasing mixture of races; in the same way we discover, also, that the East Iranians become less Iranian, and more Turanian, the farther they remove from the mother land. The relation that exists between the Burut and the pure-blooded Anatolian, the same is to be found between the Sigistani and the Tadjik of Kashgar. The latter may, indeed, be called the old inhabitant of that region, yet no one will dispute that the Turanian elements, surrounding him in such numbers, have strongly influenced him.

1. SIGISTANI OR KHAFI;

Or that Shiite population of East Iran which inhabit the eastern part of Iran, from the southern borders of modern Khorassan to beyond Bihrdjan. They are as frequently called Khafi as Sigistani, as the principal mass occupy Khaf and its neighbourhood, Ruy, Tebbes, and Bhirdjan; whilst the ancient, classical Sigistan, more traversed in modern times by Afghans and hordes of Beloochees, offers to the peaceable Persian but a very insecure retreat. Judging by historical accounts of Merv, which, in the Vendidad, is enumerated as the thirteenth locality under the name Mun, as the third spot marked, one might easily conclude that the inhabitants of modern Khorassan, especially of the northern part, might be reckoned with the East Iranians. This was naturally more or less the case before the Arabian occupation; but at this day the people of Khorassan are so powerfully intermingled with Turco-Tartar elements, that the genuine East Iranian type only begins on the other side of the southern rocky chain, behind Shehri No. Without being furnished with an especial ethnographical representation, the traveller will easily perceive that the Khafi (we preserve the appellation which is usual in the country), although brown in complexion, is to be distinguished from the Isfahani; for example: in that his complexion is more olive-brown, whilst that of the latter, tanned by the sun, appears more of a dark

21

brown. In the second place, the afore-named difference in stature and features, but especially the less fiery eye, will strike him. And in the third place, he will miss, in intercourse, that sprightliness and activity which he meets everywhere among the lively West Iranians under the same situation of climate. It can hardly be doubted, that many will be surprised that this relative difference should exist between such tribes as those in question,—of common origin, language and religion, for hundreds of years, nay, for thousands of years, of one and the same political connection. This circumstance would be with difficulty explained through an analagous case in other lands. We shall, however, recognise the cause directly, when we take into nearer view the following points:—

1st. The whole portion named of East Iran has been spared from all times the influence of the Semitic as well as Turanian nations, since the first extended themselves only toward the western side of the desert; the last, on their march westward, only at intervals passed from the high road, Merv, Nishabur, and Rei to the southern slope of the Djagatay Hills. 2nd. East Iran herself, in an earlier period, remained separated through the great desert, when the Shiite sect, the chain of solid union, embraced the Persian population of Iran; and, despite all the wildest sect-hatred, the traffic now is as great with the Sunnite Afghans and Heratis as with their western brethren. It is true that, despite all the fatigue of travel in the desert, despite all fear of the Beloochees, caravans go annually from Shiraz, Isfahan, over Yezd, Tebbes up to holy Meshed. Yet Khaf and Bihrdjan, situated south-east, are never touched upon; and then, as now, it was always the case. In the mutual intercourse of nations, language assumes foreign elements easiest and preserves them the longest. The Persian dialect of modern Iran is overloaded with Arabian-Turkish words. Fars in the south, as well as Mazandran in the north, is in this only a little distinctive. In East Iran, nevertheless, the borrowed richness of language is certainly less; and we find in much that Persian in which Firdusi, with a premeditated rejection of Arabic, wrote his great epic. In what concerns the use of old forms and words, the Persian of Bokhara is of that character, and especially we may name the Tadjiks in the first place; yet these last have too much lexicographical and grammatical material borrowed from the Turks; and this circumstance it is that has produced the conviction in our minds, that *in East Iran the purest and oldest Persian is spoken.*

As for the language, I should be inclined to cite the Khafi or the Sigistani as the primitive tongue of all the Iranians, yet, in regard to their ethnographical position in relation to the whole Iranian race, I would not venture to attribute that position to them in which the Buruts stand to the whole Turko-Tartar race. What branch of the East Iranian families may be the primitive is one of those questions to which no one could deny a high degree of importance, yet is the reply much more difficult as to the Turko-Tartar race. For the appearance of the latter on the stage of historical events is comparatively fresh, whilst the former stepped forward in a period of which we can hardly form a conception. We must, therefore, again repeat that the Sigistani or Khafi are named as the first among the East Iranians, only in consequence of their geographical position, and not from induction on the more primitive character of their branch.

TCHIHAR AYMAK.*

These are the four people or races which, from the time of the conquest of Herat, have been thus named by the Mongols. They consist of the Timuri, Teimeni, Firuzkuhi, and Djemshidi. The whole are of Iranian origin and Persian speech, and enough so to distinguish them from the Hezareh,† who, though

---

* Aimak is a Mongolian word, and signifies a people.

† Khanikoff seems to be in error when he considers the Hezareh, as formerly Œzbegs; viz., as the Berlas tribe. " Memoire sur la Patrie Meridionale de l'Asie Centrale." Paris, 1842, pp. 112, 138. I must against this cite the following arguments:—1st. Their own assertion,—that they were the remainder of the army of Djingis, and, moreover, from the statement of Abul Fazl of a troop of Mangu Khan. 2ndly. That a portion, now named the Gvbi Hezareh, which retired into the hills in the neighbourhood of Herat, and has been spared by the Persian elements, speaks a Mongolian dialect, as is proved by *Von der Gabelenz*, in a periodical of the German Asiatic Society,—vol. xx. p. 326.; and Baber affirms that in his time many Hezareh spoke Mongolian. 3rd. There is nowhere among the Œzbegs such a decided Mongolian type to be found as among the Hezareh, which is the more striking, because the first remain near their old home in more compact masses, while the latter have dwelt under a foreign climate and foreign elements.

they speak Persian, yet show their pure Mongolian type, their Turanian origin without a doubt. On the spot itself there is but a confused understanding as to its name Tchihar Aymak, because many appropriate to themselves the same, and are again opposed by others. Our travellers have most contradictory statements concerning these races, and especially this erroneous idea, that the Hezareh are to be reckoned among the Tchihar Aymak, who appeared at the Southern part of Central Asia, at a time when the latter were already indicated by the name in question.

During my abode of six weeks in the town and neighbourhood of Herat, I devoted considerable attention to this question. My knowledge is grounded, not so much on hearsay touching the race, as on their physiognomical characteristics, which are incontestably the best proof. The *Timuri*, or the Sunnite Persians of East Iran, dwell now partly on the Western boundary of Herat, as Gurian, Kuh'sun, &c., and partly also in the villages and towns situated to the east of Iran, from Turbet Sheikh Djam as far as Khaf. In the first-named region they constitute exclusively an united population, in the latter they are only to be found sporadic, for although two hundred years ago the greater number were Sunnites, yet the sect-hatred of the Shiites converted them partly by force, partly drove them into the neighbouring Sunnite city of Herat. In consequence of the frequent confusion of boundary, for Herat has endured in ancient and modern times more than forty sieges, one can easily imagine what an amalgamation has been produced by these continued movements among the solitary branches which approach so nearly to East Iran, and it is truly a wonder that the Timuri are still to be distinguished from the Shiites of East Iran.

The remarkable characteristics are first, that among them more people are to be found short and thickset than among the Sigistanis; also as regards colour, the latter are, on an average, of an olive brown, and with dark black hair, whilst among the former a whiter complexion, with chesnut brown hair, is not uncommon. As I have said, the united number of the Timuri on the East Iran boundary amounts now in its fullest extent to one thousand families, because the great majority dwell in Herat.

The *Teimeni* are hardly in any respect to be distinguished from the latter dwelling in the Northern and Southern parts of the so-named Djölghei Herat, from Kerrukh to Sebzewar: only a small part has extended as far as Ferrah, and is named by the Afghans Parsivan (Farszeban, speaking Persian). Since the Afghan rule has taken place in the Western valleys of the Parapamisian mountains, many attempts have been made to establish in the midst of the Persian population Afghan colonies, yet until this day all have failed, for the discord and strife which have wasted this neighbourhood for centuries still continue; each member of the Tchihar Aymak knowing no greater enemy than the Afghan. In consequence of this circumstance the Teimeni, although an agricultural people, are of wild, warlike nature, and there is no longer any trace of that spirit of wisdom, which in the time of the descendants of Taimur, viz., Sultan Husein Mirza, animated them.

The Sunnite Persians of former times contended in poetry, learning, and music, with the Shiite confederates in the West; at the present time they are raw barbarians in comparison with the latter.

Firuzkuhi is the name of the little people that dwell on the steep hill, north-east of Kale No, and from their inaccessible situation afflict the whole neighbourhood with robbery and plunder. To the traveller are narrated the most gloomy stories of Kale No on the summit of the mountain, and the fortified places of Derzi Kutch and Tchekseran are considered the same as the robber nests of the Bakhtiari and Luri in the environs of Isfahan. As all dwellers in mountains remain distinct from their nearest kindred in the valleys, so is this the case also between the Firuzkuhi and the remaining Aymaks, and one could almost name them the Gileki and Mazemderanis of East Persia. On the first glance they appear to have much resemblance with the Hezareh. It is even asserted that they came forth from them, yet neither has their formation of the forehead and of the chin, nor the complexion and figure of the body,—a decided Turanian character; and although it might present a strong mixture, yet does the Iranian element prevail, for, besides that they all speak Persian, the names of their dwelling-places and khans are pure Persian words.

They inhabited those hills from immemorial time, and though Taimur settled them by force in Mazenderan, they soon returned back to their old hilly home, and have lived since that time in constant warfare with their neighbours, partly supporting themselves from their scanty breed of cattle and tillage; partly also from robbery and plunder, which they perpetrate on the caravans upon the road to Maymene, or upon the scattered tents of the Djemshidi. Their total number hardly amounts to eight thousand families.

The *Djemshidi*, the only tribe of the East Iranians living exclusively in a nomadic state, inhabited from time immemorial the shores of Murgab, whither they, according to their own statement, settled out of Sigistan in the time of Djemshid, from whom they derive their descent. This national myth cannot be considered quite true, yet is it incontestable, that among all Iranians who now inhabit Central Asia the Djemshidi have the most striking resemblance with the Sigistani, which is so much the more to be wondered at, because these for so long a time have led a settled life, whilst those have led a nomadic; and the vast influence which the difference of the two ways of life has on the development of the body needs hardly be mentioned. Khanikoff thinks they approach rather the Tadjiks; but I cannot coincide in this view, because, in the first place, the Djemshidi is thinner; secondly, has a longer face and a far more pointed chin than the Tadjik; and in the third place, their language, as well in form as in copiousness, agrees much more with the Persian dialect of East Iran than with that of Central Asia. As to what concerns their method of life, they are the only Iranians who, in every respect, have taken much from the Turanians; that is to say, from the Salor and Sarik Turkomans living in their neighbourhood; whilst the other half-nomadic Aymak used a long Afghan tent, which here is named the Tent of Abraham, one sees among the Djemshidi that round, conical tent of the Tartars surrounded with felt and a reed matting; their clothing also and food is Turkomanish; indeed, even in their occupation, they copy these last. For when a flourishing position, that is, abundance of horses and arms befalls them, they are just such fearful robbers of mankind as the children of the desert. They enjoy also the reputation of the best riders and warriors amongst all Aymak, and abide, partly in service at Herat or Maymene, partly in league with one or other of the Turkoman tribes, when the immediate question among them is a large tchapao (razzia). In consequence of this aforesaid connection they were transported to the banks of the Oxus by force by Allah Kuli Khan, from Khiva, after he had conquered them with the allied Sariks. They remained more than twelve years there; a fruitful place, which was assigned to them as their new home, and rendered them well to do. Yet the longing for the poorer, but old home-like hills, was soon felt by them, and availing themselves of the confusion which a war of the Khivians with the Turkomans called forth, they packed up everything quickly and fled, without fearing the danger of pursuit, across Hezaresp, Tchardjuy, Maymene, back towards the town of Murgab. In their march one thousand Persian slaves joined them, who, in consequence of their escape, obtained their freedom; but, having reached Moorgab, were again taken in a treacherous manner and sold in Bokhara. Although the Djemshidi among all the Iranian races of the East, as well as of the West, have most truly retained the warlike spirit of old Persia, yet they are in proportion less rough in their customs and intercourse with strangers than the neighbouring Turkomans, with whom they have had relations for a long time; and, notwithstanding his wild exterior, the Djemshidi, even in the lowest class, is polite in word and manner:—the light and shade of the Iranian character are not recognisable in him, and we must not be surprised if in the customs of this nomadic people we meet with the most lively marks of the pre-Islamite time. Islam with them has taken still less root than among the other Turanian nomads, and the greater part of them use it as a veil, under which lurk concealed many features of the religion of Zoroaster; thus, for instance, fire among them is in higher estimation than among the Tadjiks; the door

of the tent is always facing the East, and the idea of
the good and evil spirit is so universal that the lowest
class of the people, especially the women, when a sheep
or goat is slaughtered, never neglect to throw certain
parts of the animal which are considered by other
nomads as delicacies, to the bad spirit as *kende*, "unclean;" and they are only eaten by the dogs. It is
worthy of remark, that among the ruins of Martchah
the same stories are in circulation, as among the Yomuts
of the old remnants of the ruins at Meshdi Misrian.
Martchah was in olden times the Kaaba of the whole
region until the wicked Turkomans appeared there,
and destroyed the whole.

This is all that I can say in respect to the Tchihar
Aymaks. I can, notwithstanding all inquiries, learn
nothing of their name before their last appellation.
According to all probability they were reckoned among
the Tadjiks, yet now they are distinct from these latter,
and form the second gradation of the Iranian race in
its extension to the North-East.

TADJIKS,

As the remnants of the Persian population of Central Asia are called, whom we meet in their largest
numbers in the Khanat of Bokhara and in Bedakhshan.
But there are, besides, many settled in the cities of
Khokand, Khiva, Chinese Tartary, and Afghanistan;
although here and there little deviation in their physiognomical outward developments are observable, in con-

sequence of the different climacteric and social relations under which the Tadjiks live. And thus, for example, the Tadjiks of Bokhara and the Afghanistan towns have much more resemblance one with another than the former with the Bedakhshanis, or the confederate races of Chinese Tartary; notwithstanding, the leading features of one common type are generally observable among them. They are usually of a good middle height, broad, powerful frame of bones, and especially wide shoulder bones. Their countenance, the Iranian type of which immediately strikes the eye at first sight, is more oblong than that of the Turks; but by the wide forehead, thick cheeks, thick nose, and large mouth, we soon perceive that this most eastern branch of the Iranian family has much that is heterogeneous, that is to say, Turanian, in its stamp of countenance as well as in the formation of body, and is in nowise to be regarded as the primitive type of the Iranian race, as M. de Khanikoff imagines.

According to the statements of the Vendidad and Greek historians, it is no longer matter of doubt that the native country of the modern Tadjik was in those celebrated regions of ancient times, Bactria and Sogdiana,—the most ancient seat of Iranian civilisation, the cradle of the religion of Zoroaster, and the source of the heroic legends of Persia. We must own, that even in the most ancient times they were inhabitants of this region, for the ancient Khorassan, which stretched far into Chinese Tartary, was, as is proved by topographical nomenclature, founded and occupied by Iranian colonies. And who is there that does not perceive the continuous stream of Scythian-Turkish elements which has overflowed Central Asia, from the valleys of the Altaic Mountains, that *officina gentium*, from 700 B.C. to 400 A.D.?

No country which was situated along the chief route of these migrations could remain unaffected by the intermingling of foreign blood; and as the northern half of Persia, the modern district of Maymene, Andchoi, and the western declivities of the Parapamisian Mountains could preserve, but in a slight degree, the primitive unity of race; so also was it equally impossible to the Iranians of Transoxiana. The inhabitants only of the mountains of Bedakhshan, namely, the Vakhani (in which name the learned writer of the article, " Central Asia," in the *Quarterly Review*, July—September, 1866, believes that he has detected the origin of the Greek, ὄξος*), can have a greater claim, from their less accessible homes, to unity of race; for all the Feizabadis† whom I have seen have more indelible marks of the Iranian type than the Tadjiks: even their very language is freer of Turanian words. And since one can imagine that a people, though in strictest retirement, can preserve for centuries its primitive type,

---

* From Vah (the river Vah), as the Oxus is called in Bendehesh, may also be derived the modern name, Vachan, Vacks-as-ird, and Vas-ab.

† During my sojourn in Kerki I lived with ten Feizabadis (Feizabad is the capital of Bedakhshan) many days in one and the same house. It was a deputation returning from Bokhara, where they wished to raise the Emir to the place of their lately-banished prince.

the Vakhani alone, and not the Tadjiks in general, must be considered the truest remnants of the ancient East Iranian.

As regards the appellation Tadjik, I have always found that those concerning whom we are speaking never use it themselves willingly; for, if this does not sound exactly in their ears as a term of reproach, people are yet accustomed to understand by it that expression of contempt with which the Œzbeg conquerors regard the subdued aborigines. By the word Tadjik, the Tartar population of Turkestan understand a man without warlike disposition, of a covetous, avaricious nature;* with crafty and vaunting ideas; in a word, everything that stands in opposition to Œzbeg frankness, simplicity, and uprightness. These relations are, moreover, to be found everywhere between Turanian conquerors and the subjugated Iranians; for as the latter, in Persia, are far inferior to the Turks in mental endowments, so is this also the case in Central Asia. And Bokhara has only become the head quarters of Central Asiatic civilisation, because here, from the earliest ages, existed the overwhelming numbers of the Tadjik population; who, continuing their previous exertions in mental culture from the pre-Islamite times, notwithstanding the oppression of foreign power, have civilised their conquerors. As in the earliest ages,

---

* Slaves prefer rather ten years in the house of an Œzbeg than five years in the house of a Tadjik, because the last, who is considered a man without conscience, makes use of them in every possible way.

after the reception of the Islam faith, all the celebrities in the field of religious knowledge and *belles lettres* were mostly Tadjiks; so, to-day, one still meets in Bokhara, Khokand, and Kashgar, the most conspicuous Mollahs and most celebrated Ishans. At the court of Bokhara, notwithstanding the Œzbeg origin of the prince, the chief ministers are always Tadjiks; nay, even in the rude Œzbeg government of Khiva, the Mehter (Secretary of State), as an officer whose qualifications must be of the highest order, is chosen invariably from the Persian population of the place. It is truly wonderful how the Tadjiks, notwithstanding more than a century of co-existence with the Œzbegs, are to be distinguished from the latter, not only in their individual nature but in their habits. A proverb says, " Look at the Œzbeg on horseback,—the Tadjik in his house;" for, the same care that the one bestows on his steed, arms, saddle and horse, the other spends on his house and attire. However poor the Tadjik, he will yet pass for a man of more substance than he is, and will always appear rich and great in public, although sparing and abstemious in his family circle. Nor is his conversation less choice: the courteous expressions, the compliments of which he makes use, sound somewhat Tartarian, to ears accustomed to Persian refinement; yet, in contrast with the Œzbeg, he is to be considered an accomplished gentleman. Attuned by nature to peaceful occupations, the Tadjiks are devoted everywhere considerably to tillage, commerce, and industrial pursuits, as they hate war; and if they are compelled to handle weapons, they are rarely valiant, but frequently cruel. They are also defective in that national feeling that strikes one so forcibly among the Œzbegs. This has best shown itself in recent occurrences in Tashkend. In a letter from General Kryjanovsky from the town above-named, (Ausland, December 4th, 1866, H. 1159), we see that, among the diversified population of that place, the Sarts were the first who drew near, in a friendly fashion, to their conquerors, and certainly rendered very readily considerable help in hard labours of pacification; and that probably to the dislike of all the Œzbegs, who certainly took no part in the pretended petition to the Russian Government.

The Tadjiks hold well together, but this is more from the mutual support of one with another in an oppressed race than a special effort for Tadjik public interest; and if they wish to distinguish themselves, which is only the case in Bokhara, then they are in the habit of showing with pride their Arabian descent. The emptiness of this last vaunt Khanikoff has shown sufficiently. He derives the word Tadjik from Tadj (crown), a head-dress, which the old fire worshippers had, and the Ghebrs wear even now;—the name Tadjik arose from it, by which the adherents of the teaching of Zoroaster were called at that time— before Mohamedanism, or else it was a term of their own adoption; for the word Tadji in Huzvari, and Tazi in Persian, which signifies Arab, has with the first no connection. It is remarkable that the word Tadjik is even found in Western Asia. There are Armenians who call Turks as well as Arabs, *i.e.*, Mohamedans, *Tadjik*, but only among themselves privately. And it seems to me to be constantly a nickname affixed by the oppression of their tyrannic rulers. Since I have found this universal among the Armenians of Asia Minor, it appears to me that they did not wish to express by it only Mohamedans, but also the adherents of a strange religion, and that this, according to all appearance, old word, has been transmitted later to the Arabians by the old inhabitants of Persia, with whom the Armenians, under the Sassanides, were in contact. That the name Tadjik has been missing among both Arabic and Persian authors of the first century, after the entrance of Islam, but existed early in Central Asia, the Uïgur MS. (Kudatku Bilig the lucky knowledge) best shows. This bears the date of 462 Heg., and we find there the word Tadjik often quoted in opposition to Turk. The above-named work, which Jaubert has mentioned in the *Asiatic Journal*, 1825, is an Uïgur version, or rather *rifacimento* of the Chinese original. The Turks themselves have always called the Transoxanian aborigines Sart, a word of which I know not the origin. M. de Khanikoff mistakes when he supposes that this is only the case in Khiva, for he must know that in the Russian Army the Persian population of conquered Tashkend at a later period was enrolled under the name of Sart, and they were so called in all Khokand. Also the above-named General Krijanovsky speaks of Tadjik and Sart as of two different races. As to this word Sart, the derivation of which is wholly unknown to me, it is a term of which the famous Mir Ali Shir, in the time of Sultan Husein Mirza Baïkera, makes use in a treaty on the Persian and Turkish language. The latter, he always calls the Sart tili (Sart language), and not the Tadjik tili. Sart is hence legally used for the Turkish appellation of Tadjik. Here and there Œzbegs busy themselves in making a distinction between Sart and Tadjik; but I cannot agree with this view, although I will not conceal the fact, that the Sarts seen in mass differ greatly in some physiognomical peculiarities from the Tadjiks. They are, for instance, more slender-built, have a longer face, and, moreover, a higher forehead than the Tadjiks; but it must also be mentioned as a qualification of the above, that they formed frequent alliances with the free Persian slaves of Central Asia, which the Tadjiks never or very seldom did.

CHAPTER XVIII.

LITERATURE IN CENTRAL ASIA.

TARTAR muse! Œzbeg Melpomene! This will to many sound passing strange! That poetry should exist in the oldest spots of rudeness and barbarism— that persons in those regions where robbery, murder, and spoliation rage most, should busy themselves with literature, may to many seem strange; but yet such a notion would be incorrect. The East was at all times the seat of poetic enthusiasm, and the more the social relations retain the stamp of olden time, that is, the nearer civilisation is to its infancy, the more general is the inclination to poetry and fables, the more passionate the sound of forced hyperboles and enthusiasm.

That the dwellers in a Kirghis tent are more disposed to poetry than the members of a polished society in Paris and London, must surprise no one. Among us it is only over a certain age that poetry indicates herself more or less; there are only certain individuals that linger round the Castalian fountains. In Central Asia those bowed down by age, as well as youthful lovers, passionately affect poetry, the warrior equally with the shepherd, the priest as well as the layman,—each one attempts the composition of poetry or devises tales; and if this attempt is probably not successful in every instance, still, nevertheless, the habit of even listening to the compositions of others may be said to be universal.

Since literature in the East is in close connection with religion, we must then divide the literary productions of Central Asia at the commencement into two parts.

1st. The Literature of Islam or the Settled Nations.

2nd. The Literature of the Nomadic or Wandering Tribes.

This distinction dates from that time when, with the entrance of Islam, foreign literary conceptions became universally diffused, which, without retaining at the present time any special national character, are in vogue among the different followers of Islam. Poetry, for this is the essence of that literature, is always the same now with Arabs, Turks, Persians, and Central Asiatics. Vainly would one seek there the stamp of a national mint; it is everywhere the same sprightly imagery of the poets; everywhere the same metaphors, parables; everywhere the stereotyped image of the rose and the nightingale, the thorn-resembling eyelashes, the fuming vapors of rising sighs, &c. Everywhere the same muse of which the learned M. de Khanikoff rightly says :—" That she comes forth free and wild, like those plants of strange forms to be met with in the calcined soil of southern Asia, covered with thistles and thorns, incrusted with salt; they diffuse through a rugged bark, here and there, aromatic, beneficent odours, and wave upon their withered stems wreaths of flowers of elegant forms and brilliant colours."—*Asiatic Journal*, vol. v., p. 297. Of this literature, however, which is well known in western countries, through many translations and learned treatises, we shall say nothing. We rather pass over the religious literature of many eccentric devotees, who, in zealous ardour towards God and the prophets, have written volumes full of pompous expressions on the subject of their love and resignation. These last productions in the three Khanats are considered as the exclusive property of the Mollah and Ishan world. The people listen very patiently to their recitals, but are not enthusiastic, for the mystical current of thought in copious language is beyond the reach of their understanding. What we wish to say, then, of the literature of Central Asia is confined, to speak correctly, to the Popular Poetry. Here we do still find something original, here some types which deserve the real name of Turkestan, and with these we wish to make our readers acquainted. The most poetically attuned people are in the Khanat of Khiva. This part of Central Asia had at the beginning of the twelfth century acquired the reputation of a special eminence in music, tuneful voices, distinguished poets and poetesses; indeed, it is hardly fifty years ago that in the courts of the Kadjars, in Teheran, a

Khivite lute-player was in great honour. Bokhara, before the ascendancy of the Turkish element, had only a few great poets, such as Rudeki and Figani; but these must be rather classed in Persian literature. To return to Khiva, I must remark that as it always surprised myself when I heard a heavy-looking, coarsely-dressed Œzbeg, with wild, sun-burnt features, sing one or another soft minor air; so, also, with travellers in general, this feeling will be found to exist on their entry among Turkomans and Kirghis. These people esteem music and poetry as their highest pleasure. After a fortunate adventure the marauder, however tired and hungry he may be, will listen in the open street with real delight to the bakhshi (troubadour), who comes to meet him. Returning home from a foray, or other heroic deed, the young warriors are in the habit of amusing themselves throughout the night with poetry and music. In the desert, where man is either ignorant of the luxuries of life, or does without them, it is, nevertheless, that the bakhshi is very seldom wanting, and besides, that the latter are found in great numbers, going about to exercise their art. The nomads have the habit of amusing themselves with poetic games.

As people regard in company the happy finding of a rhyme or cadence as indispensable to education, the young nomad girl will also, say, give the preference to him who would answer her question in a verse with happy rhymes. The poetry of the Œzbegs consists first of narratives, which either appeal to religious life or famous heroic deeds. The first are composed by the Mullah world, or by the more polished bakhshis, after Arabic or Persian sources, and adapted to native taste,—the last are genuine Tartar compositions, in which there are not wanting at times both glowing language and good metaphors. These tales of heroic exploits, which are similar to our romances, begin already to be of even greater extent, and are often recited or sung many evenings together, and although Islam plays here and there a conspicuous part, nevertheless those pieces are preferred in which home-heroes figure on well-known historic fields. Of these last-named compositions, one much esteemed in Central Asia may serve as a specimen. It bears as its title

"AHMED AND YUSUF,"

And is the history of two sons of heroes, who, after their country's fashion, even in early youth undertake a tchapao or razzia against heretical Iran, in which the leading motive is not so much the thirst for spoil as the chastisement of the unbelieving Shiites. Just at the beginning Yusuf harangues his heroes ready for the foray in the following fashion:—

"With the worthless fellow unite not, for he makes known the deepest secret. Speak no secret words in bad spots, for thy deep hidden mystery will become known. Better is the bare leaf than the faded rose. Better is dry earth than worthless grass. Better is a staff than a stupid fellow-traveller. For he makes known the direction of thy route to the foe. Do not instruct the fool, because he will, nevertheless, reach the grave of misery unconsciously. When you enter at a good-for-nothing fellow's as a guest, he attacks you like the little cur, and makes his vice known. Would that I could give you the picture of a true hero! He draws his sword only for the destruction of the unbelievers. Do not march against the enemy with a coward, since he makes known the trodden track as well as his own path. Yusuf Beg says, 'Such a time is come. This home-land is for us no longer. Fools know not their own lair; they speak angrily, and make their evil speech known.' "

They march away. The report of their heroic deeds spreads far and wide, and naturally reaches their home-land. Here governed only petty princes, each of whom would take renowned warriors into his service. The usual career of warfare proceeds, and Yusuf takes the command, but only with the consent of his comrades.

They draw out afresh for an expedition against Guzel Shah, the Governor of Isfahan. The Œzbegs are overpowered by Persian cunning. Both princes are taken and dragged in chains to Iran. This misfortune rouses deep cries from the heart of Yusuf, and as he could not turn for sympathy to his captors, he pours forth his wail to the lofty hills that surround him, and exclaims:—

"Ye snow-bedecked, many coloured hills, what has befallen me; have you seen it? I am become the slave of these unbelievers; my tarrying behind, have you seen it? No one pities my tears, the hills only throb at my tears. With lashes around my head, how must I have stepped along the way; have you seen it? Heedless were my attendants. Ah! I weep tears of blood! How captured with Ahmed Beg came I here, have you seen it? I drink blood,—in this world too heavy is my sorrow! Walking on foot, unbelievers on steeds; have you seen it? Yusuf Beg says, 'I am inwardly consumed, my sorrow is endless. Dragged with these bound hands at a horse's pleasure, have you seen me?'"

He is then thrown into prison, where he finds a fellow-sufferer in the person of a Sunnite, who as enchanter and fortune-teller by profession, had drawn on himself the displeasure of the Persian monarch; and he also finds in the daughter of the gaoler, who had become enamoured of him, a kind friend. Up to this point the strifes, the mighty hero-deeds, the religious enthusiasm, are constantly detailed. From this point love also mingles in the strain. Yusuf Beg had left at home a sister and a lady love. The former vainly waiting his return, cries bitterly, and in tears calls on her maidens to loosen her hair; the latter, in his absence, maintains her passionate regard, and sends the trained cranes of the hero with a love-letter to him. It contains the following charge:—

"Oh, ye five cranes of Yusuf Beg! Rush out and draw near to N. Strengthen yourselves and fly away over the hills! Seeing Yusuf Beg, hasten back, that the hawk see not on the plains the tips of your wings. I am deprived of half my heart. Come back, asking him of his health! Hasten back! I was once the world-rose; flown hence is the nightingale of my grove! Should my lover be living, then brush with your lively wings early back. Should the red roses have become withered; should his life have reached its end; should my lover be dead, put on mourning, and weeping return! Calling on God, shake then your wings. With ardour look forth to the heaven; burst out for the town of Ürgendj. Break out and draw towards the town of N. Gain true intelligence, and come back. Oh, hear Gul Assl's cry! Carry to him my heart-sorrow! Oh, make a pilgrimage to his grave. Bring me a little dust, and hasten back."

The birds circle around the prison of their sorrowful master with plaintive chirping. He remarks them, and sends back to his home the following message:—

"Oh, ye cranes! Fly round me, right and left, in mazy sweep in air. Go back,—say my greeting to my people! Oh, ye cranes! right and left, looking round, go back,—say my greeting to my people! The crane flies and rests high in the air. Tired are his wings with the long way. Here in prison breaks out afresh my sorrow. Oh, greet, then, my kinsmen! Kharezm town is my home. There stays my friend, my beloved, my well-wisher, my dear one, my tender one. Oh, greet her, my mother! my Kaaba! On the mountains of sorrow are pines high, high. Oh, pray for me all of you, young and old. Mournful autumn became my fate; before the life's blossoms had opened yet! Oh, greet for me my poor little sister! She from early morn waiting for me looks around. She is inwardly consumed by the torture of separation. Looking on the path in the morning with dishevelled hair, she cries: 'He is not come!' Her whole soul for me is waste and empty,—my love Gul Assl, for her I mourn. Oh, greet her! In one day, oh crane! thou wilt reach from here to Kharezm. On the way thither go over the seven mountains. Note this thou hast seen, Yusuf Beg; greet the cowardly Begs for me."

The birds depart, but the heroes languish yet long in prison. At last they are condemned to die. But the miraculous power of the Sunnee saints saves them. All the weapons employed become blunt. The Persian tyrant remarks it, and summons the heroes to his presence. As the chief condition of obtaining the wished-for freedom, Yusuf must improvise in opposition to the court fool, Kökche, and in the event of his overcoming the latter in poetic ability, then he is to be restored to his home in full liberty. Yusuf improvises in strikingly bold language. He sings not the praises of the tyrant, but his own, while he says,—

"My people is a fine people. Winters there are

continually summers, gardeners tend the gardens, the trees give their fruits. In white tents repose the aged, the youths hunt around them. In cordial companionship live the youths, spending time in delight and pleasure. Fast as the wind the steeds. In racing thy steeds lay behind them. High soaring to heaven is the flight of the birds. In scorn they carry off men. Should intelligence of me arrive in a day, in a day also an army can come. Out of six pounds of thick cord are the strings of their bows. Their princes rule in equity, partiality is far from them. Hear me, Guzel Shah, thou unbeliever, should I return to wage war on thee, then know that one wave of my arm kills 100,000 men. Of Isfahan are their swords. Their streets are united bazaars, their fields like beds of tulips. With deers, hares, falcons, the fields of my people are full. Their free inhabitants are like Hatem,* their leaders are like Behram and Rustem in the day of battle, heroes in the strife. I am a slave without power, the unbeliever regards not this; without fate the fly dies not; let not my tears flow in vain."

He conquers, goes laden with treasure to Ürgendj; and though he has to undergo some hard struggles on the road, arrives happily home, where his reception is described in many deeply-moving, highly poetical images. After an interview with his beloved and his sister they conduct him to Lalakhan, his mother, who

* The oriental emblem for generosity.

in consequence of mourning for him for several years, has almost lost her sight. They bring her the joyful intelligence, which she disbelieves at first, and says,— "My ardent desire has bent me low. Am I really to see thee, my dear child? Sunk in sorrow, I only sighed, with eyes tremulously searching for you. The whole world would I look through could I really find thee, my child. Shall I mourn like the nightingale? Shall I, like Mansur, succumb to sorrow? Shall I, like Djerdjis, weep tears of blood? Am I again to find thee, oh my dear child," &c.

Yusuf Beg is led to her. He bides apart, and when he hears the cry of his mother, his anguish bursts forth for their fatal separation in yet more sorrowful words. By the voice his mother recognises him. Overpowered by excessive joy, she yet welcomes him in the following words:—

"Oh, thou seven years' sufferer in prison! Oh, thou balsam of my wounded heart! My star of happiness brightens. Vanished is the night of misery! Oh, prince of my people and land! Thou Rustem, thou hero of the world! My Yusuf, my glorious son, my comfort, my life-power! Thou crown of happiness, thou highest grace of my life! Lalakhan has found her son, the All-powerful has shown mercy to her. Gone is all pain from my breast, all sorrow. Yusuf, my son, is come!"

Soon after this the marriage of the lovers takes place, his hero blood suffers not the adventure-seeking chief to rest. He collects an army, of which all the people of Central Asia form part. It is to take vengeance on Guzel Shah. Fortune attends his arms. The Persian is conquered; his old fellow-sufferer, Kamber, freed. He goes home crowned with glory, and the conquered Guzel Shah must pay him the following tribute.

DEMANDS OF YUSUF FROM GUZEL SHAH.

"He shall give me the whole Kharads of the town, N., —40,000 silk stuffs embroidered with gold, and 40,000 khimhal (stronger silk stuffs) shall he send. His tolls and taxes he shall collect; 40,000 magnificent dresses shall he send; 40,000 chargers, with golden saddles; 40,000 male and female camels; 40,000 young slaves with golden girdles; 40,000 youths, with beautiful eyes, shall he send; 40,000 oxen (well bred) shall he send; 40,000 rhinoceri, bound in chains, shall he send; 40,000 reins, well shod, with gold nails, and 40,000 grey falcons shall he send; 40,000 whips shall he send, the nails of which shall be symmetrically arranged; lashes, worked in silver, the handles with golden spangles; 40,000 iron greys, 40,000 foxes, 40,000 noble steeds, with snake like tails, shall he send; 40,000 ambling nags, 40,000 roadsters, 40,000 peasants, as caravan guides, shall he send; these, with black locks falling down right and left, whose faces are covered with moles; 40,000 wonderfully beautiful maidens, with golden girdles, shall he send; 40,000 caps, 60,000 turbans, shall he send. Also, 70,000 sheep and double horned rams shall he send. Yusuf Beg says he shall have all ready quickly; 100,000 Russian thalers and 10 gold dishes shall he send."

This was, in short, the material of an Œzbeg romance, of which there is an innumerable quantity, and of domestic tales also; and these are considered the most valuable portion of their literature. Here and there, one finds an union of religion and valour. The Heroes are taken out of the Islam world, as, for instance, in the story of Zerkum Shah, where Ali conquers the last named heathen prince of Persia, in wonderful engagements, which border upon the imaginative, and may be compared to the poems of Ariosto and Bojardi; finally, he converts him to Islam. There are also numerous tales of Ebu Muslim, the old Field-Marshal of the Abassides, and, later, the independent ruler of Khorassan and Kharezm. The historical facts are pretty old, and yet each Œzbeg, in the great desert which separates his home from Persia, points out many a spot where the Arabian Field-Marshal encamped, fought, and enacted supernatural deeds of valour. Finally, there are also the epics, in which the old princes of the house of Shah Kharezmian are extolled. In these, as well as in those which tell of Mohamed Emin, Khan of Khiva, Mohamed Ali Khan of Khokand, we find many an image which indicates the natural feeling and pride of the Œzbegs.

Then follow, also, on these compositions, which are

always of greater length, short poems, which tell of love, morality, heroism,—or contain special directions for handling of weapons, dressing of horses, and the duties of a good warrior. These are, for the greater part, productions of plain burghers, professional Bakhshis, people who are unacquainted with reading and writing, and leave their poetry to be written by others; or, finally, productions by women and young girls, who break out into poetic effusions from the fire kindled by passion. I brought with me a pretty collection, written on soiled paper, in a bad hand, bound in rough leather, which I found among the Turkomans at a Bakhshi's, who hid the "Opus Curiosum" in the broad leg of his boots; and it has really very strange things in it, sometimes not without beauty. We wish to produce some specimens, under the names of the writers; some of them appear to be anonymous. The first one, in the genuine Oriental style, mourns the transitory condition of humanity and the vanity of the world.

Allah Yar.

1. To build castles in this world is a fruitless thing; finally, all will become ruin, and building is really not worth the trouble.

2. Day and night, for each poor wanderer to labour and strain himself, is really not worth the trouble.

3. Friends! For idle good in this empty world,

to mourn and lament oneself, is really not worth the trouble.

4. To do homage to passion out of ostentation, to torment the poor and the sick, is really not worth the trouble.

5. To destroy the lands of Islam, and to draw the sword to annihilate, is really not worth the trouble.

6. With taxes, duties, with hundredfold griefs and sorrows to vex Molla Khodja,—nay, the whole world, is really not worth the trouble.

7. As you cannot, Allah Yar, stand the brunt of the world, why plague yourself going up and down it? it is really not worth the trouble.

Revnak.

1. I went to my love one evening, on foot, treading softly. In sweet sleep lay the dear one. I embraced her softly, softly.

2. I took a kiss from her lips and refreshed my soul by it. I embraced her tender limbs, and kissed her once more,—softly, softly.

3. I said, give me a kiss, then. What, are you not ashamed, said she? Return whence you came, quickly,—treading softly, softly.

4. I was obstinate, and would not go. She seized my arm and pushed me out. At last, I saw no other chance, and sneaked off,—softly, softly.

5. I departed; could not endure separation, and

came back. Oh, merciless one, I implore thee, give me a kiss,—softly, softly.

6. Too genial to suit European taste.

7. Revnak says, as the whole world is full of jokes and sport, so let no one blame me, and read this softly, softly.

MESHREF,

1. My soul blazes in flame, yet my mistress comes not. What said I,—Mistress! The beloved of my heart comes not.

2. I am inwardly consumed for the love of this cypress-like beauty. She is so cruel. Into her thoughts I enter not.

3. I see in dreams her ringlets, and rise deeply saddened at noon. From this lock of her hair my heart separates not.

4. Medjnun and Leila, take a lesson from me in love; my charming dear one heeds me not.

5. The life of foolish Meshref seems coming to its end, and the sad flirt heeds me not.

FUZULI.

1. Hold fast to the leading strings of modesty, for nothing is lovelier than modesty. Immodesty, mark this well, advances neither in this nor that world.

2. Oh! bird of my heart, flutter not in the air, but light on the hand of a king. The too high-flying hawk is never employed in the chase.

3. Desire treasure only from God; he has many storehouses. Should a drop only fall to thee for portion, this is amply sufficient: it ends not.

4. He, on whom the bird of happiness has rested, flies high, even without wings. He, on whom a dark lot has fallen, can scarcely raise his own hand.

5. Be always humble: strive to obtain a contrite spirit. He who suffers gold-hunger can never be satisfied.

6. You, Fuzuli, live in this world only for friendship. Winter lives in unfriendly hearts; never can it be summer there.

Nesimi.

1. *Saturday.* I met my cypress-like charmer, and she made me distracted.

2. *Sunday.* I was frantic, and a wanderer, and fell down senseless. I saw her face, and thought it was the shining moon.

3. *Monday.* At last I told her my heart-secret. Her eyes are like the narcissus, her cheeks resemble roses, her eyebrows are like a bow.

4. *Tuesday.* I became a huntsman, and went over the country (walked), yet I myself became the chased, and fell a sacrifice to the ever coy one.

5. *Wednesday.* My beauty walked in the fields; the nightingale saw her face and uttered wild cries.

6. *Thursday.* I said to my loved one: Hearken,

then, to my advice: hide thy secret still from both good and bad.

7. *Friday.* At last Nesimi saw her beauty, and drank to satiety of the sherbet of her rosy lips.

These, although through the poetic beauty of our European tastes they may not prove quite agreeable, give yet sufficient evidence that the inhabitants of Central Asia, apart from the roughness of their social relations, despite their incessant wars and forays, are not unskilled in the expression of traits of poetic feeling and tender love. The higher classes, though they do not look on the popular poetry with contempt, still wish to show traces of refined taste, a higher education, and enjoy the works of the elder Persian poets, or the books of Nevai, who stepped forward as the first of the Tchagatay poets in that kind of accomplishment, by which all the rest of the poets of the Islamitish polite world acquired renown. Nevai is a scholar of the celebrated Sheikh Abdurrahman Djami, during many years minister, field marshal, and governor of many provinces. He is of rare genius in poetry, and of great fertility; for he has produced more than thirty-two distinct works on poetry, history, morals, logic; and though his works are thoroughly Persian in spirit, and not pervaded with the spirit of Central Asia, yet the merit of having refined and ennobled the Turkish dialect of Central Asia cannot be taken from him.

Here I give a few specimens.

Nevai.

1. Oh! heart, come, let us seek out a love; the cypress-growing one, the silver-cheeked one, let us seek.

2. As the darling of our eyes has looked for another friend, we also have eyes; therefore, another let us seek.

3. She greets the glance of men only with the dust of death. Why stand longing here? Another beauty let us seek.

4. Should I not find another like thee, who destroyest all the world, then a lowly, modest, but tender one, I will seek.

5. We will hasten through field and plain for the loved one; we will search garden and meadows. Her will we seek.

6. As the wish is good, it shall not remain unfulfilled. Among small and great, through all as far as possible, we wish to seek.

7. Oh! Nevai, from this passion you will never get freed. Come, therefore, before the meeting. Patience and perseverance let us seek.

Nevai.

1. Absent from the loved one, the heart is like a land without a king. A land without a king is like a body without a soul.

2. Oh! Mussulman, what service is a body without

a soul! It is like black earth, which has no sweet smelling roses.

3. Black earth, that has no sweet smelling roses, is like a dark night, that has no bright moonbeams.

4. A dark night, that has no bright moon, is like darkness without a life-source.

5. A darkness, that has no life-source, is like a hell, which has no paradise-plains.

6. Oh! Nevai, as the loved give so much pain, it is certain that absence has its pangs, and the return no aid.

His Tchihardivan is beautiful, in which he celebrates the various ages of men, as also his adaptation of the well-known romances, Ferhad and Shirin, Medjnun and Leila, Yusuf and Zuleikha, &c. Also his versification of some stories out of the 1,001 Nights, among which Prince Seif-ul-Muluk is the most successful. The following will serve as a specimen of the latter.

How Seif-ul-Muluk sets out from the town of Tchin, and journeys to the sea.

1. Come, tale-teller, let us hear the story of the adverse fate that befel the king's son?

2. The tale-teller replied, "That is hard to do; for the sword of sorrow cleaves the breast."

3. The prince had everything prepared for his departure, and first enquired about the town of Katine.

4. Satisfactory information was soon received; all his effects brought to the ship.

5. The whole crew were on board, the officers stood prepared, and the army equipped.

6. Then the prince betook himself on board, and confided his person to the "god's device" (the ship).

7. The pilots led the way, followed by an endless host of ships.

8. There sat the prince in sweet reverie, with smiling lips and a heart free from sorrow.

9. Six months he went across the sea, with pilot carefully watching his way.

10. Soon, Fate made him feel the sting of envy, and maliciously opposed him.

11. The sea became moved and girded on the blood-thirsty sword.

12. She opened herself, and the deluge wildly burst forth,—a deluge on all sides of streams of fire.

13. Every moment she showed a fresh scene of horror—every instant makes a thousand souls tremble.

14. Wildly swelled the waves, and threatened with mighty floods: with blood-thirsty jaws rush and roar the waters of the sea.

15. Then dark fearful winds arise—the horizon veils itself in pitchy darkness, and from the surface of the sea there sounds forth wild lamentation.

16. The day, bright with the sun, becomes a pitch-dark night. What a fearful day! It is the image of the day of judgment.

17. Wherever thou lookest no man is visible, not even the hand before the eyes,—all, and over all, is water.

18. The salt waves toss and roll incessantly, and raise the ships with keels upward.

19. Ever does the mighty sea rage and roar and mount with fury from the deep abyss.

20. Wild cries of creatures break out together, you would think it was the day of Resurrection.

21. In frightful hurly-burly one ship runs into the other; they split, and sink to the bottom of the sea.

22. The yards break, the planks fall in pieces, no possibility of escape.

23. Those hundred ships, said the tale-teller; that crew, those possessions,

24. All was wrecked on the sea coast, not a trace remained behind on the surface of the waters."

Wide as the territory of Turkestan-Proper extends, so far does the literature of which we have tried to give a slight sketch in the foregoing pages. And the further we betake ourselves from the frontiers into the desert, so in like manner does Islam become weaker, and here commences the change from Mohamedan civilisation into the old Shamanism. Among the Kirghis, notwithstanding the greater part of them profess Islam, one meets here and there with a tale which was generated in the Khanats; this, however, is looked upon as an exotic plant, and never preferred to the native. The popular poetry that one finds among them forms the point of transition from the currents of ideas of one society into another. Indeed, only two days' distance from the borders of the Yaxartes, or northward from the Sea of Aral, may a bakhshi prosper, provided he can give in the best fashion tales or narratives of a purely Kirghis character. The poetry of the wild inhabitants of the steppe is more strange and odd than pretty. Here and there a happy image occurs, at other times there are only broken exclamations and solitary verses without the smallest connection. Since each person is a poet, a tale cannot long preserve its originality, either they add something new to it or cast the whole off, and few people can keep themselves from annexing to their songs the momentary influence of their fantasy. Of the love-lays of the Kirghis, Lewschine has introduced a short poem, not without charm, in his book, p. 380:—

"Dost thou see this snow? The body of my loved one is whiter still."

"Dost thou see the dropping blood of the slain lamb? Her cheeks are redder still."

"Dost thou see the trunk of this burnt tree? Her hair is blacker still."

"Dost thou know with what the mollahs of our Khan write? Her eyebrows are blacker than their ink."

"Dost thou see these glowing embers? Her eyes are brighter still."

Another specimen which follows this consists of detached sentences without any connection.

"The hawk has pounced on the ducks—on a flight of ducks—on a great flight!"

"I am very ill, and hardly ever think of eating," or "yonder is a tall pine-tree, the mist has fallen over it."

"Yesterday she allowed me to enter her house. Formerly she would come herself and caress me."

These more or less may be found among all purely popular tales of oriental people. There is even a trace of them in Hungarian, as for example,—

"Three apples and a half, I invited thee, and thou camest not," or "the crane flies high, singing beautifully, my loved one is angry, for she will not speak to me," &c.

A considerable number of tales or narratives of hero deeds exists among nomadic tribes, partly in verse, partly in prose. In these the spirit of the literature of the Turkish tribes of South Siberia is more prominent than that of their Central Asiatic neighbours; and I have heard many compositions of Kirghis Bakhshis, which I find with little variation and dialectic differences faithfully conveyed in the more recent work,—"Proofs of the Popular Literature of the Turkish tribes of South Siberia," by Dr. Radloff.

It leaves no doubt that as the learned A. Schiffner, in the myths and tales of Dr. Radloff's collection, finds traces of a Buddhist influence, so many of the irtegi (tales) of the modern Kirghis have reached them from the further south, beyond Djungaria; for Islam, coming from the south-west, could take no firm root over the Yaxartes, and now that the mighty waves of

Russian power roll down from the north, will certainly prevail no further. This kind of literature belonging rather to the Turks of South Siberia, we shall conclude our present sketch by a tale of the Kirghis, which belongs to this little horde, according to European opinion, but according to inland appellation, to Mangishlak Kazagi, *i.e.*, a Kirghis of Mangishlak. It is from the book of Bronislas Zaleski, who, as a Polish exile, dwelt nine years in the desert, and on his return, 1865, published under the title of "La Vie des Steppes Kirghizes." Paris. Fol. 1865.

The Tale of Kugaul.*

Man is, in Heaven, helpless without God; on earth, powerless without a horse.

There was once a Kirghis, named Buruzgay. He had great numbers of sheep and horses, and nothing was wanting to him if God had not denied him children. He was alone, consequently, in an advanced state of life. He said not his daily prayer (namaz), nor kept the enjoined feasts. One day, the sorrow of his childless condition overcame him, and he determined to go to the Holy places, in the hope that his prayers might obtain for him a son. He forged for himself shoes of iron, and took a staff of iron in his hand, and so betook himself on his way. He travelled

* I adopt the orthography of the original, although Kugaul (hunter) Barzagai (master lion) instead of Buruzgay would be preferable.

and travelled ten years long, and probably more. So long, so long did he travel, until his iron shoes were quite worn out, and only the handle of his iron staff remained. At last, he fell down on the ground, prostrate. Great were his sufferings, for he could neither raise himself up nor die.

Lo! before him appeared a holy man, who perceived him lying on the earth, had compassion on him, bent over him and enquired what ailed him. Buruzgay could not utter a word. The holy man fell on his knees, recited his prayer, (namaz) and prayed the Almighty to loosen the tongue of the unhappy man. Hardly had he done this, when Buruzgay began to feel his strength revive. He related his history, and on what grounds he had abandoned his aoul. The holy man withdrew a short distance, and continued in prayer until God said to him, " Thou art well pleasing in my sight. I will accomplish thy wish. But why dost thou interest thyself in Buruzgay? He pays no impost, he says no prayer (namaz), he observes no fast. How shall I have compassion on him?" " Lord," said the holy man, " in time to come he will serve Thee devoutly, and will repeat his prayers; only do not reject my intreaties. Grant my prayer and take me for an hostage." Then God said, " Depart, faithful servant, thy prayers are granted. Enquire of Buruzgay what is his desire. Will he have forty sons and forty daughters, or only one son and one daughter especially approved by me."

The holy man returned to Buruzgay. He found him quite restored, and on his knees; and he cried aloud with joy, "Oh, God, I have not lied to Thee: Buruzgay, before my return, had begun to perform his duty." He then told Buruzgay the words of God. "What shall I do with forty sons and forty daughters? If the Almighty hear my prayers, he will give me one son and one daughter." The holy man blessed him, and conveyed back to the Lord his reply. Buruzgay found his iron shoes as though unworn, and betook himself to his aoul. Approaching it, he appeared to recognize his steppe and flocks. He viewed all with heartfelt joy. Slowly and slowly regaining his recollection, he perceived that nothing had changed since his departure. He approached a shepherd, to enquire of him as to the owner of the herds. The shepherds did not recognise him, he had so fallen away, and become so changed through fasting and hardships, and his clothes were worn out. "What is our master to thee," enquired the shepherds, "go thy way." They went their way to their flocks. Buruzgay waited until their return, and questioned them afresh. The shepherds drove him away as a poor beggar (baygouche), without wishing to speak to him, till at last he uttered his name. They immediately looked at him attentively, recognised him, and told him that his wife, whom he had left in the family way, was near her confinement, and they were expecting guests in the aoul. Then, without waiting for his reply, the shepherds ran off swifter than an arrow, and coming to Buruzgay's wife, demanded the suyundji, (the customary gift for good news). They received it, and informed the wife of the arrival of her husband. She was highly delighted, and immediately afterwards Buruzgay entered. A few days after his arrival, his wife was delivered of two fine, strong children,—twins. One was a son, the other was a daughter. Buruzgay was beside himself with joy, and he kept constantly meditating on what names he should give these children, with whom God had rejoiced his old age. Whilst he was buried in thought, his former intercessor with Heaven, the holy man, came to him, and said, "Thou wilt name thy son Kugaul, and thy daughter Khanisbeg. And Buruzgay hearkened to the holy man, who immediately left him.

The children grew, and were beautiful. Four years passed away. The twins began to learn shooting, with little bows prepared for them. Kugaul easily learned to shoot, and ten years passed away. At this time, it came to pass that a mighty Sultan gave a feast (Toy). During the banquet, he gave notice that he wished a lofty mast to be erected, with a piece of gold on the summit, and that whoever could pierce with his arrow the gold piece, should be the husband of his daughter. A host of competitors presented themselves. The mast was very high; they shot in turns; none could pierce the gold piece, and the renowned archers of the Steppe missed their aim. At length, the last guest at the banquet missed also. The Sultan cried out, " are these all the young people that there are in the Steppe? Have none stayed away who will let fly an arrow for the hand of the Sultan's daughter?" "Only one remains," they replied, " Kugaul, son of Buruzgay; but he is only a little boy ten years old." "That matters nothing," said the Sultan, "bring him here immediately." They went into the aoul to seek him. He appeared on a broken-winded horse, in old clothes, with a bow at his back. He had plenty of beautiful clothes, and good horses, for his father was rich, and denied him nothing, but he wished, before the rich, to appear poor and humble. When the Sultan's wife saw him riding forward, she cried out immediately, " This shall be my son-in-law, and none other among those present." Arrived at the mast, Kugaul would not immediately draw his bow.

" You are many," said he; " I am alone, and young; and if I were to hit successfully, I might, perhaps, not then receive the hand of the Sultan's daughter. The Sultan assured him that he would give him his daughter, but only on the condition that he should shoot successfully. Kugaul prepared to pierce the gold piece. He took aim, bent his bow so powerfully, that his lean, miserable horse, sank beneath him. He struck him with his whip until he rose. Kugaul took aim again, stretched the cord afresh. This time the horse only bent the knee. The arrow went off and pierced the centre of the golden piece. Kugaul, exhausted with the effort, dismounted, unsaddled his horse, lay down on the ground, and, reclining his head on the saddle, fell asleep. He slept there three days long in his miserable attire, little as he was on a poor saddle. The Sultan had fully intended not to give his daughter to such a wretched-looking being. In vain Kugaul awaited the messengers. No one came, and he thought of some means by which he could obtain his bride. Suddenly a woman appeared before him from the Sultan's household, and explained to him fully the position of circumstances. Kugaul said to her, "Return to the Sultan, and tell him that I give him until mid-day to-morrow for consideration. If he does not then give me his daughter, and forty laden camels, and forty carpets, I will kill him and exterminate his whole family." The woman took a fancy to Kugaul, imagining him to be a great warrior (batyr), returned quickly to the aoul of the Sultan, gave the Sultana an account of the meeting, who rushed to her husband, saying, that Kugaul would become a great hero (batyr), and if he should not keep his word, he would draw on himself a disgrace darker than the earth. The Sultan's wife spoke many similar speeches, until at last her husband resolved to marry his daughter, and he gave Kugaul notice to that effect. Kugaul now attired himself in splendid robes, mounted a magnificent courser, and presented himself to the Sultan. The marriage was celebrated, and after the accustomed wedding feast (toy) Kugaul conducted his young wife home, and returned to his father's aoul. Forty camels, laden with costly objects, and covered with forty carpets followed him. This was the dower of the bride. When he reached home, Kugaul's wife lowered her veil, according to the custom of the Kirghis. But when they were in the presence of his father and mother, Kugaul lifted it for the first time. Hardly had his parents seen her countenance, when they presented her gifts of horses and cattle. Then, because they had not guessed her favourite colours for animals, the daughter-in-law did not fall at their knees to thank them. The old Buruzgay was angry at this, and cried out, enraged, "What an animal is this maiden! We have given her a host of presents and she will not humble herself before us, nor give us even the usual salute (selam)." She replied, "What are your presents to me? I do not require them. You have not given me the very best. Behind the house there is a chesnut mare, she sinks knee-deep in the sand; she alone suits me. For she will produce a stallion, which will save my Kugaul from many misfortunes, and become a true warrior's steed. Give me this mare, she is the most valuable, and I prefer her to all." "My daughter-in-law is, though young, prudent enough," said Buruzgay. This pleased him, he became reconciled to her, gave her the mare, and the young bride fell at the feet of her parents, and gave the usual greeting. A beautiful tent was erected near the old people, and the newly-married dwelt therein, and the wife of Kugaul ordered her servants to attend to the chesnut mare as the apple of their eye. They then dug a deep recess, covered it with grass, and there the mare was protected and well fed. During the night a fire was lighted around. Forty days passed and the mare brought forth a colt, a little bay stallion. The servants ran immediately to apprise the lady, and demanded a reward for the joyful intelligence. "Wait another forty days," she answered; "take great care of the stallion, give him plenty to eat and drink." The servants obeyed, and when the appointed time was passed they returned to their mistress, who informed them that from that moment they were all free, and could go where they wished. As for the young colt, a silk noose of forty fathoms was prepared,—they fed him on pure barley, milk, and kishmish (a kind of dry raisin), and he grew up with Kugaul. It happened at this time that the Khan (chief of the Kirghis) came on a visit to the old Buruzgay, and when he saw Khanisbeg and the wife of Kugaul they pleased him so much that he fell senseless to the ground. They brought him back to life, and prepared food for all. They all set to work to cut meat for mishbarmak (a Kirghis dish). The Khan did the same, but whilst his hands were occupied his eyes admired the beautiful women. He became inflamed with a mighty passion, and could not turn his looks away from her face. So absorbed was he that he did not even remark, that instead of cutting meat he had cut his own finger, and did not discover this for some minutes. Aware of it, he became so ashamed that he could cut nothing,* and not to displease his host he made belief as though he were tasting the dishes. He took leave quickly, and returned home with a concealed longing in his heart. Hardly had he reached it when he gathered his friends and relatives together, and consulted with them on the means he should take to remove Kugaul, and become possessed of his wife and his sister. Every body said that he could not kill him, for he was far too great a hero.

But they devised another plan; they resolved to send Kugaul against a hostile horde with the command to bring the Khan, who was there ruling, alive or dead. This idea pleased the love-lorn Khan. People assured him that the envoy could not return under ten years, and it was indeed very probable that he might perish. They sent for Kugaul immediately, and gave him the instructions. He returned home to his aoul and related to his wife the commands he had received. "Not on this account does he send thee," replied she, "I know the feelings of his heart. When he was here he was seized with a passionate longing for me and thy sister; he will have us and send thee

* This same episode occurs in the romance of Yusuf and Zuleikha, where Zuleikha's friends at the banquet are so astonished at the beauty of Yusuf that instead of paring the pomegranates before them they cut off the skin with their fingers.

away, so that thou mayest die; but thou hast thine horse, thou canst not fail, only return quickly." Kugaul departed, and only took with him his servants and his horse, and travelled over many steppes, until at last he reached the hostile border. Ten years, perhaps, more or less, he travelled, I do not know exactly. At last his horse stopped, Kugaul pressed him on, but the animal suddenly began to speak with a human voice. "Compel me not to advance further, we are near the enemy. Take off my bridle and saddle, I will go thither and see how many they are in number." Kugaul obeyed his horse, which began to roll on the ground, and by this means to increase his strength more than by the best food. Then he rose, shook himself, neighed, changed into a bird, and flew up into the clouds. Thus he flew for three days. At last he returned and said, "There are more enemies than hairs in my mane or tail. Consider well what thou dost. Wilt thou fight or return?" Kugaul was not terrified. He left his servants with the command that they should await him on that spot. "If you hear of my fall," continued he, "bear the news to my wife and my mother." He then offered an earnest prayer to God for help, and departed. The enemy surrounded him, but he permitted not himself to be conquered. His horse was a great help to him, for hardly did one of the enemy take aim at him with his gun than he changed into an eagle and flew far away with Kugaul towards the heaven. If he were threatened with an arrow, the horse changed into a sparrow and disappeared among the grass like a small ball. Kugaul fought thus many days and at last slew and exterminated all the men of this race, carried off the women, children, cattle, and possessions with him, brought them to the place where he had left his servants, commanded them to convey the booty home, and he himself rode forward on his faithful steed. On and on he journeyed for a long time. One evening, however, his horse would go no further, did nothing, and stood petrified. Kugaul dismounted and lay down to sleep. Towards the morning he awoke, approached his horse, and perceived that he was shedding bitter tears. "What dost thou ail, my good horse," inquired Kugaul, "why dost thou weep?" "Alas, why should I not weep!" answered the horse. "this is the spot where once I trotted in my silken halter. Here was also our aoul, and now there is not a trace remaining of it, all is destroyed." And he began again to weep. "Take off my saddle and bridle, let me take rest, and so recruit my strength, and I will make enquiry as to the doer of all this, and discover thy enemy."

Kugaul took the saddle and bridle off the horse; he began to roll afresh; and when he had regained strength he raised his head, took a deep breath with his powerful nostrils. He bounded, changed into a bird, and flew up into the air. He flew three days, without, however, discovering anything, and was already on the point of returning, when, on the opposite side, he discovered the aouls of the Khan. Hither he directed his course; flew over the tents and flocks, and saw everything. No one guessed that the bird was Kugaul's horse, only the wife of the hero (Batyr) had a presentiment that some one was coming to her, and nigh at hand, which idea she communicated to her sister. The bird returned to Kugaul, related what he had seen, that the Khan had carried off his wife and sister, taken his flocks, compelled his father to collect tezek (a fuel made of manure), his mother to tend the sheep. The horse began to weep afresh. Kugaul prayed God to come to his assistance, so that he might punish his insulting foe. He then commanded the horse to convey him forthwith to his mother. He departed, and soon found her in the steppe, occupied in tending the sheep. He threw himself into her arms. "Why dost thou thus embrace me?" said the good old woman; "can it be that thou art my son?" "If I am not thy son, am I not worth as much as he?" "Oh, no; none in the steppe is worth as much as my son." "Have you no news of him?" "I do not know where he is. The Khan has despatched him against a hostile people; since that time I have never heard talk of him. Only, to-day it appears to me that I heard the noise of his horse's wings; but I do not know whether it was reality or a trick of Satan." "And is it long since thy Kugaul departed?" "Yes, yes; a long, long, very long time." "But I am Kugaul himself. Dost thou not recognise me?" The old woman looked at him more attentively, and she did not recognise him, and said: "No, thou art not Kugaul; but if thou art his companion, or if thou knowest anything of him, then speak. But do not deceive me—do not torment me." "I am Kugaul," cried the son. "It was my horse that flew over thy head this day." But the old woman was still incredulous. He asked her if Kugaul had no birth-mark, and she replied, that he had a black spot on his shoulder, big as a hand. He then asked his mother to rub his shoulder (a common habit among the Kirghis). "But," the old woman replied, "the sheep will run about in all directions, and the Khan will beat me; for he often beats me. Go, then, and let me manage my flocks." But he insisted and pressed, and said, that if they wished to beat her, he would protect her. At last the old woman consented. She took off the khalat (upper garment) and the shirt, and proceeded to rub his shoulders. She perceived the black spot large as a man's hand, threw herself on the neck of the young man, and cried out, "Thou art Kugaul, thou art my Kugaul;" and she wept for joy. "Did you not, then, recognise me, mother?" said Kugaul. "Is it, then, so long a time that I have been? And you, my poor dear mother, how altered you are! You have grown old and grey, and your eyes are red with tears." And he embraced her, weeping. "I knew not my child," replied his mother; "how long you have been absent! But the Khan has attacked our aoul, carried off thy wife and sister, and all our effects, and reduced thy father and myself to be his slaves. I have been constantly expecting thee; but I have lost all memory: I cannot tell how long a time has passed. I know only that it is a long time, a very long time, that thou hast left us." "Be tranquil, mother," said Kugaul; " the evil days are terminating, and all begins anew to go right. God will aid me. Return to the aoul; hasten to get in thy sheep, without paying attention that it is yet early. If any one inquires about me, say that I am not far off; but not a word more." He took leave of her, and went his way. The old woman returned to the aoul, but she did not walk as usual,—she ran; she, who could hardly before catch a lamb, now chased three or four at once,—so much had her strength improved. The Khan remarked it, and said to those around him: "That old wife of Buruzgay must have received intelligence of her son." He approached her, and questioned her about her son. " He is here,—he is come," replied the old mother. "You will not be able henceforth to make me suffer any more." She spoke boldly; for her interview with her son had filled her heart with joy and hope. The Khan turned pale with fright, and soon he perceived Kugaul, who, mounted on his celebrated steed, advanced to him. Kugaul stopped at some distance, then spoke, without descending from his horse. " You have deceived me, you wished to get rid of me, to carry off my wife and sister. I thought that you acted loyally with me, and went out at thy bidding as a true man. But thou art only a hound, a perjured miscreant, a robber. We must reckon. But what shall I gain by thy solitary death. They would say, that Kugaul, the Batyr, has only killed the Khan. Gather, then, thy army together." And the Khan begged of him to grant him three days to assemble his people. Kugaul consented, and departed. The Khan sent his orders into all the aouls of his horde, and drew together a large armament of his people around him. Kugaul prayed meanwhile to God. At the day appointed he came, and said: "You are my Khan; I will not shoot first at you,—you begin." The Khan shot: missed his aim. "I will not yet shoot at thee," said Kugaul; "gather together thy best marksmen, and command them to shoot against me; if they do not hit me, then I will shoot." The best marksmen of the Khan stepped out of the ranks, and shot. Each shot an arrow at Kugaul, but his horse transformed himself into an eagle, then into a lark; protected him against all the shots, by raising himself up in the clouds—and against all the arrows, by crouching down in the grass of the steppe. They could not hit him. Three days Kugaul permitted them thus to shoot against him. On the fourth, he said to the Khan: "Well, since you are my master, you have shot against me,—you and your servants, for three days. Now comes my turn." "Do what you like," said the Khan. Kugaul placed the best hunter, and then two archers, and the Khan himself in a line behind them.

He placed himself opposite to them, and, turning to his horse, said: "My true steed, rest firm now, and change not thy position, in order that I may, with a single arrow, kill all four." The horse stayed still as a stone. Kugaul drew the string with all his might: the arrow went through huntsman, archers, and the Khan himself. When the people saw that the Khan was dead, they ran away on all sides. Kugaul followed them. He reached, on horseback, now this one, then that one, from the height of the clouds; and all that he struck, died. At last he gave over his work of extermination. He returned to his aoul, found there his parents, his wife, and sister, and seized on the possessions of the Khan. Among the women and children that the servants brought in, there was the daughter of the Khan. Kugaul took her for his second wife. He married his sister, Khanisbek, to a very rich Khan of a neighbouring tribe, and he himself became also Khan.

So ends the story. The old people say (added Mourzakay) that all this is the exact truth, and that all the events happened in the steppes. I did not see them; but we must believe what the old people tell us.

CHAPTER XIX.

RIVALRY BETWEEN RUSSIA AND ENGLAND IN CENTRAL ASIA.

IT is three years ago since, in the closing chapter of my Travels in Central Asia, I expressed my surprise and dissatisfaction at the indifference of Englishmen towards Russian progress in those regions. I then indicated not only the exact course of Russian procedure on the Yaxartes, but also its steadily approaching influence on British India. Abstaining purposely from all far-reaching political reflections, I was as brief and concise as possible, and could hardly have believed that the unassuming remarks of a European, just returned home from Asia, would be found worthy of closer consideration. Nevertheless, these few lines were discussed and dwelt upon by almost every organ of the English and Indian press, from the *Times* to the *Bengal Hirkáru*. Only a very small proportion of those various journals attached itself in any measure to my ideas; the most of them, on the contrary, rejected my good counsel; and without directly ridiculing my judgment, raised from all sides a loud-sounding Hosannah over the happy change in English politicians, who, being less short-sighted now than they were thirty years back, discovered in the advance of the Russians only a disagreeable event; nay, would even regard it with pleasure, and cry success to their march southward over the snow-capped peaks of the Hindu-Kush and the Himalayas.

In these three years, however, a great change has taken place. Far though I be from wishing as an ex-dervish to exult over the fulfilment of my prophecies, still I cannot help referring to the lines in which I happened to proclaim the progress of the Russian arms. While I was in Central Asia the furthest out-posts of the Cossacks lay at Kale-Rehim, thirty-two miles from Tashkend. Forts 1, 2, and 3, on the Yaxartes, if actually conquered, were not yet wholly in safe keeping. On the north of Khokand, too,— on the west of the Issikköl and the Narin, the Court of St. Petersburg could show but few tokens of success. The Kirghis were embittered and hostile to the strange intruders, and the Œzbeg tribes on the northern frontier of Khokand would then have deemed a Russian occupation equivalent to the destruction of the world; so much did they hate and scout the Unbelievers. Three years have passed, and what has happened in that time? Not only has Khodja-Ahmed-Yesevi, that holiest patron of the Kirghis, become a Russian subject in Hazreti-Turkestan; not only has Tashkend, the most important trading town, the great mart of Central-Asiatic and Chinese trade with Russia, been absorbed into the northern Colossus; not only does the Russian flag wave from the citadel of Khodjend, the second town of importance in Khokand; it may now be also seen on the small fortress of Zamin, Oratepa, and Djissag. The dreaded Russ has set himself up as lord-protector in the eastern Khanat of Turkestan: the Hazret, the Khan, as also the Hazret or High Priest of Namengan, strive for the favour of one who, but a year before, would have filled their very dreams with mortal terror. Nay, not Khokand only, but the Tadjik population also throughout Bokhara and Khiva, the great number of freedmen and slaves in service, and even the wealthier merchants from Mooltan and other parts of India, who once trembled before the Œzbeg power, now whisper delightedly into each other's ears that the Russians are slowly drawing nearer, and that Œzbeg lordship and Œzbeg absolutism are coming to an end.

For three years have these metamorphoses in the oasis-countries of Turkestan been carried on with sure and steady hand from the banks of the Neva. As an erewhile traveller, for whom those spots had been full of interest from my youth up, I had already kept, albeit from a distance, a watchful eye on all that went on amidst the plains of the Yaxartes. I devoured alike the newspaper reports and the scanty notices which my fellow-pilgrims from Turkestan communicated to me through their westward journeying brethren. That I took a hearty interest in everything will surprise no one, little as the utterances of the English press and the writings of British Indian diplomatists during these occurrences claimed my full attention. To the prophecies of the Dervish neither the one party nor the other gave a thought. The note of satisfaction struck three years before was kept up without a break. People were no longer content with the bare assertion, that Russian progress in Central Asia was a thing to welcome, but tried their utmost to show convincing grounds for that assertion, in order to represent the success of the Muscovite arms as tending more and more profitably for English interests.

To solve this problem the more happily, to convince all thoughtful Englishmen the more unanswerably of the profit to be gained from Russian successes, the question was debated by a light which was sure to be equally welcome to all the different classes. The scientific world was informed by the learned President of the Royal Geographical Society touching the excellent service rendered to science at large by the trigonometrical, geographical, and geological societies of Russia. Russian voyages of discovery were exalted above everything; Russian scholars were deified; nay, it was only lately that even Vice-Admiral Butakoff was presented with the large gold medal for his discoveries on the Sea of Aral. Social Reformers, on the contrary, were taught to compare Tartar savagery with Russian civilisation. The picture which I myself drew of Central Asia was contrasted with the young Russia of to-day: the emancipation of slaves, the Russian endeavours after national enlightenment, the great change in manners, the mighty strides by which Russia was approaching England in civilised ideas, were all brought into the foreground; and in every thread of this tissue was expression given to the great usefulness of Russian supremacy in Asia. The trading world was shown the advantage which must accrue from safe means of communication, now that Russian arms are on the point of smoothing a way through the inhospitable steppes of Turkestan towards India. Some journals, indeed, were carried so far away by their zeal as to point out to the honest workmen of Birmingham, Sheffield, Manchester, &c., that only English wares and English capital would travel to and fro along the new Russian commercial road to Central Asia. Even the military class had a friendly word whispered into its ear. To the sons of Mars it was needful to represent a Russian invasion of India as a ridiculous bugbear. From every stand-point, moral, physical, strategical, was such an attempt proved to be an impossibility. How, indeed, could Russia overcome the enormous difficulties of those parched steppes that stretched week after week before her; how master the warlike Afghans, or win through the dreaded Khyber Pass? And even if she succeeded in that also, how roughly would she not be handled by the British Lion, who would lie waiting leisurely for her in his luxurious palankeen? Nay, even to the Church, that mightiest of English levers, should a lullaby be chanted forth. People hinted at a happy union between the Orthodox Church of Russia and that of England. Dr. Norman Macleod is an authority; and his cry, "The Greek Church is not yet lost," has aroused the hopes of many; and very learned church dignitaries have looked forward with blissful smiles to the moment when the three-fold Greek Cross shall rise from the Neva up to the proud dome of St. Paul's in London, for the kiss of brotherhood, and the two united churches shall become a powerful weapon against Papal ideas.

Independent pamphlets and thundering newspaper articles alternated on the field of this question with the expositions above-named. The warning voice of a small minority could not succeed in making head against the Optimists, against those apostles of the new political doctrine. Sir Henry Rawlinson, whose perfect conversance with the circumstances of that region no one can dispute, a man whose practical experience is at one with his theoretic insight, has here and there in the *Quarterly Review* pointed out the errors of such speculations in solidly written essays; and though, as doubting any ultimate design of Russia upon India, he protested against all actual interference, merely blaming the indifference above-mentioned; still his words passed unheeded of the multitude. I might well say to myself that where such an authority carries no weight, my present words could but travel a very short way. I was therefore slow to speak; and yet, as I had studied this momentous question in all its aspects, and examined it from many sides with impartial eyes, I deemed it possible to show, not only to the statesmen of England, but to those of all Europe, how fatally the Cabinet of St. James errs in its way of looking at the matter; and how this cherished indifference is not only hurtful to English interests, but becomes a deadly weapon wherewith Great Britain commits a suicide unheard of in history.

How it happens that I, who by race am neither English nor Russian, have taken so warm an interest in this matter, is mainly accounted for by the fact of my regarding the collision of these two Colossi in Asia less from the stand-point of their mutual rivalry, than from that of the interests of Europe at large. Whether England or Russia get the advantage, which of the two will become chief arbiter of the old world's destinies, can never be to us an indifferent matter; for widely as these two powers differ from each other in their character as channels of Western civilisation, not less widely do they diverge from one another in any future reckoning up of the issues of their struggle. A passing glance, on the one hand, at the Tartars, who have lived for two hundred years under Russian rule; on the other, at the millions of British subjects in India, might teach us a useful lesson from the past on this point. This, however, may be reserved for later investigation. For the present we will only affirm that the question of a rivalry between these two North European powers in Central Asia concerns not only Englishmen and Russians, but every European as well; nay, more, it deserves to be studied with interest by every thoughtful person of our century.*

1. RUSSIAN CONQUESTS IN CENTRAL ASIA DURING THE LAST THREE YEARS.

First of all we will recount the historical facts of the Russian war of conquest during the last three years. Instead of going into those details about the campaigns of Perovski, Tchernaieff, and Romanovski, which were recorded partly in Mitchell's book, "The Russians in Central Asia," partly in several solid treatises in the *Quarterly* and the *Edinburgh Review*, or into the slender notices which have trickled out into publicity from the Russian State-Cabinets, or those yet scantier notices which were revealed by highly-paid English spies in Central Asia, we would cast only a hurried glance at events, in order to acquaint the reader with the latest posture of Russian arms in Central Asia.

* Up to this moment the *Revue des Deux Mondes*, alone of all the Continental press, has brought out two special articles on Central Asia. The first, without any acknowledged leaning, points out the critical conditions of the approaching conflict; the second, imbued with a Russian spirit, keeps time to the song of the English optimists; for doing which I would not blame the writer, had he not cited several passages from my book as his own property.

So successfully had the Russian operations been started in Central Asia, that after a brilliant overthrow of the Kirghis, they entered first on the conquest of Khokand, in order to gain firm foothold in the three Khanats. In those eastern parts of the three oasis-countries of Turkestan the social order has always been relatively least, the religious culture weakest, and the antipathy to warlike enterprises most strong. These were accompanied by internal disorders, for while the Khodjas through their inroads into Chinese territory on the east of the Khanat were always encountering the risk of a collision with China, which in bygone centuries did sometimes ensue, the greedy Ameers of Bokhara from the west have continually laid the country waste with their wanton lust of conquest. Before the capture of Ak-Meshdjid the nearing columns of the mighty Russ on the north had but little place in the bazaar-talk of Namengan and Khokand. At the time of the miscarriage of Perovski's expedition Mehemed Ali Khan was seated on the throne. He was beloved and honoured, and the dazzled masses were much too wanting in ideas of conquest, to think seriously of self-defence against the threatening foe on the north, or of Conolly's projected alliance with Khiva. Not till after the death of Mehemed Ali ensued the fall of Ak-Meshdjid, the first serious wound in the Khanat's existence; and the Russian success was all the easier, because at that time their fighting powers were crippled, on one side by the fierce conflict between Kirghis and Kiptchaks in the interior of the Khanat, and by the first attempt of Veli-Khan-Töre against Kashgar on the other. The storming columns of the Russians against the Khokandian fastnesses on either shore of the Yaxartes leave no cause to complain of cowardice, although the thousands of Khokandian warriors mentioned in the Russian accounts seem to rest on an over-keen eyesight.

After the capture of the last-named place, or, to speak more correctly, after a systematic restoration of the chain of fortresses along the Yaxartes, on whose waters the steamers of the Aral flotilla could now move freely about, the Russian power advanced with strides as gigantic as those with which Khokand, through the continuous working of the causes above-mentioned, continually fell away. The line of forts offered not only security against Turkestan, but was also a powerful bulwark against the Kirghis, who, being at length surrounded on all sides, could not so easily raise into the saddle an *Ished*,* as the last anti-Russian chief styled himself during the Crimean War. Thenceforth the work of occupation was pursued by the court of St. Petersburg with its wonted energy; and not till both the army corps, which were operating from the Chinese frontier to the Issik-köl, from the Sea of Aral along the Yaxartes, had drawn together

---

* *Ished*, which the Russians wrongly pronounce *Iset*, is a usual contraction of "Eish Mehemmed," which signifies "Mohammed's delight."

southwards from the north-east and the north-west
at Aulia Ata, (*Holy Father*, an ancient place of pilgrimage,) did Russian diplomacy deem it necessary
to announce, in a despatch signed by Prince Gort-
shakoff on the 21st November, 1864, that the government of the Tzar had at length obtained its long-
cherished desire to remove the boundary line of its
possessions from the ill-defined region of the Sandy
Desert to the inhabited portion of Turkestan; that the
policy of aggression was now at an end, and that its
one single aim in the future would be to demonstrate
to the neighbouring Tartar states, with regard to their
independence, that Russia was far from being their
foe, or indulging in ideas of conquest, &c. &c.

That no Cabinet save the English placed any more
faith in such assurances than the Russian Minister
himself, it is easy enough to imagine. The tale of
ever-recurring conquests from vanquished states has
long been notorious. We have instances thereof in
every page of the world's history, in every age in
which some power has set about enlarging itself. Just
as the English are vainly apologising for Lord Dal-
housie's thirst for annexation, or absorption in India,
so are all Russian notes composed in a strain of overflowing politeness. It is only the natural course of
things; and the court of St. Petersburg was right,
could not indeed do otherwise, after setting up a
government in Turkestan, than follow the southern
course of the Yaxartes; and as the waste steppe

formed at the first no defensible frontier, neither could the thinly-peopled neighbourhood of Tchemkend and Hazret furnish a better one. There was need of a well-inhabited region, to provide against being dependent merely on the means of communication from Orenburg and Semipalatinsk. Therefore was Tashkend, rich and fertile Tashkend, doomed to incorporation in Russian territory.

It would be a profitless waste of time to quote as the main cause of the Russian occupation of the last-named town, on the 25th June, 1865, the moving history of the petition of the Tashkend merchants, of the numerous deputation that came beseechingly to the Russian camp, to obtain the shelter of the two-headed Eagle, whom the Central Asiatics call the *ajder*-kite, a bird not greatly beloved of yore. Tashkend, which from time immemorial, lived at feud with the masters of Khokand, was latterly very much enraged, because its darling Khudayar was twice driven from his throne. To endamage the dominant influence of the Khirgis by means of Russian supremacy, was for it a welcome idea; but it is not at all likely that the supremacy itself should have been generally desired.

Russia has absorbed Tashkend, because she deemed it indispensable as a firm base for further operations; not, however, with a view to erecting therewith a bulwark against possessions already secured. Still it was through Tashkend that the court of St. Petersburg had embroiled itself in hostilities with the Khanat of Bokhara. The Ameer, as we know, had earned for himself, through his campaign of 1863, the nominal right of suzerainty over the western part of Turkestan; and though after his departure everything fell back into the old rut of Kiptchak lawlessness and party warfare, he still thought to make good his right over all Khokand. He therefore wrote the commandant of the newly-conquered town a threatening letter, in which he summoned him to vacate the fortress. This, however, gave small concern to the Russian general; and, hearing that Colonel Struve, the famous astronomer, whom he had sent to Bokhara for a friendly settlement of the affair, had been forthwith taken prisoner, he burst forth on the 30th January, crossed the Yaxartes at Tashkend with fourteen companies of foot, six squadrons of Cossacks, and sixteen guns, with the purpose of going straight into Bokhara and punishing the Ameer for the violation of his envoy.

This design, however, miscarried. The Russians had to retire, but did so in perfect order; and though countless hosts of Bokharians swarmed round them on every side, yet their loss was too insignificant to accord with the bombastic tales of triumph which the Bokharians thereon trumpeted through all Islam, and which even found their way to us through the Levantine press. General Tchernaieff had excused himself on the plea that his hasty advance was intended merely to baffle the movements of secret English emissaries, who were striving with all possible zeal after an Anglo-Bokharian alliance, and were also the main cause of his envoy, Colonel Struve's imprisonment. In Petersburg, however, they could not pardon his military failure: he was displaced from his high command, and General Romanofski went out in his stead. The latter moved forward with slow but all the more cautious steps. On the 12th April a flock of fifteen thousand sheep, escorted by four thousand Bokharian horsemen, was made prize of; and a month afterwards there ensued, in the neighbourhood of Tchinaz, a fierce fight, called the battle of Irdshar, in which the Tartars were utterly beaten. On the 25th May fell the small fort of Nau; and afterwards Khodshend, the third town in the Khanat of Khokand, was taken by storm; but not without a hard fight, in which the Russians left on the field a hundred and thirty-three killed and wounded, the Tartars certainly ten times that number. The battle, however, was well worth the cost, for the fortifications of this place were better than those of Tashkend or of any other town in the Khanat. This was the second resting-point for the Russian arms on their march southward; and though the "Russian Invalid," in an official report concerning further projects, affirms that the conquest of that part of Bokhara which is severed from the rest of their possessions by the steppes could never become the goal of Russian operations, while for the present it would be entirely profitless, yet progress has already been made over Oratepe, through the small districts of Djam and Yamin, as far as Djissag; whilst everywhere important garrisons have been left behind.

What has happened in the Khanat of Khokand itself during this triumphal march of the Russians, is a point no less worthy of our attention. The inhabitants, consisting of nomads,—Œzbeg, and Tadjik or Sart,—were as much divided in their Russian likings and dislikes, as they were different from each other in race, condition, and pursuits. The warlike, powerful, and widely-courted Kiptchaks, being ancient foes of the oft-encroaching Bokharians, who wanted to force upon them the hated Khudayar· Khan, immediately sided with the Russians. Their friendship was for these latter an important acquisition; and the friendly movement must have already begun, when the north-eastern army-corps came in contact with them in its forward struggle from Issikköl; for if this had not been the case, the Russian advance on that line would certainly have been purchased at heavier cost.

The Œzbegs, as being *de jure* the dominant race, had defended themselves as well as they could; yet with their well-known lack of courage, firmness, and endurance, they had but small success; and when they began to reflect that Russian rule would probably be no worse a misfortune than the incessant war with Bokhara, or their internal disorders, they prepared to accommodate themselves to inevitable fate. Only a few angry Ishans and Mollahs maintained an unfounded dread of Bokhara; the descendants, for example, of Khodja Ahmed Yesevi in Hazreti-Turkestan, who, however, in all likelihood will soon go back to the bones of their sacred forefathers, as the Russians assuredly will not hinder them from collecting pious alms among their pilgrims. Moreover, to the wealthier merchants of Tashkend, to the Sarts and Tadjiks, and a small number of Persian slaves, the Russian occupation seemed welcome and advantageous; for whilst the former expected considerable profit from the admission of their native town into the Russian customs-circle, the latter hope to be rescued from their oppressed condition through the downfall of Œzbeg ascendancy. As we may see from the correspondence addressed by General Krishanofski to a Moscow journal, it was these very Sarts who gave the Russians most help. Their Aksakals, not those of the Œzbegs, were the first to accept office under the Russians. In public places they always appear by the side of the Russian officers, harangue the people, and while Russian churches were getting built, spread about a report that His Majesty, having been converted by a vision in the night to Islam, was on the point of making a pilgrimage to Hazreti-Turkestan. From the length of their commercial intercourse with Russia, many of the Tadjiks, especially the Tashkenders, are skilled in writing and speaking Russian; they serve as interpreters and middle-men, and as many of them reach the highest places in the *mehkeme* (courts of justice) and other posts, the main motive of their adherence is easy to apprehend.

So far has it fared with the main line of operations in the Khanat of Khokand. On adjacent points likewise, both eastern and western, has the work of transformation stealthily begun. From Chinese Tartary we learn, that ever since 1864 the Chinese garrisons have been expelled, and replaced by a national government. First came disorders among the Tunganis, presently followed by the deliverance of Khoten, Yarkand, Aksoo, and Kashgar; and although these disorders may have been caused at bottom by the traditional delight of the Khokandie Khodjas in free plundering, still many of us are positively assured that the court of St. Petersburg countenanced all those revolutionary movements; aye, and that the Kiptchaks, who are now masters of Kashgar, were helped to win it by Russian arms. Such is the usual prelude to Russian interference. For a time these independent towns are permitted to carry on feuds and warfare against each other; but it is easy to foresee that their enmity will come to appear dangerous to the peace of the yet distant Russian frontier; and if haply the court of Pekin be in no hurry to restore order, the Russians are very certain to forestal it on that point ere long. The English press comforts itself with remarking, that the insuperable barrier of the Kuen-Lun mountains renders further progress towards Kashmir impossible;

and that this Russian diversion is only for the good of Central-Asiatic trade. For the moment, however, we will put aside the discussion of this question, preferring to glance at that part of Central Asia which inclines westward from Khokand. Albeit engaged in war with Bokhara, Russia has hitherto made no attack on the real territory of that State, for Djissag is the lawful boundary between the former and Khokand. About this well-known seat of the struggle with Bokhara, there is only a diplomatic skirmish, which still goes on, under whose cover the revolution of Shehr-i-Sebz holds its ground. For, even if the Russian press denies for the thousandth time all interference, yet the appearance of the Aksakal of Shehr-i-Sebz in Tashkend cannot be regarded as unimportant. It is, at any rate, noticeable with reference to the Russian plans in Khiva. The settled portion of the Khanat proper has not yet been touched by Russian influence, and only in the north, since the destruction of the fortress of Khodja-Niyaz, on the Yaxartes, have some Cossack and Karakalpak hordes, skirting the eastern shore of the Sea of Aral, been converted into Russian subjects.

2. Russia's Future Policy.

Our sketch of Russian progress in Central Asia furnishes its own evidence of the way in which the policy of the court of St. Petersburg will follow out its purpose in the immediate future.

The most southern, therefore the most advanced, outposts rest on Djissag. This word, in Central Asiatic, means a hot, burning spot, and its position in the deep, cauldron-like valley of the Ak-Tau hills entirely justifies the name. Owing to its utterly unwholesome climate, and the great want of water, the population of this station on the way to Khokand is but very small; and that the Russians have selected it for a more abiding resting-place, I cannot believe, in spite of the aforenamed asseverations of the "Russian Invalid," and in spite of the contrary opinion of the learned writer of the article, Central Asia, in the "Quarterly Review." Not only is it an unhealthy and barely tenable post; but a lengthened stay here must also be acknowledged as most impolitic. The gentlemen on the banks of the Neva know well what Bokhara is in the eyes of all Central Asia, I might even say of all Mohamedans. They know that on the Zerefshan may be sought the special fount of religious ideas and modes of thought, not only for the mass of Central Asiatics, but for Indians, Afghans, Nogay Tartars, and other fanatics. In order to achieve a grand stroke, the Ameer, who styles himself Prince of of all true believers, must be made to recognise the supremacy of the white Tzar; the holy and honoured Bokhara, where the air exhales the aromatic fragrance of the Fatiha and readings from the Koran, must learn to reverence the might of the black unbelievers; and the crowd of crazy fanatics, of religious enthusiasts, must acknowledge that the influence of the saints who rest in her soil is not strong enough to blunt the point of the Russian bayonet. The fall of Bokhara will be a fearful example for the whole Islamite world; the dust of her ruins will penetrate the farthest distance, like a mighty warning-cry. For this must the court of St. Petersburg assuredly be striving, and ready to strive.

From this stand-point it is therefore most probable that the greatest attention will henceforth be paid to the line of operations from Tashkend, Khodjend, and Samarkand. The conquest of the whole Khanat of Khokand may also follow in time, for that offers no special difficulties; but the chief interest lies in the maintenance and security of the roads of communication, on which the advancing army, in concert with the strong garrisons in the now well-fortified Tashkend and the northern forts, as also with the governments of Orenburg and Semipalatinsk, will move along a road furnished with an unbroken line of wells. The Ameer may have recourse to all possible means of gaining the friendship of the Russians, in which he has hitherto failed; he may send to Constantinople as many Job's messengers as he will; he may despatch ever so many friendly invitations to the Durbar of the Indian Viceroy: but all that will do him no good. The town of Bokhara shall, with or without his leave, be governed by an Ispravnik; for the Russians dare not and cannot rest, until ancient Samarkand and Nakhsheb (Karshi), or the whole right bank of the Oxus has been absorbed into the gigantic possessions of the House of Romanoff. That this catastrophe, this last hour of Transoxanian independence, will not be brought about so easily as the heretofore successes in Central Asia, is manifest enough. Already in my mind's eye do I behold a frantic troop of Mollahs and Ishans, with thousands of students, roaming the Khanats with holy rage, in order to preach the Djihad (religious war) among the Afghans, Turkomans, Karakalpaks; and going through scenes of the deepest, the devoutest anguish, in order to draw down the curse of God on the foreign intruder. The death-struggle will be fierce but profitless. So far as I know the Khivans and the Afghans, I deem the notion of a general alliance with Bokhara to be quite impracticable; for, if such was their inclination, they should have formed one long ago. No egotism, no political combinations, but the greatest want of principle alone, an utter recklessness of the future, will keep them quiet until Hannibal stands before their gates. In vain shall we look for any effort after a general league, either in Central Asia, or even among any of the other Eastern nations. As the very warlike Afghans could play their part with a force of disciplined auxiliaries, so also might the Khan of Khiva join the Ameer's army with twenty to thirty thousand horse. Yet this is what neither the one nor the other will do. To unite them under one command might be possible for a Timur or a Djinghiz; and even then the smallest booty might stir up rancour and dissensions in their ranks. So, too, the hundred thousand well-mounted Turkomans, who inhabit the broad steppes from this side the Oxus to the Persian frontier, are utterly useless for the rescuing of the Holy City. Their Ishans, indeed, if summoned by their fellow-priests in noble Bokhara and by the Ameer, might do their very best to stir up the wild sons of the desert to a holy warfare: but I know the Turkomans too well not to be sure that they will take part in the *Djihad* only so long as the Ameer can offer them good pay and the prospect of yet richer booty; and as they sometimes owned in Afghan-Persian offices, it is most likely that the Russian imperialists will soon turn them into excellent brothers-in-arms of the Cossacks. Enthusiasm for the creed of the Prophet existed, if I remember rightly, only for the first hundred, indeed I might say only for the first fifty years. What Islam afterwards accomplished in Anatolia, in the empire of Constantine, in the islands of the Mediterranean, in Hungary, and in Germany, was due to the impulse of a wild daring in quest of booty and treasures, and a hankering after adventures. Where these leading incentives failed, there was a failure in zeal; and I repeat that, although the struggle will be a stern one, the speedy triumph of Russian arms in Bokhara is open to not the slightest doubt.

With the fall of the mightiest and most influential part of Turkestan, will Khokand, of her own accord, exchange a protection for the manifest sovereignty of the white Tzar. Khiva however, undaunted by the example, will, to all seeming, take up the struggle nevertheless. The conquest of Kharezm, moreover, though easier than that of Khokand, is connected with remarkable difficulties. With the exception of two towns, whose inhabitants are better known through their commercial relations with Russia, the Œsbeg population of this Khanat abhor the name of Russian. In courage, they stand much higher than the men of Khokand and Bokhara, and, protected by the formation of their native land, will cause much trouble to the Russian troops from the way of fighting peculiar to the Turkoman race. As for the view upheld by many geographers and travellers, that the Oxus will form the main road of the expedition, I am bound to meet it with the same denial as before. That river, on account of its great irregularity and the fluid sea of sand borne down upon its waves, is hard of passage for small vessels, not to speak of ships of war. Not a year passes without its changing its bed several miles in the shifting ground of the steppes; and if the Russians were not quite convinced of this circumstance, the small steamers of the Aral-Sea flotilla, built as they were for river navigation, would have begun forcing their way inland by the Oxus, instead of the Yaxartes. For although the smaller forts, such as Kungrad, Kiptchak, and Maugit, which were built on the fortified heights by the left bank of the river, might do harm to a flotilla passing near; yet, owing to the sad state of the Khivan artillery, they are hardly worth considering. Attempts to pass up the river, from its mouths to Kungrad, where the stream is deepest and most regular, have already been tried; still, the fact of their remaining merely attempts, clearly shows that the navigation of the Deryai Amus (Oxus), if not altogether impossible, is a hard problem nevertheless.

These, however, are but secondary drawbacks, and in Khiva, as in Bokhara, the white Tzar will be raised aloft upon the white carpet of the Kharezmian princes, if not through the grey-beards of the Tshagatay race, at any rate by his own bayonets and rifled guns.

The conquest of the whole right bank of the Ganges once assured to them, the strip of land from Issikköl to the Sea of Aral once come into full possession of the Russians, and well provided with excellent victualling-stores, then will the game of diplomacy have begun in Afghanistan also. Among the Afghans the court of St. Petersburg will not intervene so suddenly with arms in hand; not because England's miscarriage in 1839 has made it cautious, but because such a procedure is by no means customary with the Russians. That, moreover, would be partly superfluous, partly beyond the mark, amidst the now proverbial disunion of Dost Mohammed's successors. Where brother rages against brother in deadliest feud, where intrigues caused by greed and vanity are ever in full swing; there the secret agent, the kind word, a few friendly lines of writing, are much more profitable than a sudden assault with the armed hand. Hitherto, in his brother-strife against Shere-Ali-Khan, Abdurrahman-Khan has in no way entangled himself with Russian agents, although he sought to frighten the English moonshee (agent), by bringing some such conception to his notice. That he was greatly inclined to such a step I have not the slightest doubt; but as yet the Russians have given him no encouragement to take it. For if the Afghan opponents of Shere-Ali-Khan, the Ameer accredited by England, had received but the faintest wink from the Neva, they would never have coquetted with Sir John Lawrence in Calcutta. Not only chiefs and princes, but every Afghan warrior, nay, every shepherd on the Hilmund, puts his trust in the idea of Russian trade; and I have a hundred times over convinced myself how easily, indeed how gladly, these people would embrace a Russian alliance against the masters of Peshawar. Whether the fruits of such a friendship would be wholesome, and conduce to the interests of Afghanistan, no one takes into question. The Afghans, like all Asiatics, look only to the interests of the moment, see only the harm which Afghans have suffered in Kashmere and Sindh through English ascendancy, have a lively remembrance of the last sojourn of the red-jackets in Kabul and Kandahar; and though every one knows that the Kaffirs of Moscow are very little better than the Feringhies, still, from an impulse of revenge, they all desire and will prefer an alliance with the North to a good understanding with England.

Hence it is but a friendly regard, it is only a compact upheld not by treaties, but by a strong force on the Oxus, which the Russians can aim at for some time to come.

The same kind of relation must be their object in Persia. Here too, for the last ten years, has the court of St. Petersburg been playing a lucky game. Since the appearance of Russian envoys at the splendid court of the Sofies, in the time of Khardin, until now, Russian influence has gone through many phases. At first scorned and disregarded, the Russians have risen into the strongest and most dangerous opponent of Iran. Whilst, in the days of Napoleon I., England and France, to the profit and partial aggrandisement of the Shah, vied with each other in turning to account their influence at the court of Teheran, Russia, as "inter duos certantes tertius gaudens," quietly smoothed her way to the conquest of the countries beyond the Caucasus, to the profitable treaties of Gulistan and Turkmanshay. And while the same Western Powers persevered in that policy, the Colossus of the North took up such a position on the Caucasus as well as the Caspian Sea, that its shadow stretched not only over the northern rim of Iran, but far also into the country. At the time of Sir Henry Rawlinson's embassy, English influence was near being in the ascendant; but since then it has been continually sinking; for however lavish of gold and greetings the English policy might be in Malcolm's days, it showed itself just as cold and indifferent from the time of Mac Neil downwards. Both the Shah and his ministers seem urged on by necessity to accept the Russians as their Mentor. It is not from any conviction of a happier future that they have flung away from the fatherly embraces of the British Lion into the arms of the Northern Bear; and the Shah must dance for good or ill to the song which the latter growls out before him.

If now, in accordance with the aforeshown position of the Russian power and policy in Central Asia, we cast a glance on the frontier, stretching for 13,000 versts wide, from the Japanese Sea to the Circassian shore of the Black Sea, where Russia is always in contact with so many peoples of different origin and different religion, over whose future her aggressive policy hangs like the doomful sword of a Damocles; we shall soon be driven to observe that, although the southern outposts in Asia are on the Araxes, yet the only point where, in their further advance, they impinge on a European power is to be found in Central Asia. Separated twenty years ago from British India's northern frontier by the great horde of the Khirgis and the Khanats, the space at this moment left between Djissag and Peshawar, although the difficult road over the Hindu-Kush lies midway, amounts to no more than fifteen days' journey, and in reckoning by miles to hardly a hundred and twenty geographical miles. For an army the road, though difficult, is not insuperable, while it should be tolerably easy for the development of political influence; and for all England's readiness to see a mighty bulwark for her frontier in the snow-crowned peaks of the Hindu-Kush, she forgets the ease with which a Russian propaganda from the banks of the Oxus can smooth a way hence towards the north of Sindh. From the moment, indeed, when the Russian flag waves in Karshi, Kerki, and Tchardshuy, may England regard this power as her nearest neighbour.

3. Russia's Views on India; and English Optimists.

Has Russia any serious views, then, on British India? Will she attack the British Lion in his rich possessions? Does her ambition really reach so far, that she would wield her mighty sceptre over the whole continent of Asia, from the icy shores of the Arctic Sea to Cape Comorin? These are questions of needful interest, not to Englishmen only, but to all Europeans. On the bank of the Thames as well as in Calcutta, statesmen have latterly answered them in the negative; for their organs, official and unofficial, regard the utmost danger of the meeting as a neighbourhood of frontiers, and not an aggression; a neighbourhood which, so far from imperilling English interests, will be altogether to their advantage. These gentlemen are sadly at fault, for the spirit of Russia's traditional policy,—her steadfast clinging to the schemes before indicated, the unbounded ambition of the House of Romanoff, the immense accumulation of means at their disposal for the accomplishment of their designs,—place in surer prospect the fulfilment of any aim on which they have once bent their gaze. Russia wants India first of all in order to set so rich a pearl in the splendid diamond of her Asiatic possessions; a pearl, for whose attainment she has so long, at so heavy a cost, been levelling the way through the most barren steppes in the world; next, in order to lend the greatest possible force to her influence over the whole world of Islam (whose greatest and most dangerous foe she has now become), because the masters of India have reached, in Mohamedan eyes, the non-plus-ultra of might and greatness; and lastly, by taming the British Lion on the other side the Hindu-Kush, to work out with greater ease her designs on the Bosphorus, in the Mediterranean, indeed all over Europe; since no one can now doubt that the Eastern question may be solved more easily beyond the Hindu-Kush than on the Bosphorus: for if, at the time of the Crimean War, when Nana Sahib's brother was fêted at Sevastopol, Russia had held her present position on the Yaxartes, the plans of Tzar Nicholas on Constantinople would not have been so easily buried under the ruins of the Malakhoff.

These far-reaching designs may not, perhaps, be the work of the next years, nor even of the Government of the peaceful and well-disposed Alexander; yet who can assure us that after him no Nicholas, or no yet sterner nature than his, may succeed to the throne, who will thwart the desire of a Taimur or a Nadir to come forth as a thoroughly Asiatic conqueror of the world? What a Russian autocrat can do in the present condition of Russia, in the present social position of his subjects, who, moreover, will long continue such, every one knows, and the statesmen of England best of all. It is, therefore, the more remarkable, that these gentlemen should think to put the said eventualities so easily aside, and to contest the question of a Russian invasion of India with arguments so very shallow. They usually bring forward the unpassable glaciers of Hindu-Kush and the Himalayas, and the swarms of hostile nomads which would hem in a force advancing from the north on its way southward. They console themselves with the great distance, which would bring an invading army to the Indian frontier tired and exhausted, while the English troops lying by, ready to strike at their ease, and strong in military zeal and training, awaited the shock of war with greediness. But do these gentlemen believe that Russia, in the event of her really cherishing these sort of views, would dispatch her invading armies thitherwards direct from Petersburg, Moscow, or Archangel? What end is served by the South-Siberian forts? What by Tashkend, Khodshend, and still more afterwards, by Bokhara and Samarkand? What, too, by the Persian-Afghan alliance? What did the Cossacks and the

Russian troops of the line do in Gunib, and in the rugged hills of Circassia? Were they exhausted when they reached their journey's end? And the latter station is not so much farther from the capital on the Neva, than Peshawar is from the cities just named! And why are we to assume that Russia would choose only the difficult road through Balkh to Kabul, and thence through the Khyber Pass, and none other? Without mentioning that this could have been so fatal to the English army of 1839, which fled in affright and disorder, for the march thither cost no especial sacrifices; the road through Herat and Kandahar, the proper caravan-course to India through the Bolan Pass, is far more convenient. The latter, fifty-four or five English miles in length, did indeed cost the Bengal corps of the army of the Indus many days' toil; and yet we read in a trustworthy English author that the passage of 24-pounder howitzers and 18-pounder guns caused no particular trouble. Or why should the Russians not force the Gomul or the Gulari Pass, called also the middle road from Hindostan to Khorassan, which, according to Burnes, serves the Lohani Afghans as their main road of communication, and offers no especial difficulties?

It is too hard, indeed, to scatter the sanguine views of the English optimists with regard to the strength of their fancied bulwarks. The way through Kabul would have to be taken only in case of necessity; for the chief points by which Russia could quite easily approach the Indian frontiers are Djhissag and Astrabad; from the former in a southerly, from the latter in an easterly direction. Both roads have often led armies, time out of mind, to the goal of their desires; for both, though bordered by large deserts, pass through well-peopled, even fertile districts, which can support many thousands of marching men with ease.

Indeed, even the chances of an eventual war are greatly over-estimated by the English. True, that their present army in India, numbering 70,000 picked British troops besides the strong contingent of sepoys, is not to be compared with any of their former fighting forces in those regions. To throw as strong a muster across Afghanistan into the Punjaub, would certainly cost Russia some trouble. Still we must not forget how stout a support an invading army would find in a Persian-Afghan alliance, and in the great discontent which prevails in the Punjaub, in Kashmir, in Bhotan, and among the fanatic Mohamedans of India. The ever-broadening network of Indian railways may do much to hasten and promote a concentration; but the fountain-head of military support for India being on the Thames or the islands of the Mediterranean, is not much nearer than that of the Russians, especially if we consider that more than three hundred vessels sailing down the Volga make the transport to the southern shore of the Caspian Sea considerably easier. By this road may a large army be brought in a short time to Herat and Kandahar through the populous part of northern Persia; on the one hand through Astrabad, Bujnurd, and Kabushan; on the other, by the railway as yet only projected to Eneshed. This railroad the Tzar wants to build for the relief of the pilgrimage to the tomb of Imam Rizah; yet through all the Russian promises of subsidies there gleam forth other and non-religious plans. Or would people in England, besides the no longer doubtful possibility of a Russian design upon India, measure the political constellations which the said power has called into being on her behalf, in the field of European diplomacy? The Russian-French alliance of a Napoleon I. and an Alexander I., which left noticeable traces in Teheran, would now be much easier to enter on than before, owing to the dominant influence of France in Egypt and Syria, through the commencement of the Suez Canal. And these things apart, will not the ever-increasing *entente cordiale* between Washington and St. Petersburg prove of signal advantage for Russia's purposes? People scoff at the way in which the Yankee cap entwines itself with the Russian knout; and yet the banquets on the Neva, at which American brotherhood was vigorously toasted, the journey of the Tzarovitch to New York, the mighty show made by America in China and Japan, where she threatens to turn the calm face of ocean into an American lake;—do not these things furnish ample reason for discerning in the alliance between Russia and America symptoms of the greatest danger for English interests? Indeed, when the decisive moment comes for acting, Russia will be able to avail herself of many ways and many means, which, however little worthy of notice they may seem to English statesmen, will be carefully pre-arranged without any noise.

Nevertheless, we are willing to allow that the actual shock will follow only in some very distant future. Gladly, too, will we bear to be pointed at as a false prophet. But how is it that English statesmen will proclaim as harmless the more and more manifest advance of their northern rival; how disguise and palliate the mischievous menace of that rival's aims?

The body of English politicians friendly to Russia is wont, whenever this question comes up for discussion, to reply that the neighbourhood of a well-ordered State is more acceptable to them, than several wild nomad tribes living in anarchy and plunder. An Englishman once asked me, whether I would not prefer to sit beside an elegantly-dressed fine gentleman, instead of a dirty and uncouth boor. People may wish success with all their might to a Muscovite neighbour; yet to me it is not at all clear, why those gentlemen should wish for the neighbourhood of a sly and powerful adversary in the room of an unpolished but essentially-powerless foe. What happened once in America, in the north of Africa, and even on Indian ground, between rising England on the one hand, and waning Holland and Portugal on the other, has often been and will yet often be repeated in the pages of history. As in ordinary life two strong, selfish individuals, will but rarely thrive in one same path; so does the same impossibility exist in the case of two States;—a fact, of which the long war between France and England for the superiority in India furnishes the best proof. Even if she followed the best aims, how could Russia, backed as she is by the gigantic power of the whole Asiatic continent;—she, whose policy for the last hundred years, has led her through desert regions with a perseverance so great, at a cost so lavish,—refuse a hearing at once to her own designs and to the insinuations of her abettors? Will she have sufficient self-control to forbear from profiting by the happy occasion which plays into her hands the Mohamedan population of India, more than thirty millions strong? The last-named, being the most fanatical of all who profess Islam, are filled with unspeakable hatred of the British rule. Their religious zeal, fostered on one side by Bokhara, on the other by the Wahabies, goes so far, that, in order to drain the cup of martyrdom, they often murder a British officer walking harmlessly about the bazaar, and even give themselves up to the headsman's axe.* In India, where religious enthusiasm has ever found a most fruitful soil, Islam has revealed itself in the oddest forms. The brotherhoods introduced in the days of the Taimurides, are there more powerful and important than elsewhere; and not Scoat alone, but every place has an 'Akhond of its own to show, whose summons to a crusade would be followed

* Query—Hangman's halter? (Trans.)

by thousands. In spite of the manifold blessings which English rule has secured to the Mohamedans, it is they alone who form the nest of revolutions; they alone who gave most support to the rebellion in its last disorders; they alone who take chief delight in conspiring for a Russian occupation, and proclaim in all directions the advantages of Muscovite rule.

Should we not also take this occasion to think of the Armenians, who, scattered through Persia and India, form single links of the chain wherewith the court of St. Petersburg conducts the electric stream of its influence from the Neva to the Ganges; aye, even to the shores of Java and Sumatra? The hard-working, wealthy Armenians, who in their religious sentiments are inclined to be more catholic than the Papist, more Russian, more orthodox than the Tzar himself, will assuredly not recommend the Protestant church and Protestant power to the natives of India, to the injury of supremely Christian Russia. How many zealous subjects of British rule in Calcutta, Bombay, and Madras, are not enrolled at Petersburg as yet more zealous promoters of Russian interests! Every member of this church in Asia is to be regarded as a secret agent of Muscovite policy; and if the moment came for a decision, the English would be amazed to see what kind of chrysalis emerged from this religious, moral, free and industrious people.

How, then, can England look on with indifference, to say nothing of her desire to have as neighbour a great and certainly unfriendly power, in a land where such inflammable elements are to be found? Trade will spring up, I hear from all sides; yet, to all seeming, the prospect of the commercial advantages, which British statesmen behold in Russia's oncoming, and in the removal of anarchical conditions in Central Asia, rests rather on a pretended hope than on true conviction. Is it not strange, that a people, so practical in its ways of thinking as the English, should for one moment entertain the hope that some profit would arise for England out of the plans which Russia has followed up for years with toil, and expense, and self-sacrifice; that English goods will get the upper hand in the markets of Central Asia, as soon as they have passed under the Russian rule? Henry Davies, in his commercial report, may point to the considerable figures which the export trade through Peshawar, Karachie, and Ladak, to Central Asia, has to show; and yet he must allow that this would be ten times larger, were it supported by English influence beyond the frontier of northern India. And in the same proportion will it diminish, in which the Russian eagle spreads out his wings over those regions. To Lord William Hay's plan for laying down a commercial road through Ladak, Yarkend, Issiköl, and Semipalatinsk, the Petersburg cabinet has given its seeming assent; yet, in fact, nobody wanted to support the plan, nor will it occur to any Russian statesman to carry it out. The Chinese are far superior not only to the Russians, but even to the English, in mercantile zeal; and yet they trade along the great commercial road from Pekin through South Siberia only to Maimatshin, while from Kiachta the Chinese exports are forwarded, mainly through Russian hands, to Petersburg and Europe. And how fared the Italian silk merchants, who, under Russian protection, found their way to Bokhara, but were there arrested and robbed of their goods and possessions? One of them, Gavazzi, lets us feel very forcibly in his report, that he could never place full faith in Russian letters commendatory, in spite of all after applications from St. Petersburg. The products of English manufacturing towns are wont to drive Russian manufactures out of every market. The merchants of Khiva and Bokhara still carry with them Russian articles from Nijni-Novgorod and Orenburg, which they sell to Central Asiatics under the name of *Ingilis mali*, or English wares; such being always in most demand among the latter. People in England forget that plain dealing will for some time yet be wanting to Russian policy, and that, on the commercial roads which its arms have opened out, it will throw, of a certainty, in the way of foreign interests, obstacles of a like nature, if not indeed the same, as one now meets with from Afghan rapacity, from Œzbeg lawlessness, on the commercial roads to the Oxus. In the year 1864-5 America alone disposed of more than fifteen million pounds' worth of linen and cotton goods, which was naturally possible only under the free institutions of England. Do the gentlemen in Calcutta expect any similar dealings with the Russians?

Ephemeral, alas! are the calculations formed by people in England on behalf of Russia's future policy with reference to India. Just as the fabric of security which the statesmen of Downing Street are now building within their brains, can soon be shattered to the ground; so the arguments for a future *entente cordiale* are but slight indeed. Instead of a bootless refutation, we would rather point out former mistakes, would rather touch on the means by which the danger of a direct collision,—that most perilous of all games for English interests,—may yet be avoided.

4. Russian Gains and the Disadvantages of English Policy.

In order thoroughly to understand the misconceptions of English politicians concerning their Russian rivals, it is necessary for us to consider all the advantages which the latter always enjoyed, and still enjoy, on the field of action. In Europe, we are wont to look with amazement on Russia's gigantic empire in Asia; and yet nobody thinks of the means which have rendered essential service towards the acquisition of it. The Russians are Asiatics, not so much in consequence of their descent as of their geographical position and their social relations; and it is only because with the Asiatic *laisser-aller* they combine the steadfastness and resolution of Europeans, that they have mostly been a match for the Asiatic races. In their contact with Chinese, Tartars, Persians, Circassians and Turks, they have always shown themselves as Chinese, Tartar, Persian, and so forth, according to circumstances. An English historian says, pretty correctly, if not without ill-will, that the Russians moved forward like a tiger. "At first, creeping cautiously and gliding stealthily through the dust, until the favourable moment admits of its taking the fatal spring. With smiles of peace and friendship, with soft smooth words on their emissaries' part, have they often averted every fear, every precaution, until the certain success of their schemes made all fears profitless, and baffled every precaution. Blind, therefore, and ill-advised must every government be, which can go to sleep over Russian advances towards its frontiers, be those never so slow, or the interval between the conqueror and the goal of his endeavours be never so great!" As Asiatics, they are wont to hold out less rudely against their neighbours in manners, customs, and modes of thought, than the English, for whom, on account of their higher culture, such a renunciation would be a great sacrifice, incompatible with their efforts after civilisation. They seldom offend against the national ways of thinking, and easily conform to them when their interests require it. In England the Government has hitherto disdained to place itself in direct correspondence with the Ameer of Bokhara, for what the chief city in Zarif-Khan obtained up to this date from the British cabinet was always enjoyed through the Governor-General of India. In Russia they think differently; and even the haughty Nicholas, that stern autocrat, who long shrank from calling the French emperor "mon frère," behaves, in in presence of the Tartar princes of Central Asia, not as Emperor of all the Russias, but as a Khan on the Neva. As a result of such procedure, we find the nations all along the Russian frontier of Asia, whether nomad or settled, Boodhist or Mohamedan, in such a state of intimacy at this moment, if not of actual friendship, with the Russians, as happens nowhere else in the foreign possessions of a European power.

These advantages, however, of Asiatic modes of thought, which might properly be specified as excessive slyness and craftiness, are, even in political intercourse, far more profitable than the open and upright language employed on principle by Englishmen from of old. It is only Great Britain's foes in Europe, only the enviers of her power, who can find fault with the English in India; and yet whoever is sufficiently informed as to their political dealings with native princes and neighbours on the border, whoever is thoroughly conversant with Asiatic character, will, in the utter absence of this very defect, discover the one great fault of English statesmen.

From the largest province on the Amoor, to the smallest of the possessions latest won by Russia on Asiatic ground, may we always find one same procedure of intrigues and wiles,—a scattering of the seeds of discord, bribery and corruption, through the vilest means,—all serving as forerunners of invasion. Men come first through commercial relations in contact with foreign elements; then the slightest differences come to be readily employed as *casus belli*; failing these, the ground will be undermined by emissaries, the chiefs bribed by presents, or bemuddled with lavish draughts of vodki (Russian brandy), and drawn on into the dangerous magic circle. A well-founded cause of war and of invasion would nowhere be easy to discover; and certainly the gigantic empire of the House of Romanoff has been builded up more through the wiles of its Asiatic statesmen than by the might of its arms. Moreover, in consequence of the qualities lately named, Russia is more conversant with the relations of Asiatic peoples, far better informed of all that is passing in the border-states, than the English and other Europeans. To the great watchfulness of her emissaries, to the unwearied zeal of her diplomatists, is she indebted for the fact that her cabinet is often more quickly and fully informed of the most private doings of her neighbours, than the particular native government itself. Passing over the fact that, in Petersburg, a company of the cleverest men can make money out of their experiences through the different parts of Asia, there is here and there a Kirghis, a Buryat, a Circassian, or a Mongol, who, after being trained in Russian learning and modes of thought, becomes a most serviceable tool against the wholly or half-subjected land of his birth.

In England we meet everywhere with the sharpest contrasts. Whoever is aware of the great ignorance of public opinion in England about events in India, about the relations between those great possessions and the neighbouring States; whoever in the course of a year has noted down those absurd and ridiculous news, those telegraphic despatches in the English papers, which reach Europe and England through Bombay and Calcutta; whoever is aware of the very small number of English statesmen who are so carefully informed on Asiatic relations, that they can pass a sound judgement on questions of Eastern policy;—such a one must surely be amazed at the way in which Great Britain founded her foreign possessions, to say nothing of her being able to hold them until now.

And just as even those among the English public who have lived any time in India have kept aloof from the natives, in accordance with their national character, and are but seldom conversant with their language and manners,—so, too, can the English Government entrust to naturalized Levantines, and not to Englishmen, the Dragomanate, that necessary organ of mutual intercourse, in such important embassies as that, for instance, of Constantinople. While Russia, France and Austria, have long had Oriental academies for diplomatic beginners; in England, with her rich dower of colleges, schools, and universities, no one has ever thought of such an institution. And so again in the legislative body as well as in the ministry, where the smallest questions often have a special advocate, there are but very few men competent to discuss the important relations in Asia; and even these, on account of the prevailing nepotism, are but seldom allowed to turn their experiences to account.

This indifference must surprise all foreigners. Still more amazed will they be to hear men of the liberal party say: "What does Asia concern us; what the swarm of barbarous races that cause us more trouble than profit; what the wealth of India, whose income has long ceased to cover her expenditure, to say nothing about the costs of the conquest?" I have often heard remarks of this kind from the most famous leaders of this party. The sincerity of their confession defies questioning; and yet they have always left me without an answer, when I have asked them how they would make up for the loss of that political influence which springs from a great colonial empire. People seem wholly to forget that a large number of young Englishmen, of all ranks, are pursuing military and political careers in India; they seem to be unaware how many sons of clergymen and officers, to whom no sphere of action offers itself within their island home, earn wealth in lucrative offices on the Ganges and the Indus, with the view of spending at home in a calm old age the outcome of their earlier years. They seem to leave entirely out of their reckoning the enormous number of merchants dwelling in their great Asiatic dominions amidst the most extensive commercial interests, through whose hands English capital multiplies by millions. Those liberals are very short-sighted, who deem the possession of such a colony as India an indifferent or superfluous matter. That they should wish to see the greatness of their fatherland founded on the flourishing condition of inland manufactures, and not on their dominion over foreign peoples, can no longer be regarded as a view generally valid in England, now that more than sixty millions pounds sterling are laid out in Indian railway undertakings alone; for that neither manufacturing industry nor the enterprising spirit of English merchants can succeed, to any great extent, without the supporting hand of English rule, is amply shown by the circumstances of British trade in Algiers, Central Asia, and other non-British territories.

It is faulty views like these which neutralise all the advantages of English individualism in the presence of Russian policy, which always acts with steadfast consistency. To these errors may be ascribed the fact that Russia, having grown up into a powerful rival in a space of time incredibly short, is treading so close on the Achilles-heel of Great Britain. With the position she holds on the Aral and the Caspian Seas, after conquering the whole of the Caucasus, after her enormous successes in Central Asia, it would now be useless to try and force back that giant power. What might with no great trouble have been attained twenty years ago, it is now far too late to attempt; but if England would avoid the usual lot of commercial states,—the doom of Carthage, Venice, Genoa, Holland, and Portugal,—there is but one way left to her: a policy of stern watchfulness, a swift grasp of the measures still at her command.

5. Advice to England for the Purpose of Averting the Danger.

To think of moving out in open hostility to the growing power of Russia, were now, on England's part, just as great an error as the strange inaction she has displayed for the last twenty-five years amidst all the occurrences beyond the Hindu-Kush. Russia will establish herself on the right bank of the Oxus, will absorb the three Khanats, and perhaps Chinese Tartary, will make everything Œzbeg to acknowledge her supremacy. That can no longer be prevented; but thus far and no farther should Englishmen allow their rivals to advance.

All that lies between the Oxus and the Indus should remain neutral territory. Through her physical conformation, through the warlike character of her inhabitants, and specially through their great aptitude for diplomacy, Afghanistan would be altogether suited to form a military and political barrier against any possible collision between the two giants. That country would cost the conqueror, coming whether from North or South, a tenfold harder struggle than did the Caucasus. Besides, the possession would not for a long while make good the material advantage of an expensive war; and although the continual disorders that prevail in the mountain-home of the Afghans may be of no advantage to either neighbour, still the danger is not so great as to justify any schemes of conquest on one side or the other.

How, then, in case Russia continues her policy of aggression, may England secure the neutrality of Afghanistan? What must she do to set up with her influence there a solid barrier, without coming forward as a conqueror?

That is the work of a skilled diplomatic intercourse, the work of an uninterrupted alliance, carried on by agents, who, acquainted with the Afghan character, and eschewing English modes of thought, can conduct themselves as Asiatics.

The same fault which Lord Auckland committed in 1839, by his active interference in Afghan affairs, that fault and one far greater still did his successors prove guilty of, through their utter withdrawal from the scene, through their strange indifference in respect of the concerns of the neighbouring State. The English resemble a child which, after having once burnt itself at a fire, will not for a long time venture to draw near its warmth. The catastrophe of the Afghan campaign, the thirty millions sterling in costs, dwell even now, after a quarter of a century, with such fearful vividness in the eyes of every Briton, that he trembles at the very thought of political influence beyond the Hindu-Kush. Have we not here two sharply-opposed extremes? First, armed to the teeth in support of the interests of a prince so little loved as Shah Sujah; and then, after the annexation of the Punjab, scarce willing to give one more thought to Kabul! And why should the frontier above Peshawar be so dangerous a barrier for every Englishman and European? If several thousands of Kakeries, Lohanies, Gilzies, and Yusufzies, yearly pass over the northern frontier of Hindostan,—some for mercantile purposes, others to graze their flocks,—why should British travellers not be allowed to venture over the Hindu-Kush, let alone a few hours' journey beyond Peshawar? Afghan merchants drive a flourishing trade with Mooltan, Delhi, Lahore: why, from the English side, may not one mercantile firm or another betake itself for the same end to Kabul?

In truth, this state of things has always astonished me; the more so, when I heard that the officer whom Sir John Lawrence sent to Kabul to offer welcome to Shere Ali Khan had to be always escorted there by a strong detachment of troops, to guard himself from the rage of a fanatic population. This is surely a mode of proceeding at once wrong and ridiculous, for giving Asiatics a lesson in European magnanimity and European love of justice. England, who has long dealt with the Asiatics after this fashion, resembles a person trying with all his might to make a blind man comprehend the beauty of one of Raphael's cartoons. In this respect Russia is far more practical. She knows that such proofs of magnanimity and humanity are only ridiculed by the Orientals; that, so far from taking the example to themselves, they misuse those proofs for their own special ends; and, instead of wasting moral preachings on them, England would act shrewdly by helping herself to the same weapons, and treating Orientals in Oriental fashion.

At the time when the martyrs Conolly and Stoddart were pining in cruel imprisonment, out of which they were afterwards delivered only by the headsman's axe, there happened to be in British territory a number of Bokharians, Khokandies, and other Central Asiatics, by whose arrest the lot of the English officers might have been alleviated, and their deliverance from death assured. In such cases Russia is wont to clear herself from the dilemma by the law of retaliation. England acts differently. She would play the high-minded part; and what has she gained by it? When I was in Bokhara, I heard how this very act of British generosity had missed its mark. England, said the Bokharians, dares not awaken the wrath of the Ameer of Bokhara: her weakness commands this moderation.

Do the gentlemen in Calcutta imagine that the Afghans think otherwise? No; and they likewise say: protected by the might and greatness of Islam, our indigo and spice merchants, our camel-hirers, can venture unharmed on British ground; whilst not one infidel soul dares show himself among us.

The same unpardonable weakness did the Viceroy

of India show in 1857, when he was sent by Lord Canning to Peshawar to conclude, in conjunction with Edwardes, an offensive and defensive alliance against Persia with the then reigning Dost Mohamed Khan. At that time the Afghans were hard pressed; they wanted arms and money: the grey-haired Barukzie chief, attended by his sons, betrayed this fact in every word; and yet his demands were fulfilled in every point, without his yielding in the least to any of England's leading claims. Four thousand stand of arms, with bayonets, sabres, pouches, and twelve lakhs of rupees a year, were promised him, so long as England was at war with Persia. Of this large sum they received, even after the conclusion of peace at Paris, a considerable instalment; and yet the chief end of the negotiations at Kabul and Kandahar—the appointment of a permanent English representative—was not attained. Dost Mohamed Khan avowed, as Kaye tells us in his " History of the Sepoy War," that he would not take on himself the responsibility of such a step; that he could not protect English agents against Afghan fanaticism; that every step of theirs might compromise, &c., &c. I cannot comprehend how John Lawrence, one of the few men acquainted with Eastern character, could yield to the endearments of the grey Afghan wolf,—how he could believe those false apprehensions. If even Dost Mahomed could say that an English mission might tarry in peace at Kandahar, why could it not fare as well in Kabul? The British commissioners were greatly in the wrong if they doubted even for a moment the supreme power of the Afghan ruler. With a very little more persistency, the English, who then appeared as helpers in need, might have obtained not two but several posts of embassy. The Afghans would soon have grown used to their presence, and the diplomatic alliance, once made easy, would have been maintained unbroken.

In a semi-official article, which appeared in the *Edinburgh Review* for January, 1867, Sir John Lawrence now strives to show how hard and vain it is to enter into diplomatic intercourse with neighbours so wild and turbulent as those who surround India on all sides. Still, I cannot understand why the Viceroy should not take example from Russia, who, with the same elements on her frontier, sends envoy after envoy, knows how to obtain for them respect and safety, and so keeps moving forward to her wished-for goal. Why does not England pursue, in this case, the same policy which she once began in China, Japan, and other Asiatic countries? It seems to me that people are less convinced of the difficulty of carrying out such a purpose, than of the extreme remoteness of the consequent gain. Or are these gentlemen really unaware of the permanent support thus rearable, not only for English interests in Afghanistan, but even for the special welfare of the Afghans themselves?

Sir Henry Rawlinson's diplomatic bearing in Kandahar, which enabled him so long to maintain himself there with his suite in the most difficult position, at a period the most critical, is a splendid proof that even the rudest Asiatics are not unmanageable. And if the said officer could accomplish so much in the threatening attitude of a conqueror, what might not first have been attained through political tact and friendly persuasion?

The tangible results of uninterrupted diplomatic intercourse would, if we mistake not, be:—

1st. A greater impulse given to trade; for, as English goods have long enjoyed a good name in Central Asia, English products, imported direct from England, could certainly drive similar but less-prized Russian products out of the market. At present this is naturally not the case: at this moment, in the bazaars of Kabul, Kandahar, Herat, and other places, there is much more sold of many Russian articles,—such as ironware and working tools, coarse cotton and handkerchiefs,—than of English ones; solely because the former, owing to the lower price at which they were first saleable, are not raised by the additional payments to so high a figure as the English goods, whose value, originally dear, is raised twofold in the transit. Moreover, in Bokhara, here and there in Khiva and in Karshi, Russian traders may be found who, secure in the energy of their government, can of course advance their own interests better than foreign mercantile agents. In vain should we seek for a better apostle, a better pioneer for civilisation, than trade; in vain, for a better teacher to turn men to our own ways of thinking, than the silent bales of goods which are carried over from Europe; and England, apart from her commercial interests, is bound, for the ends of humanity also, to help forward trade in Central Asia.

2. The Afghans, who, under the name of Ingilis or Feringhi, have hitherto been acquainted with but one armed power, one conquest-seeking neighbour, will easily, in the peaceful garb of diplomatic intercourse, in well-meaning counsels, accept the teaching of a better one. In the year 1808, when the Afghans had little fear of an English invasion, the ambassador, Mountstuart Elphinstone, with a numerous following, whose escort amounted to only four hundred Anglo-Indian soldiers, was well received throughout Afghanistan, for fear and mistrust had as yet taken no root. Down to the beginning of this century the same state of things might be found in all parts of the Ottoman Empire. European and enemy were deemed identical things; but now, after our embassies and consulates have pushed themselves, spite of the Porte's reluctance, into many places, will Osmanlis and Arabs no longer cherish the same sort of views? They have clearer notions about the generic term, "Feringhi," and know for certain that Russia, for instance, feels just as friendly to the Porte as England feels inimical; that this government has one set of plans, the other another; and so on. Without consulates such a result could not have been attained. And so the Afghans, until they have

been brought into nearer and peaceful intercourse with the English, will never understand what England or Russia may do for their weal or woes; whose friendship will render them the more or the less service.

3. The Afghans, most warlike of all Central Asiatics, might, with the powerful support of English counsels, easily be raised into a military power of some importance. What the *Instructeurs Militaires* of their day accomplished in the army of Sultan Mahmood and Mehemed Ali Pasha; what English officers accomplished with the troops of Abbas Mirza,—would be as nothing in comparison with the consequences of a similar undertaking among the Afghans; out of whom, so far as one may judge from the military bearing and manœuvring of a Kabul regiment drilled by Sepoy deserters, a regular army will very easily be formed. Such a result may also be attained with the fortresses of Herat and Kandahar, whose fortifications, in the event of their coming under the charge of a second Pottinger, would certainly prove a far harder prize for Russian besiegers than if they were given over to the warlike skill of Afghans alone.

4. The prime gain, however, which we look for from a permanent agency is, that England, being accurately informed of proceedings in Central Asia, of the military and political movements of Russia, will no longer be exposed to the danger of finding herself suddenly surprised on one point or another, and, through the continual uncertainty in which she wavers touching

the true state of things, of being disabled from taking the right precautions. At this moment, the Viceroy maintains a few Moonshies without any official character in Kabul, Kandahar, and Herat; Moonshies, that is, scribes, and Mohamedans, who, being among other things well paid, are engaged to furnish occasional news. Besides these, there are also spies, or secret emissaries, despatched in this or that direction on special conjunctures, who roam in the disguise of a merchant or a pilgrim through Turkestan, and furnish tidings of political events. Letting alone the fact that I regard both the former and the latter class as alike unfit for such an office, because they never enter in their memorandum-books anything but bazaar-reports and the politics of the caravan, I may, as one who has lived whole years among Orientals, be allowed to place the very smallest faith in those people. Do persons in Calcutta consider what Mohamedan fanaticism is; are they aware that no amount of gold will succeed in turning one Mussulman to the account of the Feringhie against another Mussulman? To all appearance these emissaries and spies will display the greatest diligence, the most reckless loyalty, the most forward zeal; and yet in the interior of Central Asia they will fulfil the commands of their order by squatting on the self same carpet with those religious comrades, with whom they repair to one common mosque. On this point British statesmen will certainly not agree with me, though that is the very reason why they are so little acquainted with what goes on in Central Asia,—why the absurdest stories spread through India into Europe,—and why they can regard the affairs of the Khanats in the light which Russian diplomacy has kindled for them.

Far as I am from wanting to set up as a political advice-giver, I find that these unpretending counsels point out the only means whereby Afghanistan's neutrality can be secured, and herself erected into a powerful barrier against Russia's further progress in Central Asia. In view of so weighty a question as the possession of the East Indies is for the greatness and continuance of English power, it were too dangerous to seek a false protection in palliative measures. Political errors, however trifling, form in time so many links in one unbroken chain of disasters,—a chain which, presently, the greatest struggles, the most clear-eyed statesmanship, may trouble themselves to break in vain.

6. THE GENERAL INTERESTS OF THE QUESTION.

It still remains to answer the one further question, why we cannot look with indifference on the danger for English interests from Russian ascendancy, and for what special reason it is that the decline of England's power seems to us so detrimental, that we see in Russia's undue influence a bar to the advance of the spirit of our age.

The answer is very simple: Russia was, is, and long will be Asiatic. The cheering prospect that the overgrown body of Russian power will, according to the laws of nature, necessarily break up hereafter into two or more sections, and the danger that threatens us be thereby lessened, is one which we cannot for a moment entertain. We need only fix our eyes on the character of political life in Russia, its social circumstances, the relation of the people towards the upper castes of the governing circle, the general state of popular culture, and the modes of popular thought, to see how everything there is Asiatic, aye, wildly Asiatic in tendency; and how little, in spite of the long struggle after European civilisation, has yet been taken in, to speak comparatively, from what we call European or Western life. Without repeating the well-worn adage, "Scrape a Russian and you will lay bare a Tartar," it is none the less impossible, whether from personal experience, or the reports of later, and to Russia most friendly travellers, to help acknowledging how much may yet be found, on the Neva and in other large Russian towns, of that surface civilisation which many Asiatic governments bring successfully to bear on short-sighted Europe. No doubt this pretence of civilisation succeeds better in Petersburg, wielded by a government containing a strong admixture of Christian and European elements, than in Cairo, Constantinople, and Teheran. The Russian noble, in appearance a finished European, thoroughly versed in our language, manners and modes of thought, will certainly cut a better figure than the semi-European Effendi on the Bosphorus, or the Persian Mirza. A government which draws towards itself, at a cost so heavy, so many scientific and artistic forces, which has lately advanced with so much zeal in founding schools, universities, scientific associations, which hires persons in Europe to blazon forth the progress of Russian civilisation,—can assuredly reap for itself greater credit than the Porte or the Persian ministry, which, engaged in upholding their weakly existence, cannot bestow so much attention on the needful pageantry.

No wonder, then, if to a superficial glance Russia seems more European, more imbued with the spirit of our civilisation, and can easily win the sympathy of those who would love her with all their might. But if once we try impartially to lift up the outer covering and peep into the inside of the great Russian community, what shall we behold?

Great, indeed, is the disenchantment that awaits us at every step, when we seek to discover in the majority of the Russian people those traces of progress, which ought to exist according to the statements of Russian hirelings in the European press. The Englishman who, in 1865, in a pamphlet called " Russia, Central Asia, and British India," sought to indoctrinate the English public with the same idea, and, inferring the commencement of many reforms from the bearing of such innovations as slave emancipation, placed such a conversion in the foreground, though even Russian writers like Herzen and Dolgorukoff are doubtful of it, would in all likelihood have thought very differently, if he had drawn the parallel, not between persons of intelligence, but between the Russian people and the Asiatics.

On that immense frontier where Russia touches Asia, we shall everywhere find the Russians standing on a markedly lower level of development, and in freedom of manners far behind those Asiatic peoples to whom we would impart the advantages of our younger European as compared with their old Asiatic civilisation. Alexander Michie, a traveller from Pekin to Petersburg, and so great a friend of Russia that he calls Siberia a second Paradise, and deems the exiled Poles enviably fortunate, cannot, however, help proclaiming aloud the superiority of the Chinese to the Russians, wherever he finds the two holding intercourse with each other. And this is the case not only in Maimadshin and Kiachta, but even among the Mussulmans. The Russian, as a northerner, will display more energy than the Asiatic *de pur sang;* but his remarkably dirty exterior, his drunkenness, his religion bordering on fetishism, his servility, his crass ignorance, his coarse, unpolished manners,—are characteristics which make him show very poorly against the supple, courtly, keen-sighted Eastern. Just as I have heard a cultivated Moslem Tadjik in Bokhara speak with contempt of the uncivilised Russians, whom he set above the Kirghis only, so in all likelihood will every Chinaman, every Persian in Transcaucasia, and every well-educated Tartar in Kazan, say the same. What can these nations, then, learn from Russia?

Can her forms of government awaken any envy in Asiatic races? The corruptibility of the placemen, their tyrannical and arbitrary conduct under Nicholas, the mass of more than fifty million peasants who occupied the lowest of all positions beside the caste of placemen and nobles,—all this really is not particularly alluring for those among whom the wildest autocratic institutions are yet combined with patriarchal mildness.

Yes, it is hard, not only at present, but even in the distant future, to discover in Russia's craving for conquests the prospect of a profitable change in the social life of the Asiatic peoples, a change in the direction of European ideas. If we ask ourselves what has become of the Tartars, who for more than two hundred years have dwelt under Russian protection; what of the great number of Siberian tribes,—such as Bashkirs, Voguls, Tzeremisses, Votjaks,—which have been or are on the point of being absorbed into the Russian nation, must we not everywhere regard the Russianising as the chief result?

Russianising is naturally a step from Asia towards Europe, as the government of an Alexander II., so far as it has gone, may even be called a turning-point: and yet who will blame us, if to this wearisome process, whose results seem always doubtful, we prefer the English scheme of civilisation, which has at this moment such splendid and surprising results to show in India, and wherever else it deals with Asiatics?

That the peoples of broad India, of the land which

has been the cradle and the fountain-head of that Asiatic civilisation which we show up and fight against as unfit to live, hold very persistently to their old usages, to their own ways of thinking, no one will dispute; and yet how great a change has come over India, even since the beginning of the last century! Methinks, even the worst enemies of Great Britain will be unable to deny that the caste-system of the Hindoos and their many inhuman customs have suffered a mighty blow from English influence. No one can deny that these wild Asiatics, in spite of all their stiff-necked bearing, are advancing with wonderful strides on the path of our civilisation. We find at this moment in India a great number of people thoroughly convinced of the blessed influence of their conqueror: numerous schools and institutions spread the light of the new world abroad through all classes of the population. Not only are there many well versed in the English tongue; they also take an active part in our scientific discussions, are enrolled as members of learned European societies, and sometimes even take up the pen to emulate the writers of the West. Rajah Radakant Deb Bahádur, Maharajah Kali Krishna Bahadur, Baboo Rayendra Lala Mitra, a good many pundits (priests), and other learned gentlemen, may be found on the list of French, German, and Anglo-Asiatic societies, and are known in distinguished circles by their works. Strong in their own sense of nationality, the Hindoos are now better acquainted with their language, history and philosophy, than ever they were in the days of their inland princes. Societies are formed, as in England, for the extirpation of certain prejudices, for doing away with so many shameful habits and customs, for the advancement of social intercourse; and if we consider how much the reading world increases day by day, how large a circle has been procured from among the natives for such Hindustani papers as the *Hirkara Bengála* ("Bengal Messenger"), the *Suheili Panjábi* ("Punjaub Star"), the *Audh Akbar* ("Oudh News"), *Khairkah Panjábi* ("Punjaub Wellwisher"), and how greatly the press is rising day by day into a powerful factor of Europeanism, we shall be obliged to own that England's subject races stand, in respect of culture, not only above their yoke-fellows in Russia, but even above many of the Russians themselves.

If to the above-named unfitness of Russia for civilising India we superadd the important circumstance that Russia, in thus absorbing half the world, and blending many millions of Asiatics into her own body, presents herself in an attitude of powerful menace, not to Great Britain only, but to all Europe as well, we shall find this immense predominance more hurtful to our own existence than advantageous to the leading Tartar races of Asia. Russophobia, we are told, is a foolish crotchet; and I am willing to think so myself. Still, if we contemplate the mighty influence of the Russian two-headed eagle in all parts of Asia; if we reflect, that through its position on the Hindu Kush the court of St. Petersburg will solve, in its own favour, the Eastern question on the Bosphorus, it is hard to feel perfect peace of mind with regard to the future destiny of our own hemisphere. The diplomacy of to-day, which pays more homage to fashion than to good sense, makes merry enough with Napoleon's prophecy regarding Cossack rule in Europe. But people forget how much may be accomplished with our present means of communication by a power which will extend from Kamshatka to the Danube, or perhaps to the shore of the Adriatic,—from the icy zones of the North Sea to the burning banks of the Irawaddy. Visionary as it may seem to many, it is in nowise impossible that some hundred thousands of Asia's wildest horsemen may readily follow the summons of such a power into the midmost heart of Europe. In the beginning of this century the possibility of such an inroad, à la Djinghis Khan and Taimur, was shown by the Don Cossacks on the banks of the Seine. And why might this not be repeated now-a-days, with railroads and steamers at their disposal? Our European war-science may overcome this savage power: no member of the House of Romanoff could long play among us the part of a Djinghis or a Taimur. Yet a struggle of that sort, however momentary, would evolve mournful issues; and it is now a matter of pressing need to keep off the approach of such an event, while measures of precaution are still within our reach.

Apart, however, from these far-reaching calculations,

can any one doubt that England's power and greatness are of more advantage than Russian supremacy to the general interests of Europe? England has many foes, or perhaps we should rather call them, enviers. Certain voices in the continental press will always, under the sway of passion, discover in her conduct selfishness, greed, and pride. Enthusiasts will see the blindest materialism in every move; and yet people must be blind and carried away by prejudice, not to see the triumphs won by English greatness, English capital, and English endurance, for our civilisation and our scientific researches. Is it not England alone, whose powerful flag has opened Eastern Asia to our trade? Who else but English travellers have been driven by a daring spirit of inquiry into the farthest regions, in order to enrich our geographical and ethnographical knowledge; and what happens on the Thames, what in every other town of that ever-stirring and busy island-realm? Do those haughty spirits who are continually finding fault with English materialism, ever consider that these brokers, in spite of their lively interest in trade and money-making, still render the greatest service in the advancement of science, in the enlightenment of the world? What country is there, in which Government gives its millions so readily for an institution like the British Museum; where a hundred thousand pounds is laid out with so free a hand on the mere catalogue of a library, as lately happened in London; where Government fits out ships and expeditions in quest of an imperilled traveller, as they have lately done in behalf of Livingstone?

Yes; in spite of all her faults, from which no country is free, we must allow that England, whether in consequence of the materialism thus strongly censured, or of the thirst for power so often laid to her charge, anyhow stands at the top of European civilisation. For if France and Germany furnish indispensable aid in diffusing the light of our higher civilisation, still, the chief agent is England alone. With her flag emerges the day-dawn of a fairer era in every zone, in every part of the world. What the enviers of Great Britain tell us of her tyrannical behaviour, is mainly an untruth. It is not at the writing-table and in easy arm-chairs, but in the countries of the Asiatic world, that these sentimental fault-finders should inform themselves about England's influence; and if they saw how the march of our western civilisation drives out the vices of the old Asiatic, how it seeks to upraise the downtrodden rights of man, and freeing millions from the absolute sway of a single tyrant, leads them on towards a better future, then assuredly they could not remain indifferent to England's influence in foreign lands.

And would it not be grievous, if Muscovite ascendancy should do harm to such a State? The strong will of a free people governs on the Thames; on the Neva the ambition of an Asiatic dynasty, a system of government so framed that its capacity for reform in the future remains doubtful, while its great perniciousness in the present is all the more assured.

Yes; only in Russia's approach towards India, that Achilles-heel of British interests, may we discover the infallible sign of serious danger for England. A greater struggle than that which the British Lion had to encounter in the south with France, for the establishment of its power on the Ganges, it has still to look for in the north. The first-named foe, weaker in numbers and endurance, had but a small fleet, and a sea at that time unnavigable behind her back, and could easily be overcome. The last-named, on the contrary, will be supported by an unbroken chain of fortresses, garrisons, guarded roads; her weapons are a boundless ambition, the blind devotion of millions of subjects, and the sympathy of rude neighbour-states. Victory over such a power will be far less easy, and the consequences of defeat far greater.

Be on thy guard, therefore, Britannia! For if the star of thine ancient fortune should now begin to wane, then will that verse—

> "The nations not so blest as thee
> Must in their turn to tyrants fall,
> While thou shalt flourish great and free,
> The dread and envy of them all,"

—have to remain unread in the different zones.

LEWIS & SON, Printers, Swan Buildings, Moorgate Street, London.